WHEN ECONOMIC
CRISES ENDURE

WHEN ECONOMIC
CRISES ENDURE

Jacques Mazier, Maurice Baslé, and Jean-François Vidal

Translated by Myriam Rosen

M.E. Sharpe

Armonk, New York
London, England

Library of Congress Cataloging-in-Publication Data

Mazier, Jacques.
[Quand les crises durent—English]
When economic crises endure / Jacques Mazier, Maurice Baslé, Jean-François Vidal ;
translated by Myriam Rosen.
p.   cm.
Includes bibliographical references and index.
ISBN 1-56324-568-X (hardcover : alk. paper).   ISBN 1-56324-569-8 (pbk. : alk. paper)
1. Economic history—20th century.   2. France—Economic conditions—20th century.
3. Depressions.   I. Baslé. Maurice.   II. Vidal, Jean-François.   III. Title.
HC54.M3513   1999
330.944′08—dc21   98-30972
CIP

Printed in the United States of America

The paper used in this publication meets the minimum requirements of
American National Standard for Information Sciences—
Permanence of Paper for Printed Library Materials,
ANSI Z 39.48-1984.

∞

BM (c)	10	9	8	7	6	5	4	3	2	1
BM (p)	10	9	8	7	6	5	4	3	2	1

CONTENTS

LIST OF TABLES

LIST OF FIGURES

ACRONYMS AND ABBREVIATIONS

CEPII: Centre d'Études Prospectives et d'Informations Internationales, Paris

CERC: Centre d'Études des Revenus et des Coûts, Paris.

CIS: Community of Independent States

ECU: European Currency Unit

EEC: European Economic Community

EFTA: European Free Trade Association

EMS: European Monetary System

GATT: General Agreement on Tariffs and Trade

GDP: Gross domestic product

GRESP: Groupe de Recherche et d'Études sur les Systèmes Productifs, Université de Rennes 1

ILO: International Labor Office

IMF: International Monetary Fund

INSEE: Institut National de la Statistique et des Études Economiques, Paris

MIMOSA: Modèle Intégré Mondial pour la Simulation et l'Analyse, OFCE and CEPII, Paris

MITI: Ministry of International Trade and Industry, Tokyo

OECD: Organization of Economic Cooperation and Development

OFCE: Observatoire Français de Conjoncture Economique, Paris

OPEC: Organization of Petroleum Exporting Countries

R&D: Research and Development

SMEs: Small and Medium Enterprises

UK: United Kingdom

USSR: Union of Soviet Socialist Republics

VAT: Value Added Tax

PREFACE TO THE
ENGLISH TRANSLATION

This book is an abridged and reworked version of a monograph first published in French, by Economica, Paris, in 1984, with a second edition in 1993.

The approach adopted is that of economic history and comparative economics. The authors are associated with the French Regulation School. This school puts the emphasis on institutional change, the development of productive systems, and the social relations of production in trying to explain economic growth and macroeconomic trends.

The economic crisis of the 1970s is analyzed in its long-term context by comparing the different growth phases of the five countries that have dominated the world economy since 1890. The book looks at the differences between the respective economies, their international links, and the economic policies that followed.

Particular attention is paid to the years 1980 and 1990. Some countries, especially in Europe, became stuck in crisis; while others such as the United States were able to restore the momentum of growth. European macroeconomic policy is critically analyzed from the inception of the European Monetary System in 1979 to the run-up to Monetary Union at the end of the 1990s.

Translation of any work is always fraught with difficulties. The authors wish especially to record their thanks to Robert Guttmann, professor at Hofstra University in New York, for his invaluable help in this awkward task. As always, they take full responsibility for the many flaws that remain.

INTRODUCTION

The world economic crisis of the late twentieth century has lasted more than twenty years now, and questions about the risks of stagnation or prolonged slowdowns of growth reemerge continually. The crisis has hit the industrialized countries all the harder because it followed nearly thirty years of rapid growth. But the trajectories of individual countries appeared increasingly different in the course of the 1980s, even within the limited group of OECD members. Japan managed to create a new form of growth and surmount the crisis at the end of the 1970s, but since the early 1990s it has been confronted by a new and wide-ranging crisis. Until recently, the unemployment level remained very low in the Alpine and Northern European countries, while mass unemployment continues to hit the countries of the EEC, and medium-term employment prospects remain very unfavorable. The United States has seen its industrial competitiveness decline sharply, but has returned to an unemployment level close to that of the 1960s. The situation in the countries of the South is just as diverse. The new industrialized countries of Southeast Asia have undergone sustained growth and a remarkable process of industrialization. In spite of factors of weakness, notably an overly great dependence on the outside, their results seem much more favorable than those of most other countries of the South where the 1980s were a "lost decade" and the social situation is particularly serious. In this context, economists have proposed divergent and often contradictory analyses.

The followers of Keynes have offered several readings of the crisis. Some of them invoke a synthesis with the neoclassical schema; this is well represented by the usual macroeconomic forecasting models, the most recent versions of which, in the form of multinational models, give a useful representation of the world economy. The current crisis is thus perceived as a conjuncture of unfortunate events: oil crises, the rise in the American interest rates, or the absence of a concerted recovery on the European level. More appropriate economic policies would thus have allowed the crisis to be resolved.

This thesis is not unfounded. Certain authors have emphasized that the 1980s had seen the triumph of Keynesian ideas with the success of the

Reagan recovery in the United States or, conversely, the cumulative process of blocked European growth generated by the austerity policies autonomously conducted in each country. However, this thesis must be criticized in two respects. In its neo-Keynesian version, it has the disadvantage of underestimating, or indeed ignoring, the importance of structural factors that are characteristic of this period, such as the introduction of new technologies, the transformation of the wage relation, the movements of globalization and financial liberalization. In its neoconservative version, well illustrated by the studies of the OECD, it provides a basis for the adjustment and liberalization policies that will be discussed below.

Other Keynesian writers, in particular those of the Cambridge School, are opposed to such an approach. They have placed the accent on the articulation between productivity and growth, growing returns, and the decline of profitability with its consequences for capital accumulation. They have stressed the perverse effects of policies inspired by neoconservatism and monetarism. They have also played a pioneering role in modeling the world economy. Kaldor was representative of this current of thought until his death in 1986. In France as well, this perspective partly dominated a whole series of studies developed within the government itself during the 1970s.

The neoconservative economists, who first denied the reality of the crisis, were later to attribute it mainly to factors of rigidity blocking the natural functioning of the markets: the rigidity of the labor market first of all, but also the burden of regulations in many sectors, the weight of compulsory tax and social security deductions, and government's excessive interventionism. Consequently, it is by reducing these factors of dysfunction and restoring market mechanisms that the crisis can be surmounted. The result was a fairly coherent policy of neoconservative inspiration that overcame certain national specificities to emerge as the norm in the 1980s. One part of the Keynesian current rallied behind this approach in order to arrive at a synthesis that is probably best expressed by the OECD's studies and policy proposals.

Marxist-inspired approaches, for which crises are an integral part of the functioning of the capitalist system, were in principle better placed to describe lasting blockage of growth. In practice, since the end of the 1960s, Marxist writers were the first to speak of a general crisis. Through a significant renewal of the analysis, in particular with the "Regulation School" in France and radical economists in the United States, original studies on accumulation regimes, the transformation of the wage relation, or international growth regimes went beyond the old and often rather antiseptic debates. Although these works have not yet led to a completely structured, formalized synthesis that can respond to the neoclassical/neo-Keynesian synthesis, they shed an interesting light on the crisis in the medium run.

The present study must be placed in this last perspective. Because of its scope, the current crisis cannot be correctly understood without being placed in a long-term perspective. A rapprochement with the crisis of the 1930s and a comparison with the modes of growth that prevailed before and after the Second World War are fruitful for bringing out the nature of the changes now under way. Certain preliminary definitions must, however, be introduced on the methodological level.

Growth and Crises: A Few Issues of Methodology

On a theoretical level, we situate ourselves between the Regulation School and the Cambridge School analyses of the accumulation of capital, and we round out our analytical tools with the contributions of quantitative history and applied macroeconomics. The crisis of the late twentieth century must be analyzed on the basis of a general explanation of the capitalist dynamic identifying, on the one hand, all the forces that generate growth and constitute the accumulation regime and, on the other hand, all the forces that guarantee the cohesiveness of the capitalist system and allow it to reproduce itself from one era to another, as designated by the term "regulation." These ideas will first be discussed in national terms before considering how they are articulated with the phenomena of internationalization. This is the general framework for our analysis of the crises, which argues that they reflect the inability of regulation to ensure the reproduction of the system as a whole and that they emerge as a transition between two successive accumulation regimes.

Accumulation Regimes and Institutional Forms

The accumulation regime approach was founded in France by the work of Aglietta (1979) and Boyer (1977, 1979a). It diverges profoundly from the traditional theories of growth that dominated until the beginning of the 1980s. These were based on simplistic hypotheses that could hardly take into account the multiplicity of relations and conditions determining the long-term evolution of economic systems. With their stable parameters and their uniform growth rates, they could not integrate either the notions of rupture and change or the role of institutions and structural factors, phenomena that are present in any process of growth and crisis. The traditional theories, with their hypotheses of constant yields of scale and decreasing marginal returns, could only explain growth through an exogenous motor—technological progress. And because they presumed that the same laws applied to all economies, atemporally, they could not explain the specific features of different countries and different periods.

Rather than this overly reductive approach, we prefer the concept of the accumulation regime. This relates first of all to the basic idea that the forces generating growth are linked to processes of capital accumulation, which are conceived simultaneously as a group of capital goods to be combined, a relation between social classes, and a sum of money to be exploited for profit. However, we shall not refer to magnitudes expressed in terms of labor value. These may well allow the functioning of the capitalist system to be described on the highest level of abstraction, but they only refer to an objective notion of value and are of little use for describing changes in market prices.

The concept of the accumulation regime also relates to that of periodization. It is based on the observation that structural changes and the emergence of new institutions are at the heart of long-term growth and that each country presents significant specificities. Thus, the forms of competition between firms have undergone profound change over the past century, as have relations between banks and firms. The forms of government intervention have also been considerably renewed and enlarged over time (e.g., social policy, public financing, planning). But the most profound transformation was perhaps that in the relations between employees and employers under the combined influence of social struggles and technological changes. On that basis we attempt to delineate successive periods, each one presenting its own regular features that attest to a certain stability of economic structures, institutions, and regulation procedures.

For each complex historical period, the accumulation regime can be characterized by five major institutional forms: the monetary constraint, the wage relation, the forms of competition, the nature of the State, and the articulation with the international regime.

- The monetary constraint is the most global because it defines the nature of formalized relations between the different agents. Money is not a good but a social relation that carries with it certain norms (Aglietta and Orléan 1982). It is a common unit of measure governing all contracts and ensuring the equivalence of different products resulting from individual labors. It has a transactional function that permits operations to be concluded without obstacles. The person who sells merchandise is required to accept payment for it in legal tender. Thus, money must also be able to serve as a repository of values for the accumulation of capital, but this function cannot be imposed by the authorities because no one is required to keep the money he or she has on hand. And when it is associated with a system of credit, money offers the possibility of surpluses and deficits, and the issuing of money, along with the functioning of the financial system, contributes to defining a monetary constraint that determines the scope of possible deficits.

- The wage relation is the most important structural form because it designates all the conditions governing the use and reproduction of the labor force. This concept simultaneously covers the social and technical division of labor, the forms of mobilizing employees, the production techniques implemented, the determinants of the wage income, and the wage-earners' lifestyle.

- The forms of competition describe how relations between a group of decentralized, autonomous centers of accumulation are established. The existence of a system of prices reflecting relative scarcities is in itself inadequate to allow the adjustment between decisions that are independent of one another. It is necessary for different forms of competition to be set up according to the scale of the installations, the nature of yields of scale, the individual or collective nature of the product. The adjustment of the structures of supply and demand implies a more or less complete mobility of capital and has consequences for the organization of the financial system.

- The nature of the State corresponds to a group of "institutionalized compromises" that are gradually elaborated and create regularities in government interventions, marking a break with the strict market logic (Delorme and André 1983). The State's interventions interact in multiple ways with the other institutional forms that they help to shape, without the State's being either completely autonomous or completely predetermined.

- The forms of articulation with the international regime constitute the last basic feature of an accumulation regime, whether in the form of exchanges of goods, movements of capital, or direct investments, namely the choice of the production site. Contrary to received wisdom, internationalization has always been a major feature of capitalism, and is not a recent development. But obviously, the articulation between internal dynamics and the world economy takes place according to the particular forms of each major period and each economic system.

Two major accumulation regimes based on specific forms of the wage relation can be distinguished. Extensive accumulation corresponds to a growth of capital that occurs in a series of large waves periodically coming up against problems of outlets, without disrupting production conditions and with very low productivity gains. The wage relation is competitive, and wage consumption plays a limited role as an outlet for capitalist production.

Growth depends on the employment of a growing number of wage-earners. Yields of scale are very reduced. The limits of such a regime are clear.

Intensive accumulation, by contrast, involves a major transformation of the conditions of production with increasing yields linked to mass production. Productivity gains are high and may permit the distribution of a rapidly increasing wage revenue if the wage relation transforms itself and establishes a link between an increase in wages and in productivity. In such a hypothesis, the rapid growth of a new consumption standard is encouraged and the resulting increase in outlets helps to bolster accumulation. A virtuous circle of growth and productivity is thus initiated, with increasing outputs playing a privileged role.

The two accumulation regimes are not mutually exclusive, but over fairly long periods, one of them may appear dominant. This was the case, for example, during the 1950s and 1960s with the gradual affirmation of intensive accumulation. These considerations show that in order to characterize the accumulation regimes, it is necessary to analyze carefully the modes of distribution and consumption. This point goes back to an earlier line of thought, very present among the members of the Cambridge School, who have always insisted on the importance of the link between accumulation and mode of distribution.

To conclude this brief survey, it may be noted that recent developments of the theory of endogenous growth have attempted to go beyond certain weaknesses of traditional neoclassical theory by reintroducing increasing returns with the help of external effects on the store of knowledge, modeling of innovation activities, or an analysis of the impact of infrastructures. Since the two pioneering articles of Romer (1986) and Lucas (1988), a vast literature has emerged. This approach reflects an important break. It indicates an interesting return toward a Schumpeterian conception of technical progress. Through the interplay of external effects, it also marks the beginnings of a recognition of institutional factors, notably the State and the social conditions in which the accumulation of knowledge and innovations takes place. In this sense, a parallel can be drawn with certain concerns of the Regulation School, but the two approaches are based on very different methodologies.

Growth and Regulation

The accumulation regimes thus defined enjoy fairly stable dynamics. What remains to be understood is how, in complex market economies, the coordination of the multiple decisions made by individual agents who are aware only of local constraints takes place. In attempting to reply to this question, the Regulation approach marks its distance from the theory of general equilibrium.

One of the main postulates of neoclassical theory is that any phenomenon can be analyzed in terms of individual supply and demand. The Regulation approach, by contrast, assumes that there are laws determining overall reproduction and translating necessary relations between the elements of the system. In no case do these laws result from a simple accumulation of individual choices. They appear as a product of history and impose their constraints on the decision-makers, so that most behaviors are determined by the overall functioning of the economy. In general, these laws are valuable only for a given period, and they should not necessarily be interpreted in terms of supply and demand. They reflect the functioning of institutions, the codification of the balance of power, or the state of the productive apparatus. A wage equation thus reflects both a group of rules determining the modalities of wage negotiation and the balance of power between firms and unions. In addition, the neoclassical approach is based on the notion of equilibrium. While it admits the existence of temporary disequilibria, the flexibility of prices is supposed to permit a return to equilibrium. In the Regulation approach, the core of the analysis is not the equilibrium value of the variables but the process of adjustment that governs the dynamic of these variables. Nor is it assumed that prices necessarily play a role in establishing equilibrium. Rather, there is an attempt to define the mechanisms that determine the evolution of social supply and demand and to show how the coherence of these changes is ensured during periods of growth or, conversely, how it is absent during periods of crisis. This coherence, however, has nothing to do with a static equilibrium. It is guaranteed through successive adjustments that generate economic fluctuations. The study of these fluctuations is useful for bringing out the regulation procedures at work and identifying their development over time.

It is clear that the stability of the regulation is only relative because the very play of regulation continually modifies the basis of these relations and the state of the underlying economic and social structures.

The stylized regulation procedures that can be identified always remain at a certain distance from the concrete processes, but they constitute the basic schema according to which capitalism reproduces itself during a given period. Following the studies of Boyer (1977, 1986c), two major types of regulation are analyzed: competitive regulation, where adjustments result from the interplay of a group of markets and the flexibility of prices and incomes, and monopolistic regulation, where these mechanisms are profoundly modified by the appearance of new institutional structures and forms. Such an approach allows us to attempt formalizations and establish a bridge between historical analysis and the explanation of short-term adjustment mechanisms. The analyses of regulation made in this study bear throughout on the distribution dynamic, which determines both consumption and investment, and on the supply dynamic, which is studied on the basis of the accumulation rhythm and productivity cycles.

The Regulation School: Some Definitions

Accumulation regime: "The whole of the regularities ensuring a general and relatively coherent increase in capital accumulation, i.e., allowing the absorption or distribution over time of the distortions and disequilibria that are continuously generated by the process itself" (Boyer 1986c).

Mode of regulation: "The whole of the procedures and individual and collective behaviors having the threefold property of:

- reproducing basic social relations through the conjunction of historically determined institutional forms;
- supporting and directing the accumulation regime in force;
- ensuring the dynamic compatibility of a group of decentralized decisions without requiring the economic players to interiorize the adjustment principles of the whole of the system" (Boyer 1986c).

Mode of development (or **mode of growth**): "Conjunction of an accumulation regime and a kind of regulation" (Boyer 1986c).

International growth regime: "Configuration of economic spaces and their connections based on the existence of firmly established complementarities guaranteeing the increasing accumulation of capital" (Mistral 1986).

A more complete presentation of the Regulation School may be found in Boyer and Saillard (1995).

National Space and Internationalization

The preceding approaches have been limited to the national space considered as an entity endowed with a certain autonomy. Such a position is justified to the extent that the most important structural forms underlying the regulation procedures are in fact defined on the national level: wage relations, procedures for issuing currency, instruments of economic policy, lifestyles, industrial and financial structures. Even so, national economies have never constituted entities functioning autarkically. International exchanges have always played an essential role at the different stages of the history of capitalism. But the way that national economies have been integrated into the global arena and the organization of that area have greatly changed. A predominantly vertical international division of labor (where the manufactured goods of the center are exchanged for the primary commodities of the new countries) has given way to a predominantly horizontal international division of labor (where the exchanges of manufactured goods between advanced capitalist countries predominate). Institutional forms have undergone profound transformations: if protectionism was the dominant form until the end of the Second World War, free exchange has taken over (in principle at least) since then. The international monetary system has weathered periods of great instability to go from the gold standard to the gold exchange standard and then to flexible exchanges. Drawing on the work of regulationists such as Mistral (1986), Aglietta (1986), and Bernis (1977), we shall try to adapt the concepts initially developed for the study of national dynamics to the analysis of international relations.

The International Growth Regime

International exchanges are linked to the comparative advantages enjoyed by the different countries. But in the context of a dynamic analysis, such advantages should not be seen as "falling out of the sky." On the contrary, they are created in the course of the growth process itself. International exchanges developed under the impetus of the most industrialized countries. Their main trends, which we shall designate by the term "international growth regime," are shaped by the forms of accumulation in these countries. These international growth regimes are characterized by several features.

The first results from the gap between the dynamics of supply and internal demand by product in the most advanced countries. We shall not designate here the relationship between global supply and demand, even though there are countries with structural surpluses or deficits in their current operations. These balances, which are sometimes considerable, represent only a slight proportion of the total world trade. On the other hand, differences by product are likely to be very great, especially on a disaggregated level. The accumulation regime determines a dynamic of social demand for the various goods, and the domestic supply may develop in a different way. The impossibility of adequately developing the production of basic goods is a prime example. Likewise, for certain manufactured goods, the firms may obtain increasing yields of scale and high productivity gains, so that their production capabilities largely surpass the size of the domestic market. These differences strongly influence the development of international demand.

The second feature bears on the way that exports respond to international demand. This implies the emergence of a correspondence between the accumulation dynamic in the center and that of the supplier countries. The expansion of international trade is associated with a reinforcement of the international division of labor. Since the productivity levels and growth potentials of the different branches vary greatly, the specialization conditions the income level per inhabitant and the growth rate of each country. The adjustment of supply to international demand helps to determine the rank among growth rates in the different countries.

The last major feature of the international growth regime is the configuration of bilateral trade. The intensity of bilateral relations between countries varies greatly, as demonstrated by intra-European trade or that between Latin American countries on the one hand and the United States and Europe on the other. These preferential relations result from both the advantages of geographical proximity and the necessity of regulating international trade. The colonial empire was an old form of regional consolidation in which the metropolis imposed its norms on the colonized countries. The EEC is a more recent form, where the regulation of exchanges results from an agreement among partners. The changes in regional configurations are a significant element of the international growth regime.

The international growth regime is also structured by two major institutional forms—international networks and international institutions per se:

- The international networks include a first group of infrastructures (trade outlets, transportation and telecommunications networks, banking establishments) that ensure the material connection between the different spaces and permit markets to be enlarged while reducing uncertainty and costs. They also include multinational firms, which play a determinant role in the localization of production and the international allocation of investment.
- The institutionalization of international economic relations takes place through two main channels: formal or informal compromises covering the development of exchanges (tariff or non-tariff barriers, colonial empires, GATT, free-trade agreements); an international monetary system providing private agents and international regulations with a framework for guaranteeing the multilateralization of payments and sustaining and stabilizing the international creation of currency in harmony with changes in productive activities.

The cohesion of the international growth regime is not automatically guaranteed. In order for trade to increase, the main traders have to develop their exports and imports at similar rates in order to avoid the emergence of unbearable external disequilibria. The limit of the tolerable disequilibria depends, as we shall see, on the forms of international regulation. Regional configurations must also be compatible with trends in international supply and demand, which may have implications for the foreign trade policies of the different countries. In general, the stability of the international regime depends on the degree of compatibility between the state of the international division of labor and the forms of international regulation.

Forms of International Regulation

Once international trade was regular and sufficiently intense, which has been the case since the second half of the nineteenth century, forms of international regulation have emerged alongside the national forms. These consist of groups of procedures and behaviors that compete with the reproduction of the international regime. They are subject not only to the same tensions affecting national regulations, but also to the weaknesses of the international regimes, most notably the absence of a supranational power endowed with the legitimacy and means of coercion proper to the national powers. Indeed, there are periods when a dominant economy is able to impose an international order through its technological, financial, and military superiority. The best example is the case of the United States between 1945 and 1965. But the supremacy of the dominant economy can always be challenged by the emergence of new powers.

International regulation, moreover, imposes norms on the national economies. These can enter into contradiction with the conditions of reproduction of the national social formations. This retroactive impact of the international on the national corresponds to what is generally called the "external constraint." The intensity of this constraint is that much stronger when the national dynamic, with its modes of regulation, does not manage to adapt to the international growth regime. The intensity of the international norms has to be moderated so as to tolerate a certain diversity in the national dynamics so that a sufficient number of countries can participate in the expansion of world trade and in the international regime.

International regulation implies the existence of a key currency which will serve as a common instrument of measurement and transactions. This poses several problems, beginning with the legitimacy of the international currency that all countries must accept using. The issuing of the key currency, along with the degree of international mobility of capital, defines the norm of creditworthiness. It depends on the dynamic of the dominant economy, which can expand or diminish the tensions of the world economy. The coexistence of several currencies implies the definition of a regime of exchange and forms of adjustment of the balance of payments in which the interaction of movements of goods and capital plays an essential role.

The adjustment of supply to demand for different kinds of goods shows the entire difference between a unified national market and the international market. On the latter, the conditions of competition are far from being totally harmonized. Governments can impose different forms of protectionism, often corresponding to internal social compromises. Even if the protectionist mechanisms are abandoned, factors compartmentalizing the national markets remain: tax laws, social legislation, public aid, and public markets. International negotiations within the framework of the GATT or the EEC show that the harmonization of the conditions of competition imply a questioning of national regulation procedures and a considerable development of international law.

On the world scale, the adjustment of demand to production capabilities must also be ensured. In the short run, this implies that the transmission of short-term economic fluctuations remains limited so that tensions in the opposite direction emerge simultaneously in the different countries and counterbalance one another. In the long run, international regulation must allow the various countries to achieve their potential rates of growth. But if they are pushed too far, the divergences in the national dynamics are likely to call into question the cohesion and stability of the international economy.

Crisis, Regulation, and Profitability

It is commonplace to speak of the contradictory nature of the growth and accumulation process. This seems to be punctuated by phases of slowdown or crisis that are more or less durable according to the period and whose nature remains to be defined. The origin of these crises may indeed lie in the spontaneous interplay of regulation procedures. In this way we can speak of a "minor crisis" or "crisis of regulation," where the crisis appears as one regulating element among others. This was the case with the crises of competitive regulation during the second half of the nineteenth century and until 1930. The spread of intensive accumulation after the Second World War had made this kind of crisis give way to simple slowdowns. But crises may have another, more profound origin: they may result from a growing disequilibrium between the forms of regulation and the state of the structures at a given point, including in their international dimension. Ultimately, regulation can become incapable of ensuring the reproduction of the system. In this case we can speak of a "major crisis" or a "crisis of mutation" or a "structural crisis," that leads over time to a questioning of the main features of the former growth and ensures the emergence of new regulatory mechanisms. Despite their profound differences, the crisis of the 1930s and the current one both fall into that category.

Beyond this distinction between the two forms of crisis, which is essential but very general, the way that the disequilibria reflect themselves must now be specified. Within the Marxist or Cambridge line of thought, a central but non-exclusive role is attributed to the rate of profit, which is both the result and one of the main determinants of accumulation. Through its synthetic nature, it allows the integration of the combined effects of the regulation procedures affecting prices, wages, and productivity; the identification of the impact of the other partners in the distribution; the recognition of the effects of technological changes or transformations in the organization of work; and the assessment of the states of the outlets. The interest of such an approach is not so much to bring out a downward movement of profitability or its stagnation at an inadequate level which, in itself, would be an element of crisis (and which may be the case in certain situations). What is involved, rather, is taking the formation of the rate of profit as a guiding element, bringing out the tendencies and countertendencies intervening on this level, and thus identifying certain essential factors in the crisis.

If the rate of profit plays a central role, it cannot sum up by itself all the disequilibria competing to set off a major crisis. Alongside the national factors by themselves, the international dimension of accumulation seems to be a basic source of disequilibria. It may intervene as a simple amplifier of national disequilibria, but it may also have its own logic, creating a growing disparity in relation to the forms of regulation and the institutional forms that only have meaning on the national level.

The current crisis is manifestly a "major" one that is increasingly calling into question the very foundations of the former pattern of growth. It cannot be analyzed without being resituated in a historical perspective. The originality of the accumulation regime set up after the Second World War must be defined in order to understand the limits it faced. The changes under way for more than twenty years must be compared with the ruptures that occurred during previous crises in order to arrive at a better understanding of their impact. The two parts of this work are conceived within that framework: the first is devoted to the main features of the predominant growth regimes since the beginning of the twentieth century, and the second to the origins and issues of the two major crises of this century.

Part I

Growth and Regulation

CHAPTER ONE

From Extensive to Intensive Accumulation

The links between accumulation and productivity are at the heart of the growth process. The wave of accumulation in the 1950s and 1960s was accompanied by an exceptional growth in labor productivity and a total disruption of the conditions of production, through the intensification of the capitalist division of labor and the spread of assembly-line work. This development contrasted with much slower transformations during the first half of the twentieth century. Similarly, the slowdown in the growth of labor productivity since the 1970s raises a major question with regard to its origins: did it reflect a simple effect of the stoppage of growth and the freezing of accumulation, a crisis of labor, or an "exhaustion of technical progress"? A new technological transformation is now under way, especially with the spread of computerization and biotechnologies. One of the questions emerging from the current crisis would thus seem to be the future impact of these new technologies on work conditions, employment, and productivity.

As we have already indicated in the Introduction, capital accumulation can take two very different forms, extensive or intensive, and these have profoundly different effects on the conditions of production, employment management, and productivity. This chapter will address such links between accumulation, employment, and production in an attempt to identify their long-term logic. First of all, a general framework will be sketched out to recall the major stages of growth in the leading economies since the beginning of the century. The opposition between intensive and extensive accumulation will then be studied in detail. We shall show how, after a first attempt in the United States during the 1920s, the intensive accumulation system did not really flourish throughout the leading economies until after the Second World War.

Growth and Accumulation: An Initial Overview

It has often been argued that since the beginning of the century, the leading economies have experienced two major periods of growth interrupted by two world wars and two structural crises. Obviously, such a presentation must be qualified. The two world wars hardly affected all economies in the same way. The crisis of the 1930s somewhat spared Japan and gave the illusion of being more rapidly overcome in Germany (at what price!). The two periods of growth were quite different both quantitatively and qualitatively. Even during the rapid growth of the postwar years, there were sharp disparities from one country to another. And since 1974, the various economies have hardly reacted to the crisis in the same way.

With the memory of the Belle Epoque foremost in everyone's mind, the years before the First World War seem prosperous. There was sustained growth throughout the major industrial countries, particularly in the United States and Germany once their heavy industry had been set up. Only Great Britain, confronted by sharper international competition, seemed to fall somewhat behind after the beginning of the century. The First World War was to affect these economies in different ways. Its impact was most direct in France and Germany. By contrast, the United States experienced a strong recovery, but its investment rates declined relative to the record levels of the previous decade. It was above all Japan, a "semi-industrialized country" at the time, that drew the most profit from the war by increasing its exports and experiencing an initial boom in accumulation (see Table 1.1 and Figure 1.1).

The postwar period seems even more contrasted. The United States continued its rapid growth with high rates of investment; this was to be the first wave of intensive accumulation. France also experienced a vigorous recovery that lasted until 1930 and was accompanied by fairly sustained investments, especially during the second half of the 1920s. Germany, on the other hand, had a more difficult time recovering from the war, owing to the hyperinflation of 1923, unstable growth, and weak investment. Great Britain's difficulties continued after the war with a sharp monetary constraint, a slowdown in growth, and insufficient accumulation. Japan meanwhile underwent a serious reconversion crisis throughout the 1920s.

The crisis of 1929 thus arose in considerably different contexts. Originating in the United States, it spread throughout the economies. It was more lasting and profound in the United States, in spite of the New Deal implemented after 1933; five years later, production and above all investment had not yet regained their 1929 levels. Only the Second World War was to guarantee a real end to the crisis. Germany was very harshly

Table 1.1

Average Growth Rate of Production (at constant prices—private Ssector—in %)

Country	Period						
	1900–1913	1913–1929	1929–1938	1938–1955	1955–1973	1973–1979	1979–1989
France	2.1	1.7	1.0	+2.2	5.7	3.0	2.4
United States	4.0	3.1	−0.5	3.7[2]	3.6	2.6	2.6
Germany	3.0	0.5	2.9	—	4.7	2.4	1.9
United Kingdom	1.3	0.8	1.8	1.8	3.2	1.4	2.8
Japan	2.4[1]	3.4	5.7	—	10.7	3.5	4.2

Source: 1900–1973, GRESP-Rennes; 1973–1989, OECD.
[1] Average for 1905–1913.
[2] Average for 1938–1950.

affected, but the policy of the Nazi government, based on rearmament, led to a recovery that, whether in spite or because of the war, would continue until 1944. The crisis hit France later and less profoundly, but for a longer period of time; in 1938, production levels were still below those of 1929. The war, which led to significant losses, only aggravated the situation. Paradoxically, Great Britain was less affected by the crisis and experienced a moderate recovery after 1932, because of the depreciation of the pound on the one hand and the revival of investments on the other. This growth continued during the war. Japan quickly overcame a sharp recession in 1930–31 and threw itself into a policy of armament, development of heavy industry, and territorial expansionism. As in Germany, this rapid "growth" lasted until 1945.

Following the Second World War, the industrialized countries found themselves in fairly different situations. The United States launched a new growth regime based on mass production and consumption. In spite of the widespread destruction it suffered, Germany inherited a significant industrial potential. France, on the other hand, was limited to a production system that was extremely outdated after fifteen years of frozen accumulation. Great Britain, in spite of severe war damage, found itself in a relatively more favorable position because of a certain effort to renew its productive apparatus. As for Japan, with the loss of its foreign possessions, it was forced to turn back to its domestic market. During the 1950s and 1960s, the industrialized countries as a whole experienced the same growth regime based on mass production and consumption and the spread of Fordism. Nonetheless, there were differences between more advanced countries, such as the United States or Great Britain, and those countries that were less industrialized to begin with, such as France and

6

Figure 1.1 **Long-Term Investment Rates in the Leading Economies** (0%; constant prices; for the United States and the United Kingdom, private sector; for Germany, France, Japan, private sector, except agriculture)

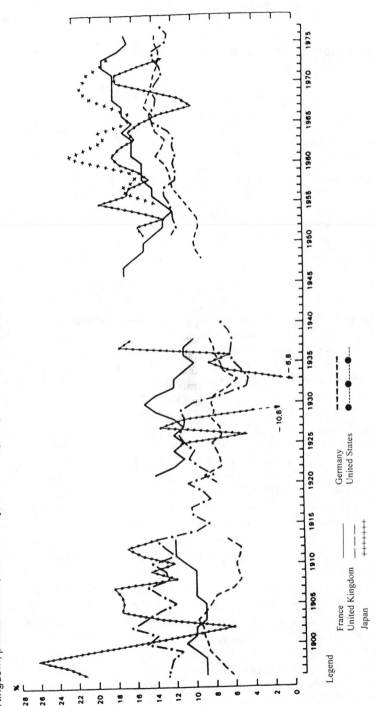

Legend

France
United Kingdom – – –
Japan +++++++

Germany
United States

Source: GRESP-Rennes, France.

especially Japan. From the beginning of the 1970s, various indices suggest that the postwar growth pattern was coming to a halt. The oil price shock that began at the end of 1973 was to become the second major crisis of the twentieth century. In the case of France, this brief survey may be complemented by more detailed data concerning sectoral growth and employment.

Extensive or Intensive Accumulation?

Understanding how labor productivity, employment management, and capital accumulation are linked in the long term requires a precise analysis of the nature of the successive accumulation regimes since the beginning of the century. Two major accumulation regimes may be distinguished. A predominantly extensive accumulation is characterized by a growth of capital occurring in successive waves without any major disruption of production conditions and with moderate productivity gains. By contrast, the intensive accumulation regime is marked by a rapid transformation of the productive processes; the growth of investments is more regular and accompanied by planned obsolescence of equipment. Productivity gains are considerable. The organization of work is restructured along Fordist lines. These two modes of accumulation are not mutually exclusive, but, according to the state of the economic and social structures and production norms proper to each period, one or the other appears dominant, thus conditioning the nature of the links between accumulation, employment, and productivity.

The Aims of Taylorism and Fordism

The problem of seeking new production conditions was first raised at the end of the nineteenth century, which was a period of renewed strength for the unions. The United States played a pioneering role insofar as the last waves of immigrants were for the most part unskilled, their employment posed specific problems, and their integration was becoming more difficult. Experimentation with new methods of production based on the development of repetitive work and output norms, the elimination of slack periods, and an intensification of labor was both possible and necessary. This was the task of Taylorism (Frederick Taylor, b. 1856; d. 1915, was a well-known American engineer), which sought to replace worker control with management control (Coriat 1979; Aglietta 1979). Taylorism developed considerably in the United States from 1900 on, and it continued to expand until 1930. The capitalist division of labor became more acute, the compartmentalization of tasks and repetitive work more widespread. The timeclock made its way into the shop. Those industries most affected at the outset were metal conversion, heavy equipment, and, especially, automobiles.

A new stage was reached with Fordism, which extended and complemented Taylor's efforts in at least three respects: the introduction of conveyor-belt systems that permitted the elimination of a large part of the handling workforce; the development of the assembly line, which pushed the compartmentalization of tasks to an extreme; and the placing of workers at work stations where fixed rhythms could be imposed. The American example was not without influence on Europe, and notably France, especially given the fact that the First World War had encouraged a rationalization of production conditions and led to the mass production of certain goods (munitions, weapons, etc.). While references to the American example were numerous in the 1920s, and production-line work developed in certain branches (automobile manufacture), the real impact of this movement in France during the first half of the twentieth century nonetheless remains open to question.

Whatever the case, in the period just after the Second World War, Fordism underwent an unprecedented expansion in all of the leading economies. Assembly-line work spread. The need for maximum utilization of greatly increased quantities of equipment led to the growth of continuous or semicontinuous production processes. Continuous work in successive shifts resulted in extraordinary productivity gains relative to earlier periods. This trend was closely tied to the appearance or rapid expansion of new products: mass-consumption goods, modern capital goods, the growth of electronics, the standardization of intermediate goods, the gradual replacement of coal by oil. The class composition of the labor force underwent radical changes: the number of specialized workers increased sharply at the expense of unskilled workers and especially skilled workers with a real trade. This shift was facilitated in the United States by the proletarianization of Blacks and in Europe by the recourse to immigrant workers, the proletarianization of peasants, and the use of the female workforce. At the same time, the category of workers, managers, and technicians advanced, while artisanal activities declined or were integrated into the capitalist production process, notably in services and businesses (subcontracting, new services for households and firms, distribution activities).

But Fordism was not limited to work processes. The growth of mass production, if it was really to flourish, presupposed a simultaneous transformation of wage-earners' living conditions and the rapid rise of a new standard of working-class consumption. Such transformations implied profound changes in the nature of relations between employees and employers and in the conditions determining wage formation. This idea was already taking root in Henry Ford's wage policy (the $5 day). But in practice, its concrete implementation and expansion came up against many obstacles that we shall address later on.

Finally, Fordism was marked by multiple internal contradictions: the problem of coordinating overly fragmented tasks and different work rhythms, the necessity of multiplying the number of specific work stations and bonuses in order to divide the whole of the workers more effectively, the workers' difficulty in obeying a uniform rhythm without self-regulation. From the end of the 1960s, a problem of resistance to compartmentalized, repetitive work flared up in most of the leading economies. This was manifested by greater absenteeism, higher rates of turnover, increased manufacturing defects, and finally, greater numbers of strikes that were often quite localized but all the more significant insofar as production apparatus was very vulnerable to the obstacles posed by a few dozen specialized workers. This opposition to the Fordist model of industrial work played a significant role in the crisis of intensive accumulation. One of the issues today is again the search for a new capitalist organization of work oriented toward a reconstitution of tasks and more automatic control of production. This question will be discussed in greater depth in the second part of this book.

Limited Productivity Gains in France Until 1938

On the level of the French economy as a whole, per capita labor productivity showed relatively limited growth until 1938. Beyond the simple effect of catching up after the First World War, no acceleration seemed to manifest itself during the 1920s, and the per capita growth of capital even showed a slight slowdown. It was only after 1950 that notable productivity gains appeared and the intensification of capital showed a sharp increase (see Table 1.2, page 12.)

A sectoral approach allows further definition of these initial observations. With the exception of energy, where sharp productivity gains were tied to the development of new energy sources (electricity and then oil), the performances of the so-called modern sectors, which until 1930 experienced a more consistent rhythm of accumulation (intermediate goods, capital goods, transport), were astonishingly mediocre. Until 1930, the growth of labor productivity in these sectors was no more rapid than in the rest of the economy, and capital per worker showed practically no increase. On this point, we are in agreement with the observations of economists as different in their orientations as Bettelheim (1947) or Divisia, Dupin, and Roy (1956) when they stress the breakdowns produced in certain key sectors such as aeronautics, automobile manufacture, or chemicals, where the French industry had enjoyed a considerable advantage before 1914. The crisis of the 1930s accentuated this phenomenon, with consumer-goods industries better resisting the crisis while production goods and transportation were more severely affected.

These observations give us an initial reason to think that the intensive accumulation regime was only beginning to take shape during the 1920s. To be sure, between 1920 and 1930 there was a sharp reduction in working time that affected all the branches in practically the same way. This decrease was related to significant protest movements in the 1919–21 period. Its effects on the organization of work appear to have been rather limited, and it can hardly be considered a sign of an intensification of labor. It should be noted that, even in terms of hourly productivity, no acceleration can be observed during the 1920s in the so-called modern sectors with the exception of chemicals and energy. Taylorism showed considerable expansion in certain areas, notably following the impetus given by war production and the spread of mass-production work. The examples of the automobile industry and mining are significant but remain relatively isolated. Far from penetrating the whole of the manufacturing branches in France, Taylorism remained in a state of incubation during the 1920s. It seems clear that the weight of small production activities, the place of the rural world, the existence of skilled workers with a real trade, the lack of initiative among one portion of the employers, and the relatively rigid structure of cities built for another era and little suited to the appearance of a new mode of consumption prevented any notable changes from taking place rapidly.

Such a halt was the continuation of what had already taken place during the last third of the nineteenth century, when the French industrial system was modernized much more slowly than that in Germany or Great Britain (Bouvier, Furet, and Gillet 1965). Between 1870 and 1900, the coal mines underwent only a very limited mechanization, and productivity gains were low; metallurgy plants set up near the mines were rare. Likewise, the iron and steel industry made no attempt to diversify toward mechanical infrastructures or constructions. For a long period, the low level of employees (often female) in the consumer-goods industries offered no incentive for mechanization.

The domestic market remained rural and offered little demand for industrial goods, and, unlike the case of Great Britain, the foreign markets and the colonies played only a limited role. This situation lasted until the Second World War. Moreover, in order to impose the break that permitted the expansion of intensive accumulation, voluntarist actions were required: the intervention of the State and the establishment of a planning process, productivity missions to the United States, the gradual opening of the borders, and so on.

The period from 1950 on saw the emergence of a new accumulation regime characterized by the spread of Fordism, an acceleration of the rhythm of capital intensification, and a rapid, regular increase in labor productivity, along with the growth of mass production.

The Pioneering Role of the United States and the Unequal Development of Intensive Accumulation

The examination of the way that intensive accumulation took hold in the other leading economies sheds additional light on the question. The United States undoubtedly played a pioneering role. From 1916 on, the growth of Taylorism was sufficiently important to have generated a clear acceleration of labor productivity both in industry and overall. In the case of the United States, it is possible to speak of a first boom in intensive accumulation during the 1920s, notwithstanding the fact that no acceleration in the growth of capital per worker is observed (see Table 1.2). The accumulation dynamic could not continue, however, and the crisis of the 1930s marked a significant break, the origins of which merit consideration (see Figure 1.1).

Like France, the other industrialized economies seemed very far behind. In Germany, productivity gains remained limited until 1929, and capital per worker even showed a decline between 1913 and 1929, which suggests that the mode of accumulation remained largely extensive and that Germany had difficulty overcoming the consequences of the First World War. The detailed studies of G.W. Hoffmann (1965) confirm this theory. In the production and conversion of metals and in chemicals, which had been the principal growth sectors of the German economy since the end of the nineteenth century, labor productivity rose less quickly between 1913 and 1929 than between 1890 and 1913. The low level of accumulation during the 1920s did not allow the introduction of new production processes. Even during the 1929–38 period, which, in Germany, was generally marked by an increase in production, there was no acceleration in productivity gains relative to the long-term trend.

Great Britain offers certain particular features: the increase in labor productivity was lower than that in all the other countries from 1900 to 1929, and there was no acceleration during the 1920s. The growth of capital per worker as well as the accumulation dynamic remained limited throughout the entire period. This situation reflects in part a hidden crisis of accumulation going back to the beginning of the century. The adaptation to new technologies was not easy, and Great Britain had difficulty recovering from the loss of its hegemony over the world economy. On the other hand, it seemed better able to surmount the crisis of the 1930s, in terms of renewed accumulation and productivity.

Japan constitutes an even more special case. During the first half of the twentieth century, it was not a leading economy but a country undergoing rapid industrialization. The years from 1910 to 1920 were marked by a boom in accumulation and productivity, partly brought on by the effects of the First World War. If the beginning of the 1920s appeared to be

Table 1.2

Labor Productivity, Capital Productivity, and Capitalistic Intensity (annual average growth rate in %, private sector)

		1900–1913	1913–1929	1929–1938	1938–1955	1955–1973	1973–1979	1979–1989
Germany								
	Y/N	1.9	0.2	2.2		3.9	3.1	1.6
	Y/K	0.1	0.7	1.1		−1.8	−1.0	−0.8
	K/N	2.0	−0.4	1.1		5.6	4.2	2.4
France								
	Y/N	2.7	1.9	0.5	1.7	5.9	2.9	2.5
	Y/K	0.1	0.1	−2.6		0.1	−1.1	−0.2
	K/N	2.6	1.8	3.0		5.8	4.1	2.8
United Kingdom								
	Y/N	0.3	0.9	0.7	1.2	2.8	1.5	2.4
	Y/K	−0.2	−0.4	0.8		−0.7	−1.6	0.6
	K/N	0.5	1.3	0		3.5	3.1	1.8
United States								
	Y/N	1.2	1.4	0.4	2.5	2.4	0	0.7
	Y/K	0.2	0.8	0.2		0	−1.3	−0.6
	K/N	1.3	0.6	0.2		2.4	1.3	1.3
Japan								
	Y/N					10.3	2.9	3.0
	Y/K	−0.8[1]	−0.7	0.4		0.1	−3.7	−1.4
	K/N					10.2	6.8	4.4

Source: 1900–73, GRESP–Rennes; 1973–89, OECD.
Y = production   *N* = employment   *K* = capital
[1]Average for 1905–1913.

a period of reconversion and halted growth, Japan quickly surmounted the sharp recession of 1930–31 and, for nearly fifteen years afterward, experienced very sustained accumulation. Overall, during the 1913–39 period, Japan was marked by significant structural changes. The First World War allowed the country to diversify and considerably strengthen its production system. Foreign trade, which most often showed a deficit between 1895 and 1914, recorded considerable surpluses between 1915 and 1919. The growth of the chemical, heavy equipment, and electrical industries surpassed that of textiles. During the long crisis of the 1920s, chemicals and metal conversion took over from textiles, which had been the principal sector of the first burst of industrialization between 1880 and 1913. The trend toward concentration was significant. The large firms set up the labor relations system that prevails to this day and which is based on the principles of lifelong employment and employee promotion through seniority. It is impossible, however, to conclude that an intensive accumulation system was established in the 1920s. The traditional sector (craft industry and agriculture) remained very important until around 1960, and many observers admit that until 1950, production techniques were still far from modern.

Outside the case of the American economy, the real development of intensive accumulation in the leading economies began only after the Second World War. There was thus greater convergence during the 1950s and 1960s, but each economy nonetheless retained its own features, reflecting the state of its economic and social structures. Accumulation was less sustained and productivity gains more limited in the United States after 1950 because of the advantage already held both in the 1920s and during the war-induced recovery after 1940. Unlike the other leading economies, the United States showed no acceleration in labor productivity after 1950.

In Germany, extremely high investment rates in the 1950s, the existence of a very considerable industrial potential inherited from the Nazi period, and the use of an abundant, skilled workforce (partly related to the influx of refugees from the East) all allowed sharp productivity gains resulting in positions of leadership, notably in intermediate and capital goods. In Japan, successive waves of accumulation led to a disruption of production conditions and an unprecedented transformation placing the country in the position of a leading economy from the end of the 1960s. As for Great Britain, it occupied a specific position, with accumulation rates still low and productivity gains limited, partly because of the difficulties encountered by British firms in setting up new production methods in the face of union resistance, and partly also because of the financial strategy of the "City" (the world's largest financial center located in London.)

The end of the 1960s marked a turning point in the intensive accumulation regime, as first signaled by the protest movements challenging the working conditions proper to Taylorism. Among the indicators reflecting the slowdown of the postwar growth mode, the rhythm of accumulation fell off in the United States and Germany at the end of the 1960s and the beginning of the 1970s. There was a reversal in Japan as well, and the rapid growth of productivity was not sustained in all the economies.

Although the development of Fordism and Taylorism is probably one of the major phenomena since the 1950s, it must be recognized that there are no quantitative evaluations that can be compared with data on labor productivity. On the one hand, there is no overall series on labor intensiveness. On the other, data on work conditions and the workforce are not sufficiently continuous to be directly connected to the national accounts. In an ingenious attempt, Weisskopf, Bowles, and Gordon (1983) have used this data to widen the impact of production functions. These three authors explain the development of American labor productivity by four main factors: the rate of utilization of production capacities, capital per worker, the effort to innovate resulting from the pressure of competition, and labor intensiveness. This last variable, which is not directly known, is evaluated on the basis of several factors: the extent of surveillance, which is compared to the proportion of office workers and managers in relation to workers; the likelihood of being laid off, which depends on unemployment rates and the power of the unions; and income losses resulting from being laid off. According to the authors, the slowdown in productivity gains observed in the United States at the end of the 1960s resulted above all from declines in innovation efforts and labor intensiveness. This explanation is based on the hypothesis that the trends observed from 1950 to 1979 can be explained within a single equation, which ultimately excludes the idea of an exhaustion of the potentialities of intensive growth.

The Long-Term Output per Capital Ratio

The output per capital ratio is used in numerous studies despite the fact that it remains much debated. An initial problem emerges on the level of its statistical weakness. This is already considerable for the period after the Second World War and even more so for the last seventy-five years, notably because of the conventions used to establish the accounting standards for the valuation of capital (depreciation, equipment life expectancy).

On the theoretical level, the ambiguities of this ratio are just as great, whether they involve the concept of global capital or the interpretations in terms of efficiency that are sometimes proposed. In particular, this relationship must not be considered as a purely technical reflection of the efficiency of production processes. Indeed, the very conditions in which these processes are transformed closely depend on the whole of social relations and in no way constitute an autonomous or purely technical given. Finally, the output per capital relationship is a flow–supply ratio that poorly describes fluctuations in magnitudes. The reversals that can be observed in its development should be interpreted with caution because they only bring out the effects of trends that have been at work for several years. Nonetheless, this ratio remains a useful indicator because of its synthetic nature, which allows the joint effects of labor productivity and intensification of capital to be summarized. In addition, it plays an important role as a determinant of the profitability of capital. These are the two aspects that will be examined here.

Over the long term, this ratio is stable in France, the United Kingdom, and Germany (see Figure 1.2). The case of the United States appears exceptional in this respect, because of the sharp rise that occurred during the 1940s. Beyond this initial observation, it can be ascertained that until

1913 the extensive accumulation regime predominated everywhere, and the output per capital ratio showed little change. After 1920, it was only in the United States that the establishment of intensive accumulation and the resulting productivity gains gave rise to a slight increase in the output per capital ratio, interrupted only by the crisis of 1929. In the other economies, extensive accumulation remained dominant throughout the 1920s. In Germany, the relative stability of the output per capital ratio that is observed can be related to the difficulties of the economy after the war (low productivity gains, sluggish investments). The creeping crisis experienced by the British economy since the beginning of the century was reflected in the slight decline in the efficiency of capital, tied to the low productivity gains. During the 1930s, the changing output per capital ratio only reflected the uneven intensity of the crisis and the fairly late nature of the recovery.

Here too, the spread of intensive accumulation throughout the leading economies after 1950 is clearly recognizable. It is initially reflected, as in France, by a considerable increase in the output per capital ratio relative to the prewar level. The scale of this development, however, varies from one country to another. Very pronounced in Japan, Germany, and France, it is practically nonexistent in Great Britain. Indeed, the financial strategy of the "City" and the restrictive practices of the British unions (control of hiring, defense of trades, limits on immigration, etc.) constituted an effective brake on the organization of new production methods. These practices prevented English industrialists from sufficiently intensifying labor, and the output per capital ratio could not increase.

In all countries, however, the intensification of production processes more than compensated for productivity gains, ultimately leading to the decrease in capital efficiency that got under way at different times according to the country involved: in the early 1950s in Great Britain, in 1960 in Germany, in the mid-1960s in Japan (if we speak of the branches as a whole). This decline was the least pronounced in the United States and France. The deterioration of the physical conditions of growth constituted a new sign of the gradual halt of the postwar mode of accumulation.

This brief analysis of the links between accumulation and productivity has allowed us to compare the regimes of extensive and intensive accumulation. A periodization for all of the leading economies has been outlined. An econometric approach should now allow us to verify some of our conclusions in the case of the French economy.

Econometric Analysis

If labor productivity is a key variable in the growth process, it is also one of the most difficult concepts to analyze because of the multiplicity of

16

Figure 1.2 **The Long-Term Output per Capital Ratio** (%; constant prices; for the United States and the United Kingdom, private sector; for Germany, France, Japan, private sector excluding agriculture)

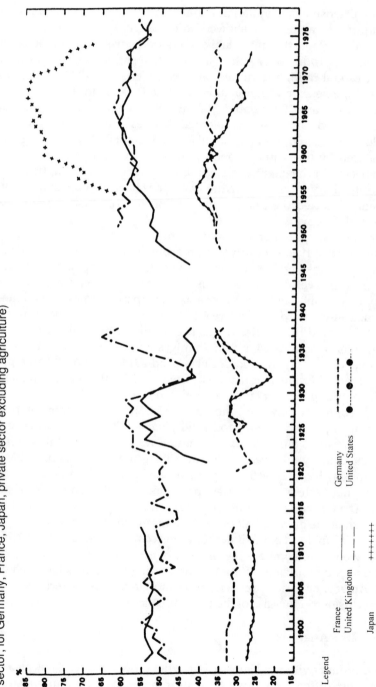

Legend

France ——
United Kingdom — — —

Japan ++++++

Germany —·—·—
United States ·····●·····

Source: GRESP-Rennes, France.

determinants involved. The links between productivity and capital are far from being perfectly explained. The measurement of capital stock is a subject of theoretical debates and presents practical difficulties, notably in the valuation of capital depreciation. Econometric tests of the production functions often prove to be uncertain, even if taking into account the various generations of equipment seems more satisfying than introducing a homogeneous capital stock into the functions.

Given these difficulties, we shall limit ourselves to partial results and simple econometric methods. We shall examine the links between labor productivity and capitalist intensity, first of all in the case of France, where a more detailed analysis of sectoral data will be carried out, and then in the case of the other leading economies. Certain conclusions from the preceding section, notably with regard to the ways of setting up intensive accumulation and the nature of the breaks following the two world wars, can thus be verified.

Nature of the Breaks in France Following the Two World Wars

The comparison between the 1921–29 period on the one hand and the 1945–73 period on the other takes on a certain significance because of its consequences for the interpretation of the 1929 crisis in France. According to several authors, including Boyer (1977, 1979b), the considerable acceleration of labor productivity gains observed after 1920 in France resulted in large part from an initial spread of the methods of labor intensification, which would then have come up against an inadequate expansion of demand at the end of the 1920s. According to this interpretation, there would have been a break in the long-term growth pattern of labor productivity because of the spread of Taylorism after the end of the First World War.

In the preceding section, we took a considerably different point of view, and this for several reasons. First, it is not certain that the 1921–29 period has been properly delimited, since in 1921 hourly productivity was at an abnormally low level. For all branches except agriculture, the 1921 level was 11 percent lower than that of 1913, eight years earlier. To be sure, from 1913 to 1929, the average annual growth rate of hourly productivity was 2.3 percent for all the branches except agriculture, as compared to 1.7 percent from 1896 to 1913. But this result was obtained through an acceleration in the consumer goods, service, and business sectors. Conversely, a deceleration can be observed in intermediate goods, capital goods, and transportation, which, apart from energy, were the most modern sectors.

Furthermore, in terms of per capita productivity, a deceleration can be observed during the 1913–29 period relative to the preceding period from 1896 to 1913. These results have inclined us toward the hypothesis that the gains recorded between 1921 and 1929 would be linked above all to a recovery of losses and delays accumulated during the First World War. But the other thesis (initial spread of Taylorism) cannot be totally excluded, and detailed monographic studies would in fact be necessary.

To take the analysis further, we have attempted to see whether the labor productivity gains between 1921 and 1929 can be explained apart from the trends observed between 1896 and 1913. This was done with econometric tests of productivity equations in the form:

$y - n = a\,(k/n) + bz + c$
where
y = annual growth rate of the value added by volume
n = annual growth rate of employee numbers
k/n = annual growth rate of capital per worker
z = indicator reflecting the short-term situation.

The tests were carried out on the annual data for the 1897–1913 period, which permitted estimates of the parameters a, b, and c. With the help of these equations, labor productivity was calculated by introducing the annual growth rates observed between 1922 and 1929. These productivities calculated from the functions observed between 1896 and 1913 were compared to the labor productivity observed between 1922 and 1929. Table 1.3 shows the results for 1929.

For the 1922–29 period, the observed productivity is less than or equal to the calculated productivity in all sectors. This means that the productivity gains were lower than what might have been expected on the basis of the relationship observed in the preceding period and in view of the accelerated growth of production after the First World War. This would suggest that there was no break in the productivity dynamic before 1929, at least not in the case of the French economy.

In order to verify these results, the same calculation was carried out for the 1949–73 period, taking as a base the productivity equations tested on the 1896–1938 period (with the exception of the years 1913–23). The results are presented in Table 1.4, where it can be seen, on the contrary, that for the 1949–73 period, observed productivity is greater than calculated productivity in five out of six sectors, the only exception being construction and public works. The difference is particularly significant for energy, which suggests that this sector was undergoing the greatest break in its dynamic. For the majority of sectors, the acceleration in productivity gains after the Second World War seems to reflect a break with earlier trends.

There would thus appear to be a qualitative difference between the 1921–29 period and that of 1949–73. In the first case, labor-productivity

Table 1.3

Productivity Gains During the 1920s in France

	Labor productivity in 1929 (1922 = 100)	
	observed productivity	calculated productivity
Consumer goods[1]	122.3	120.7
Capital goods	145.7	150.2
Intermediate goods[2]	121.1	151.8
Construction and public works (2)	133.8	142.4
Energy	114.1	119.7
Transportation	119.4	117.1

Equations used and tested on the 1897–1913 periods
$$y\text{-}n = a\,(k/n) + bz + c$$

	a	b	c	R^2 DW
Consumer goods(1)	1.15	0.98	−1.8	(0.51)
	(0.6)	(3.6)	(−0.6)	2.8
Capital goods	1.34	0.57	−3.15	(0.91)
	(2.2)	(8.8)	(2.9)	1.5
Intermediate goods(2)	−0.84	0.35	1.7	(0.31)
	(−0.6)	(2.2)	(0.6)	2.6
Construction and public works(2)	0.08	0.30	−0.25	(0.53)
	(0.2)	(3.3)	(−0.3)	2.6
Energy(1)	−0.03	0.76	−1.58	(0.51)
	(0.1)	(3.3)	(−1.7)	2.3
Transportation(1)	−0.18	0.84	0.01	(0.51)
	(−1.10)	(2.9)	ε	3.0

Note: [1] $z = (y + y_{-1})/2$
[2] $z = I$, investment growth rate

gains seem to result in very large part from a phenomenon of rapid recovery following the First World War. On the contrary, during the 1944–73 period, labor-productivity gains appear to reflect a real break that can be attributed to the spread of intensive accumulation.

The Case of the Other Major Countries

In the same way, productivity equations were tested by subperiods on the level of the economy as a whole. The results are presented for the two periods of stable growth, 1891–1913 and 1955–73. Those for the interwar period are less significant because of the variations in the rate of adjustment of employment during the deflationary periods, which modifies the scope of short-term fluctuations in capital per worker (see table 1.5).

Table 1.4

Labor Productivity in France, 1949–1973

	Labor productivity in 1959 (1949 = 100)		Labor productivity in 1973 (1949 = 100)	
	calculated	observed	calculated	observed
Consumer goods	115.7	156.3	141.4	326.7
Capital goods	132.8	135.0	214.9	307.5
Intermediate goods	119.1	169.3	128.8	377.3
Construction and public works	124.2	106.9	183.0	187.3
Energy	142.6	192.5	253.3	660.0
Transportation	122.7	162.9	164.9	286.9

Equations used and tested on the 1897–1913 Periods

$$y/n = a\,k/n + b[y - Y] + c$$

	a	b	c	R^2 DW
Consumer goods	−0.28	0.90	2.8	0.69
	(−1.2)	(7.6)	(4.7)	(1.1)
Capital goods	−0.13	0.84	3.8	0.57
	(−0.4)	(5.8)	(2.6)	(0.83)
Intermediate goods	−0.4	0.72	3.3	0.51
	(−1.6)	(4.5)	(3.3)	(0.89)
Construction and public works	0.10	0.87	2.3	0.52
	(0.4)	(5.3)	(1.8)	(1.3)
Energy	0.23	0.88	2.6	0.66
	(1.3)	(7.1)	(3.9)	(1.3)
Transportation	0.23	0.93	1.35	0.66
	(1.3)	(7.2)	(1.3)	(1.0)

Y = average annual growth rate for the period.

According to these results, it is not the residual trend that explains the productivity gains, since the constants are for the most part close to zero. On the other hand, the capitalist intensity elasticity of productivity increases, and the relations between these two variables becomes more significant after 1950. An analogous result was obtained for agriculture and the manufacturing sectors in France. It is likely that after the Second World War, the investment effort was more oriented toward productivity gains than before 1914; the accumulation of capital was more closely linked to the radical disruption of the organization of work.

The breaks in the productivity dynamic can be highlighted by comparing observed and calculated productivity on the basis of relations from the 1891–1913 period, which include the growth rates for capital per

Table 1.5

Productivity Equations

		a	b	c	R^2	DW
United States						
	1891-1916	0.36	0.78	0.77	0.96	2
		(3.8)	(17.1)	(3.0)		
	1951-1968	0.76	0.79	0.59	0.87	1.3
		(5.9)	(10.1)	(1.7)	0.92	1.1
United Kingdom						
	1891-1916	0.74	0.85	0	0.92	1.1
		(10.5)	(14.4)	(0.7)		
	1951-1968	0.77	0.86	0.1	0.96	1.4
		(12.3)	(18)	(1)		
Germany						
	1891-1916	n.s.	0.71	1.9	0.9	1.4
			(14.1)	(4.9)		
	1951-1968	0.8	0.92	0.4	0.87	1.0
		(3.6)	(7.2)	(0.3)		

Equation: $y/n = a\, k/n + b[\,y -Y] + c$
Y = average annual growth rate for the period

worker. The results for the interwar period are presented in Table 1.6.

In the interwar period, for the United States, the gap increases regularly, reaching a peak in 1938. In the United Kingdom, the change is much more limited. The German dynamic calls for another interpretation: the peak in fact occurs between 1930 and 1932 and declines sharply afterward; the productivity differential was transitory and linked to the period of violent deflation at the beginning of the 1930s. It basically results from the increase in the speed of adjustment of the numbers of workers at the beginning of the crisis. We shall return to this point further on.

For the 1950s, the same kinds of calculation bring out an exogenous acceleration—relative to the preceding periods—of productivity gains in France and in the Federal Republic of Germany. In the case of the latter, the break appears rather late, toward the end of the 1950s; the reconstruction, which really began only in 1949, lasted until 1957. It resulted in part from restarting of existing equipment and the hiring of a workforce that was abundant because of immigration; at the outset, the intensification remained relatively limited. The United Kingdom constitutes a case apart, as the only industrialized country in the West that did not go through a process of catching up to the American level, and it clearly fell behind relative to the other European countries.

Table 1.6

Relationship Between Observed and Calculated Productivity

Year	United States	United Kingdom	Germany
1920	100	100	—
1923	105	103	—
1925	108	104	100
1927	110	105	101
1929	112	106	103
1932	126	108	126
1935	135	110	117
1938	138	110	110
1954		100	100
1957		99	101
1960		97	108
1963		95	117
1968		91	144
1972		88	160

These calculations as a whole clearly show that there was a break in the labor productivity trends. This occurred during the First World War in the United States and perhaps in the United Kingdom, and during the 1950s in France and Germany. At its origin, the intensification of labor developed without an equivalent acceleration in the intensification of capital, which permitted a rise in the productivity of capital and an increase in profitability. Parallel to these new forms of work organization, new forms of employment and remuneration of the workforce were set up.

❖

The examination of the macroeconomic data on productivity brings out the fact that between 1916 and 1950, the United States took a clear lead over the other countries in the development of intensive accumulation. To be sure, from the 1920s on, European business circles were aware of the American methods and imitated them in the most modern firms. But on the scale of the economy as a whole, its effects remained limited. The sharp rise in productivity gains depended on both the possibilities of transforming production processes and work organization within the firms and the intensity of demand on the macroeconomic level. The intro-duction of Taylorism implied the imposition of very strong constraints on workers, with timeclocks and detailed instructions dictated by the depart-ment of planning and programming. At the beginning of the twentieth century, the American workforce seemed less capable of opposing the disruption of work methods: the unions were weak and had few measures of legal protection. Above all, the mass of workers was largely composed of low-skilled immigrants who were ready to accept trying work conditions.

During the 1920s, France enjoyed the most favorable macroeconomic conditions among the three major European countries. The reconquest of Alsace and Lorraine had strengthened the industrial apparatus. Demand increased steadily after the war, with the needs of reconstruction and the rapid rise in exports; this trend was facilitated by the depreciation of the franc, while the United Kingdom practiced policies that were systematically restrictive in order to defend an overvalued currency. These favorable factors allowed France to make up for part of the losses in productivity resulting from the war. But intensive accumulation remained limited, because the industrial structures were still marked by the split between the dynamic, modern branches and a multitude of traditional firms and activities. This structure was reinforced, moreover, by an attitude particular to the leaders of the Third Republic, who sought to limit major disruptions in order to preserve political and social equilibrium.

In Germany, macroeconomic conditions were unfavorable during the 1920s. Territorial losses had drastically reduced the capacities of the capital-goods sectors and weakened foreign competitiveness. The defeat and collapse of the imperial regime in 1918 had brought about a grave social and political crisis linked to the destruction of traditional values, and such a context was hardly favorable to the reinforcement of work discipline. Above all, foreign monetary and financial constraints prohibited Germany from showing any sustained growth: from 1927 on, the authorities were forced to put a halt to it, just when the recovery was beginning.

In continental Europe, the Second World War eliminated these blockages. In France, the defeat and the Occupation discredited the former elites and the ideology they transmitted. Growth and modernization became the primary objectives of the leadership. After a slight hesitation, the Allies decided to encourage German recovery, with considerable aid from the United States. From 1951 on, the Federal Republic showed current account surpluses that allowed it to increase its trade reserves quickly and to enjoy rapid growth without being subject to external constraints.

The backwardness of the United Kingdom has been variously interpreted. It is clear that after the relative recovery of the 1931–37 period, the country entered a vicious circle. Low productivity gains limited increases in real wages, which did not prevent the share of wages in the national income from increasing, at the expense of profits and investment. In addition, losses of world-market shares were both considerable and ongoing. The low levels of supply and demand fed each other. The trade-based union structure led workers' organizations to extend the field of negotiations to the content of work stations and to slow down changes in work methods. Furthermore, the capital-goods sector, which played a driving role in the development of

Fordism, saw its share of investment and capital stagnate while it was rising considerably in the other European countries. The mediocre performances in this sector functioned as a buffer limiting overall growth.

There is no doubt that the exceptional productivity gains registered in continental Europe and Japan during the 1950s and 1960s were in large part tied to a mechanism of catching up to the American model, which had gained an advantage during the preceding period. The OECD countries show a clear (inverse) correlation between their relative level of productivity in 1950 and their subsequent gains. This process was encouraged by the attitude of the United States, which, much more systematically than before, exported its growth regime. On the one hand, the authorities considered that it was in the country's interest to encourage the recovery of Europe and Japan by spreading their own model. On the other hand, the large American firms, which until 1940 had mainly been interested in their sphere of influence in Canada and Latin America, massively exported their capital goods, technologies, and capital toward the other industrialized countries. These exchanges of merchandise and capital made for the spread of a new form of growth on an international scale.

The real rise of intensive accumulation and Fordism in the whole of the leading economies dates only from the beginning of the 1950s. A greater similarity and a certain convergence thus appear in the forms of growth: the boom in accumulation led to an unprecedented acceleration in productivity. But this productivity is also linked to the acceleration in growth permitted by the emergence of mass consumption and new modes of income formation. Nonetheless, each economy manifests sharp particularities: the dominant nature and considerable "advance" of the United States; the dynamism of German industry that ensured very strong positions in capital goods from the 1950s on; the gradual halt in accumulation in Great Britain, where the new production methods penetrated less than elsewhere, partly because of the restrictive union practices, which helped to trap the English economy in a vicious circle; the disruption of production conditions because of very rapid accumulation in Japan, leading to a transformation that had no equivalent elsewhere.

The end of the 1960s, however, marked a turning point that can be perceived in terms of the deterioration of the physical conditions of growth: accumulation became increasingly costly in capital, and productivity gains no longer compensated for increasingly expensive production processes. Sharp social tensions developed in reaction to Fordist-type industrial work. This is one of the origins of the present crisis of intensive accumulation.

But the accumulation regimes cannot be analyzed independently of the forms of global reproduction and notably the modes of income formation and consumption that, in large part, condition the growth process.

CHAPTER TWO

Wage Formation and Consumption Standard

At the same time that the postwar period saw the gradual creation of a new accumulation regime characterized by the intensification of capital and an acceleration in the growth of labor productivity, regulation procedures underwent a profound transformation. Competitive regulation was replaced by regulation based on imperfect competition including monopolistic structures and administered pricing. Direct wages underwent a long, durable upward trend, while the indirect wage spread with social transfers. Likewise, the wage relation was considerably modified, in terms of both production conditions and social relations, leading to an improvement in the individual work contract, the recognition of unionization, and the appearance of collective agreements. Wages came to obey new laws: the rhythm of industrial activity exercised a less direct influence; a de facto wage–price index gradually came into being, and certain sectors assumed leadership roles. In sum, this more regular and sustained rise in wage income allowed the rapid advance of a new consumption standard from the 1950s on.

Wages and the Transformation of Wage Relations

Key Stages in the Evolution of the Wage Income

In France, there have been three notable changes in the long-term evolution of wages. After 1950, the nominal wage was less sensitive to the short-term economic situation than before, and the growth of real wages was markedly more sustained (see Table 2.1). It was also much more stable. In terms of annual data, the real wage declined six times between

Table 2.1

Real Wage Rate in the Leading Economies (annual average growth rate in %)

	Period						
Country	1896– 1913	1913– 1929	1929– 1938	1938– 1950	1950– 1973	1973– 1979	1979– 1989
France	2.5	2.4	2.7	–4.0	5.5	3.2	1.1
United States	1.9	1.7	0.8	2.6	2.4	0.3	0.0
Germany	1.3	1.5	–3.9	–	5.9[1]	2.8	1.2
United Kingdom	0.4	0.4	1.3	1.5	3.1	1.6	2.3
Japan	2.6	2.8	5.7		7.0[2]	2.7	1.6

Sources: 1896–1973, GRESP–Rennes series.
1973–1989, OECD series.
[1]Germany: 1951–73.
[2]Japan: 1953–73.

1897 and 1913 and nine times between 1923 and 1938; by contrast, the same annual data reveal no decline between 1952 and 1978. The regularity and forcefulness of the growth of real wages were thus able to stimulate the rise in the consumption standard.

The "social" wage was instituted, moreover, through an indirect income that served as a guarantee against certain risks (illness, maternity, old age, on-the-job accidents, unemployment), with wage-earners contributing to this benefit. In France, employers were long divided over the social regulations and the organization of social protection systems, while on the union side, there was ongoing antagonism between reformist and revolutionary unions. This probably explains the rather belated appearance of the trend toward the "social" wage. Until the passage of the social protection and family allowance laws of 1928, 1930, and 1932, the indirect wage remained negligible, representing less than 2 percent of the total wage. As a result of the crisis and the political change of 1936, this proportion was to reach 4.6 percent in 1937, but social protection did not really develop until after 1946. Thus, by 1952 the indirect wage represented 20.5 percent of the total wage, and by 1977, 30.2 percent.

The differentials among average sectoral wages also declined between 1896 and 1970. The reduction of the spectrum basically occurred after the two world wars. However, the hierarchy among the sectors remained stable. The decrease in wage differentials was another factor encouraging the spread of the consumption standard proper to Fordism.

Similar changes can be observed in the other leading economies (see Table 2.1). Until the Second World War, the nominal wage underwent frequent decreases, especially in the United States and Japan. This dependence in relation to short-term fluctuations diminished markedly after

1950. Likewise, the growth of the real wage rate became more rapid and more regular. Only in the United Kingdom did purchasing power stagnate for several years. The emergence of the trend toward the "social" wage varied from one country to another. In Germany, which was somewhat of a pioneer, a modern system of social protection was created at the end of the nineteenth century. In Great Britain, a wide range of health and unemployment insurance was set up after 1911. The social context was very particular in these two countries, where modern employers coexisted with a highly structured workers' movement. In the United States, on the other hand, somewhat as in France, social policy developed later, from the 1930s on. Nonetheless, the social-wage system was different, and indirect wages represented a smaller proportion of total wages than in France.

The Transformation of Wage Relations

With the transformation of the mode of accumulation, the expansion of the wage-earning class gave greater power to its members. The State was increasingly led to intervene in wage relations by instituting regulations (expanded labor and social laws) and encouraging the negotiated settlement of labor conflicts through collective agreements, in the same way that it had expanded social transfers and the indirect wage. A new social compromise could thus be instituted.

At the turn of the century, the expansion of the industrial wage-earning class and the rise of unionization went hand in hand with urbanization, even if these trends were less powerful and later in France than in Great Britain and Germany. This expansion continued until the 1930s. In 1931, factory and office workers in France constituted three-quarters of the industrial workforce and more than 54 percent of the total workforce. Pressure from the growing number of wage-earners was reinforced by that from the emergence and spread of unionism, held in check by management resistance. This development began at the turn of the century: in 1892, there were 140,000 union members in France; by 1909 the figure had reached 945,000. One specific feature of this unionization should be noted. The union movement at this time opted for a relatively elitist and minority approach, notably because of the anti-worker repression that had followed the Paris Commune, the weight of agricultural structures, and the survival of organizations close to guilds and crafts in cottage industry. Union federations were mainly established in the traditional occupations, and there was no development of a mass-based, reformist unionism. This situation left lasting traces until after the Second World War. Thus, in spite of the changing face of French unionism, the membership rate remained lower in France than in most other countries of northern Europe, unlike the situation that was to prevail in the 1950s and 1960s with the growing power of the major union organizations. Labor conflicts were to increase between 1890 and 1908 and again at the end of the First World War, although at that time, there were few conflicts concerning the organization of work. During the crisis years, from 1931 to 1940, the number of strikes reached a peak; the trend resumed after 1947 and at the beginning of the 1950s, then declined in the following years. At the end of the 1960s, wage demands reemerged in France, as elsewhere in Europe, and remained at a high level until 1975. These were most often related to disputes over forms of work and processes of deskilling; the crisis of industrial work was one element in the economic crisis.

In Great Britain, collective bargaining goes back to the beginning of the nineteenth century, and the tradition was solidly established after 1860. First introduced on the regional level, it spread after 1914 in order to avoid competition from low-wage areas.

In France, collective bargaining appeared for the first time at the end of the nineteenth century, but its real development came later. An 1892 law encouraged government conciliation and arbitration in case of collective disagreements between management and employees (mining conflicts). But the unions were only recognized legally in 1919 in accordance with the promise made during the war. The spread of such negotiations and collective agreements in France was nonetheless limited. There was frequent recourse to strikes, and these rarely led to collective agreements (in 5 to 8 percent of the cases from 1919 to 1929). In 1939 the International Labor Office (ILO) was able to note "the growing importance of collective agreements as an element of the society's social and economic framework." This observation holds true for Great Britain, the Netherlands, Norway, Austria, and Sweden. In France, it was only in 1936 that there was mutual recognition between employer and employee unions and real negotiation got under way. Overall, it was mainly after 1949, the year of the international convention on the right of organization and collective bargaining defined by the ILO, that negotiations and collective agreements became widespread in the private sector, paralleling the expansion of social policy.

Until the mid-1970s, the spread of collective bargaining predominated, with a greater number of issues addressed (length of work, training, monthly pay of workers, hours, profit sharing). The agreements were increasingly applied on the interoccupational level and concerned sectors where they had previously occupied little place (the public sector). This was the era of the progress contracts, rather typical of the wage-formation regimes adapted to the mass production and consumption system. Thus, significant breaks appeared in the long-term evolution of wages, while wage relations underwent profound transformations. What, then, were the consequences in terms of wage-formation laws?

Wage Formation: From Competitive Regulation to Administered Regulation

Different elements have already been cited to support the thesis of a shift to a new form of wage regulation. More stable direct wages, complemented by indirect wages, and more negotiated social compromises leading to collective agreements are the new forms that developed at various moments according to the country. A systematic study of the changes in the regulation procedures can now be added to these elements, first of all by examining the impact of employment adjustments on wage income, then by studying the transformations of wage formation in each of these countries. Significant differences can thus be singled out.

Wage Income and the Adjustment of Employment

In competitive regulation, the wage income depends largely on the rhythms of economic activity, while in administered regulation, this link tends to disappear (Boyer 1978). This gradual separation can be explained by three groups of factors going back to the different components of the wage income. First of all, employment adjusts more quickly to economic fluctuations in competitive regulation than in monopolistic regulation, which shows certain rigidities. The increase in per capita wage rates, meanwhile, becomes more independent of the short-term situation. And the growth of the indirect wage makes the wage income more autonomous relative to the rhythms of economic activity.

The adjustment of employment relative to fluctuations in production is traditionally analyzed by comparing the observed numbers of employees (N_t) to the numbers of technically efficient employees (N_t^*), where the latter is calculated with the help of a production function or, more simply, on the basis of a long-term pattern of labor-productivity growth (π^*).

(1) $\quad N_t/N_t^* - 1 = (N_t^*/N_{t-1})^\lambda$ with

(2) $\quad N_t^* = N_0 Y_t^{\alpha} e^{\gamma t}$

(to keep things simple), or

(2b) $\quad N_t^* = Y_t / \pi^{*\alpha}$

or, after differentiation:

(3) $\quad n_t = a y_t + b n_{t-1} + c$

with $b = 1-\lambda$, where λ designates the speed of adjustment of employment.

Econometric analysis thus allows the speed of adjustment of employment to be measured indirectly, but the direct method, by means of the productivity trend, while more imprecise, offers the advantage of being applicable to shorter periods.

Table 2.2

Adjustment of Employment to Production

		a	b	c	R^2	DW	λ
United States							
	1892-1913	0.35	0.11	0.63	0.79	2.7	0.89
		(8.8)	(1)	(1.6)			
	1920-1940	0.6	−0.23	−0.8	0.87	2.7	1.23
		(10.6)	(−2.4)	(−2.0)			
	1952-1965	0.61	0.11	−1.2	0.64	2.6	0.89
		(3.6)	(0.5)	(−1.4)			
	1966-1979	0.5	0.43	−0.5	0.65	2.3	0.57
		(4.6)	(2.4)	(−0.8)			
United Kingdom							
	1892-1913	0.49	0.06	0.21	0.48	2	0.94
		(3.8)	(0.3)	(0.6)			
	1922-1938	0.38	0.24	−0.11	0.81	2.1	0.76
		(7.6)	(4.1)	(−0.4)			
	1951-1969	0.64	0.04	−1.7	0.77	1.6	0.96
		(6.7)	(0.3)	(−3.6)			
	1969-1980	0.4	0.47	−1.3	0.64	2.1	0.53
		(3.9)	(2.1)	(−3.2)			
Germany							
	1892-1913	0.15	0.41	0.33	0.39	1.5	0.59
		(2.7)	(2.4)	(0.9)			
	1927-1938	0.48	0.22	−1.2	0.94	2.6	0.78
		(10)	(2.6)	(−2.4)			
	1952-1969	0.41	0.4	−2.1	0.87	2.3	0.6
		(7.3)	(4.2)	(−5.5)			
	1969-1978	0.44	0.4	−1.9	0.9	1.1	0.6
		(6.4)	(3.2)	(−5.7)			
France							
	1898-1929[1]	0.01	0.73	0.26	0.41	1.3	0.27
		(0.7)	(2.6)	(1.0)			
	1930-1938[2]						0.59
	1954-1973	0.42	0.28	−1.46	0.39	2.1	0.72
		(3.2)	(1.6)	(−1.7)			
	1974-1977[2]						0.14

$n_t = ay_t + bn_{t-1} + c$

$\lambda = 1 - b$ (whole economy except agriculture)

[1] Except 1914-23

[2] Direct computation with the productivity trend.

Interesting results, in line with those already obtained by Boyer and Mistral (1983), can thus be obtained, and these permit the opposition of competitive and monopolistic regulation of employment. But significant differences emerge from one country to another (see Table 2.2). The speed of adjustment of employment increased during the crisis of the 1930s in the United States, Germany, and France, while it decreased during that of the 1970s in the United States, the United Kingdom, and France. This pattern helps to explain the decline in prices during the first crisis and, conversely, played a role in the acceleration of inflation during the first phase of the current crisis. Likewise, the adjustments in employment that were carried out at the beginning of the 1930s can be related to the cumulative process of decline observed during these years. Conversely, it was the defense of employment during the 1970s that helped to limit the extent of the recession.

The United Kingdom was an exception during the 1930s because deflation there was less serious than elsewhere. On the other hand, Germany stood out in the 1970s because it was very quick to make disinflation a priority. A second result raises more of a problem with regard to regulation theory. In the United States, Germany, and the United Kingdom, the adjustment of employment took place at the same rate before the First World War and after the Second World War. In the case of France, it was even faster after 1950. The transformation of the growth regime does not seem to have led to the expected slowdown. Nonetheless, it is true that growth was very regular during the 1950s and 1960s, which made the necessary adjustments less significant.

Wages in France: From Competitive to Monopolistic Regulation

Over the long term, wage regulation in France underwent a double evolution that was very characteristic of the shift from competitive to monopolistic regulation. The link between wage rates and fluctuations in economic activity tends to diminish over time (see Table 2.3). From the 1960s on, the effect of short-term pressures on nominal wages clearly diminished and became less significant. This analysis is also confirmed in a Phillips-type curve, where it can be observed that the unemployment rate, representative of disequilibria in employment, exerted a significant negative influence on wage rates before 1913 and during the interwar period. After the Second World War its influence decreased considerably (see Table 2.4). It must also be noted, following Boyer (1979b), that the wage–unemployment relation shows a very pronounced separation after 1933 and during the 1970s, which suggests that the regulator effect of the unemployment rate is altered by massive unemployment.

The second characteristic of the shift to a monopolistic-type regulation is the spread of the indexation of the nominal wage to prices. This only began to appear after the First World War. Econometric tests on the 1896–1913 period show that no significant wage–price correlation can be obtained regardless of the specification used (see Tables 2.3 and 2.4). The hypothesis of an indexation of wages to prices, even partially, must thus

Table 2.3

Determinants of Wage Rates in France

	a	b	c	R^2	DW
1897-1913[1]	0.32	0.62	0.8	0.67	2.8
	(-0.6)	(1.6)	(0.8)		
1923-1938	0.71	0.27	1.1	0.78	1.7
	(6.3)	(2.5)	(1.0)		
1953-1969	0.71	0.7	1.2	0.77	1.7
	(6.5)	(4.4)	(1.1)		
1959-1977	1.1	0.39	2.1	0.83	2.0
	(8.0)	(1.9)	(1.2)		

$w = apc + by + c$
with w = wage rate
      y = production at constant prices
      pc = consumer price index
(annual growth rates)
(whole of economy except agriculture)
[1]with one mute variable in 1906.

Table 2.4

The Phillips Curve in France

	a	b	R^2	DW
1901–1913	0.006	−0.06	0.44	1.9
	(0.5)	(2.5)		
1920–1938	0.63	−0.03	0.80	1.5
	(7)	(1.9)		
1951–1985	1.1	−0.02	0.86	2.0
	(12.6)	(−3.6)		

Source: P. Villa (1993).
$w = apc + b \log U + c$
U = rate of unemployment

be rejected for the years prior to the First World War. After 1923, variations in prices intervene significantly in the formation of nominal wages.
The parameters of the price elasticity of wages are estimated with enough
precision for us to conclude that during the 1923–38 and 1952–69 periods,
indexation of wages to prices remained partial. According to the adjustments, the indexation coefficient ranges between 0.6 and 0.7, with no
basic difference between the two periods in this respect. On the contrary,
from the 1960s on, the adjustments show that elasticity is very close to 1
and that a mobile scale based on cost-of-living adjustments emerges. In this

respect, the results obtained here agree with those presented by Boyer (1979b).

The last characteristic of monopolistic or administered regulation of wages is the social wage and the spread of social transfers from the 1950s on, which contributed to the separation of the wage income from fluctuations in economic activity.

United States: Precocious Indexation but Persistence of More Competitive Regulation

From the 1892–1916 period on, the indexation of wages to prices was already fairly strong, while the sensitivity to employment growth rates, used as an indicator of pressure from demand, was high (see Table 2.5). These results are close to those obtained in the American studies, all of which conclude that before 1916 wages were linked to prices. For Eckstein and Girola (1978), elasticity is taken to be 1.3 in the short term and 1 in the long term; for Bathia (1961), between 0.6 and 0.9; and for Gordon (1975), equal to 0.61. Price rises have considerable repercussions on wages. The estimates obtained for the 1892–1929 period (including the war years) yield parameters very close to those for the 1892–1916 period. The wage regulation of the 1920s is the same as that before the war, with an almost total indexation and a workforce strength elasticity of employee wages close to 1. The stability of the wage dynamic contrasts with the shift to intensive accumulation that occurred from the 1920s on. The equation for the 1923–38 period yields coefficients fairly close to those of the preceding periods. In spite of the reforms adopted during the 1930s, the wage dynamic underwent few modifications. However, in 1934 and 1935, the deliberate reinflation measures led to sharp rises in wages.

After the Second World War, the aggregate demand elasticity of wages showed a clear decline but nonetheless remained significant. This suggests a weakening of the link with pressure from demand. Sachs (1980) arrives at an analogous result by using the separation of industrial production from its trend as an indicator. On the other hand, Gordon (1975) and Eckstein and Girola (1978) conclude a stable relationship between wages and unemployment rate. But the unemployment series for the period prior to 1914 were established by extrapolating the results of the ten-year surveys and do not constitute reliable data for long-term comparisons. According to our results, wage indexation is less strong than before the war and, above all, slower. In the prewar period, most price rises impacted on wages within one year. From the 1950s on, there was a delay of two to three years, and by the beginning of the 1960s, nominal wages had become rigid. This result, which is confirmed by most recent studies on the United States, must be related to the nature of the collective agreements.

Table 2.5

United States, Wage Equations

	P	P_{-1}	$0.5\,(P + P_{-1})$	N	Constant	R^2 and DW
1892–1916	0.8	0.24		0.78	−0.2	0.81
	(4.2)	(1.0)		(4.4)	(−0.4)	2.4
1892–1929	0.77	0.29		0.78	0	0.91
	(9.7)	(3.1)		(4.6)	(0)	2.5
1920-1938			0.77	0.83	1.1	0.94
			(5.7)	(7.8)	(2.5)	2.2
1952-1969			0.65	0.33	2.1	0.44
			(2.5)	(2.9)	(2.5)	1.4
1965-1980			0.8	0.19	2.6	0.77
			(6.5)	(1.8)	(3.2)	2.3

P = consumer price index
N = employment
(annual growth rate)

The passage of the Wagner Act in 1935 strengthened the unions. The 1945–47 period was marked by numerous social conflicts, leading in turn to a concentration of worker demands. By 1947, however, the Taft–Hartley Law limited the right to strike, along with the influence of the unions. In 1948, the heads of General Motors and the United Auto Workers signed a three-year agreement, and this kind of settlement was subsequently applied in many other industries. As a result, wages became less sensitive to demand, the indexation mechanism slowed down, and the exogenous trend of wages increased: the agreements were signed with the implicit or explicit assumption that productivity gains would permit a rise in real wages. In the United States, the monopolistic regulation of wages is not accompanied by a sharp indexation in the short term. There, it implies the rigidity of the nominal wage but not that of the real wage, whereas in Europe, indexation is more rapid, which is apparently related to the fact that wage negotiations are carried out on an annual basis. During the 1970s, indexation grew slightly stronger, which is normal for a period of accelerated inflation because the agents seek increasing protection from price rises. The sensitivity of wages to the pressure of demand continued to decline.

United Kingdom: Precocious Monopolistic Regulation

For the United Kingdom, the unemployment rate and the growth rate of the gross domestic product are the two most significant indicators of pressure from demand (Table 2.6). Before 1914, the influence of the unemployment rate was quite significant, which corresponds to the conclu-

Table 2.6

United Kingdom, Wage Equations

	P	log U	Y	Constant	R^2 and DW
1892–1913	0.59	−1.97		3.1	0.57
except 1907	(2.7)	(−2.7)		(2.8)	1.8
1892–1913	0.91		0.41	−0.3	0.55
except 1907	(4.3)		(2.5)	(−0.8)	1.6
1923–1938	0.98	0.27	0.77	0.4	0.63
	(4.5)	(0.1)		(0)	3.6
1923–1938	0.94		0.2	0.5	0.68
	(4.8)		(1.5)	(0.9)	3.2
1952–1969	0.57	−0.8		4.9	0.57
	(3.9)	(−0.1)		(6.7)	1.7
1952–1969	0.78		0.2	3.3	0.60
	(4.5)		(1.5)	(3.9)	1.8
1965–1980	0.95	−1.1		4.9	0.79
	(5.8)	(−0.5)		(2.2)	2
1965–1980	0.86		−0.2	4.8	0.79
	(5.6)		(−0.4)	(2.2)	1.9

Note: P and Y = consumer price index and gross domestic product (annual growth rate).
U = unemployment rate.
1907: Sharp wage increases obtained following the threat of a general strike of transport workers.

sions of Phillips (1958) and Lipsey (1960). Wages were partially indexed to prices. Lipsey has obtained lower elasticities, between 0.21 and 0.37, but his estimate covers the 1862–1913 period. From 1923 to 1938, the influence of unemployment disappears, while indexation is nearly total, which corresponds rather well to Lipsey's results. The link between wage and activity, which was strong during the 1920s, breaks down in 1931–32. This can be interpreted by supposing that when unemployment is high, its fluctuations no longer affect wages. But the insensitivity of wages continued after the Second World War, which suggests a structural rather than a short-term change. It should be noted that the United Kingdom broke definitively with the gold standard in 1931, which meant that monetary policy was no longer exclusively determined by the desire to stabilize money and prices. British unions had grown much stronger before and after the First World War, but they were weakened by the failure of the 1926 general strike, which confirmed the victory of deflationary policies. From 1933 on, the number of union members was again on the rise, and this trend accelerated sharply during the Second World War.

The characteristics of the 1930s were to continue after the war: wages showed little sensitivity to demand and were strongly indexed, but the exogenous trend showed a clear increase. Indexation grew with the rising inflation of the 1970s.

The evolution of wages since the 1960s has been the subject of a fairly large number of comparative studies dealing with the main OECD countries (see especially Coe 1985; and Grubb, Jackman, and Layard 1983). These generally conclude that in Europe, real wages are rigid because of sharp indexation, and little affected by unemployment, while nominal wages are sensitive to the short-term situation in Japan and rigid in the United States. This European-style monopolistic regulation developed very early in the United Kingdom, a phenomenon that seems partly related to the characteristics of the union movement. From the beginning of the twentieth century, union organizations had a large number of members, and they increased their influence by encouraging the birth of the Labor Party, with which they maintain organic ties. Government authorities gradually recognized them as valid interlocutors and no longer sought to limit their activity. Although the different organizations are grouped together on the national level in the Trade Union Congresses (TUCs), within the industries and the firms, management has to negotiate with a multiplicity of trade unions and sectoral unions that may compete with each other and rarely accept a single discipline. Negotiations do not result in stable compromises; in the United Kingdom, they are one aspect of social conflicts in which there is constant pressure for higher wages. During the 1980s, the Conservative government tried to reduce the influence of the unions, but among all the European countries, the United Kingdom was the one in which the purchasing power of the average wage showed the greatest increase.

Germany: Growing Indexation but Persistence of Greater Wage Flexibility

For Germany, significant results have been obtained on the basis of equations with a specification close to those used for the United Kingdom. The interwar period, which is not homogeneous, is not dealt with here (Table 2.7).

Before 1914, wages were partly indexed to prices and very sensitive to pressure from demand. In spite of the growth of social protection and the strengthening of the unions, regulation was largely competitive. During the first half of the 1950s, unemployment was high, and the exceptionally good economic situation was above all linked to reconstruction, with the result that the German economy developed under particular conditions. Over the 1958–80 period, indexation was considerably higher than before 1914, but wages remained sensitive to the economic situation, even in the 1970s; from 1974 on, the crisis led to a slowdown in wage increases. This last feature distinguishes the evolution of wages in the Federal Republic of Germany from that noted in France and the United Kingdom. The

Table 2.7

Germany, Wage Equations

	P	P_{-1}	$0.5 (P + P_{-1})$	U	Y	Constant	R^2 and DW
1892–1913			0.41	−0.64		3.5	0.70
			(3.3)	(−4.4)		(7.7)	1.4
1892–1913			0.61		0.34	0.6	0.54
			(4.2)		(2.5)	1.1	1.6
1958–1980[1]	0.82	0.31			0.66	1.3	0.66
	(3.6)	(1.1)			(4.5)	(1.0)	1.5
1965–1980[1]	0.82			−0.75		6.3	0.67
	(4.2)			(−2.9)		(6.0)	2.0

Note: P and Y = consumer price index and gross domestic product (annual growth rate). U = unemployment rate.

[1] Except 1970, when there was a sharp rise in wages following numerous conflicts.

choices of economic policy were different in these three countries. Once the war was over, France accepted inflation in order to stimulate growth, and the United Kingdom hesitated between recovery and austerity. In West Germany, where the memory of the instability of the interwar period remained strong, the authorities and public opinion were more attached to respecting the major equilibria. Even during the 1960s, a severe austerity plan was implemented in 1965–66, which resulted in the sharp recession of 1967. This position was accentuated at the beginning of the 1970s with the rise of inflation. The central bank subjected firms to a strict monetary constraint, which meant relatively high real interest rates and the appreciation of the mark. This policy led industrial firms to undertake significant workforce cutbacks and to resist requests for wage increases.

German unionism also offers certain specific features. In the United Kingdom, for reasons of organization, and in France, for ideological reasons, the different unions are in competition with each other, and this often leads them to multiply the pressure they exert through their demands. In Germany, a single organization exercises significant influence, and its decision-making procedures, as in the Scandinavian countries, are centralized. This allows negotiations to be concluded by taking into account macroeconomic data, where the opposition to inflation plays an important role.

In the main industrialized countries, it has fairly often been the case that the evolution of wage regulation does not coincide with changes in the accumulation regime. This is due to the fact that the evolution of methods for organizing work largely depends on decisions made within the firms, while the evolution of wages depends above all on world political and social conditions. In the United States, the acceleration of productivity gains appeared, on the macroeconomic level, during the First World War, but wage regulation remained unchanged until the 1930s. Conversely, in the United Kingdom, monopolistic wage regulation appeared during the 1930s, while productivity gains remained limited. In France and Germany, the transformation of the accumulation regime and that of wage regulation developed almost simultaneously from the 1950s on, with the result being that these two countries benefited from sustained, stable growth until the crisis of Fordism. On the other hand, even during the 1960s, when Fordism was triumphant, there were differences from one country to another concerning the indexation of wages and the sensitivity of wages to the economic situation. In terms of wage equations, the shift to monopolistic regulation led in all four countries to a revival of the exogenous trend resulting from the fact that high productivity gains were at the basis of the wage dynamic. This coherence was called into question in the short term by the import levies on oil and, in the longer term, by the slowdown in labor productivity gains.

Wage Relation and Consumption Standards

After the Second World War, the new forms of wage income formation created sufficient demand to guarantee the rapid rise of mass production and consumption at the same time that lifestyles as a whole were radically altered.

The Emergence of a New Consumption Standard

Until the end of the 1930s, the structure of worker expenditures remained remarkably stable in France. The proportion of food expenditures declined only from 70 to 60 percent between 1856 and 1930 (see Table 2.8). Most of the reproduction of the labor force thus took place outside the capitalist sphere of production, properly speaking. The improvement of the workers' standard of living occurred mainly through a diversification of their food expenditures, notably with a sharp decrease in grain consumption. The shift became even clearer in France from the 1950s on, and the same development can be observed throughout the leading economies (see Table 2.9). The proportion of food expenditures showed a sharp drop, while those related to housing, transportation, and health and personal hygiene increased. The change in the consumption structure was closely linked to the spread of intensive accumulation, the accelerated rise of wage income, and the accompanying trend toward urbanization. Expenditures for household goods increased with the construction of new housing units, while the spread of suburban housing projects led to a sharp rise in transportation expenditures (mainly individual, moreover).

The spread of a new mode of consumption did not eliminate inequali-

Table 2.8

Long-Term Evolution of Worker Expenditures in France (1856-1930) (% of total consumption in current prices)

	1856	1890	1905	1930
Food	70.7	65.0	63.6	60.0
including grains	21.8	13.8	12.1	7.2
Clothing	12.2	12.6	10.5	12.6
Housing	15.2	15.7	17.1	17.8
Health-hygiene	1.3	4.0	4.7	3.9
Transportation	—	0.4	1.0	0.9
Other	0.6	2.1	3.0	4.7

Source: J. Singer-Kerel (1961).

ties, however. Between 1856 and 1971, gaps were considerably reduced in France; thus, the level of total consumption in 1956 was 4.2 times greater for executives than for agricultural workers. This figure declined to 2.9 in 1971, but greater inequalities continued to exist (3.6 for domestic spending, 11.3 for vacations). Outside of such income differentials, other factors particular to each category, such as lifestyle and social standards, also intervened.

The analysis of changes in household expenditures must be taken further. Along with individual consumer goods likely to arise from mass production, the consumption of collective goods (culture and leisure activities, education, and above all, health and personal hygiene) rose just as quickly, if not more so. Health and education expenditures constitute a separate category because their mode of financing varies from one country to another. The former experienced the most rapid growth in the United States, while their advance was more moderate in West Germany and the United Kingdom. Since the beginning of the crisis, certain shifts have emerged because of the decline in revenues and the pattern of relative prices, without, however, marking a break in the mode of consumption. Certain factors (housing costs, health, transportation) underwent less of a change than others that came to represent a smaller share (clothing, consumer durables).

Relative Prices, Production Conditions, and Consumption Standard

The impact of mass production on the structure of consumption emerges more clearly when constant prices are used. Thus, the products showing the most rapid growth by volume in France from 1959 to 1973 are automobiles and household goods, along with furniture (see Table 2.10). The

Table 2.9

Changes in Budget Coefficients (in current prices)

	France			Germany			United Kingdom			United States		
	1960	1973	1979	1960	1973	1979	1960	1973	1979	1960	1973	1979
Food	38.3	28.3	26.4	37.7	29.6	27.9	32.7	24.8	24.9	24.0	19.9	18.9
Clothing	11.2	9.0	8.1	11.7	10.6	10.0	10.5	9.1	8.0	9.8	8.9	7.9
Housing	12.2	16.8	18.2	13.2	17.0	17.5	14.6	18.6	19.8	20.6	21.5	23.2
Household goods	11.9	11.6	11.1	13.1	12.9	12.0	8.6	7.9	7.3	8.7	9.1	8.4
Individual transport	2.5	3.7	3.8	2.4	3.5	4.5	3.5	4.2	4.4	5.9	7.0	7.1
Transport and communications	8.6	9.9	11.2	6.9	10.2	11.5	6.8	9.5	10.0	10.4	11.1	11.9
Entertainment	5.8	6.8	7.3	7.3	7.7	7.6	7.6	9.1	9.2	6.0	7.7	7.7
Miscellaneous goods and services	9.5	13.8	14.0	7.7	8.5	9.0	15.8	16.9	16.4	14.5	14.8	14.9

Source: F. Gardes (1983).

Table 2.10

Structure of Household Consumption in France for Certain Household Durables (1959-1979)

	1959	1973	1979
Constant prices			
Automobiles	1.6	3.3	3.1
Household Equipment	1.6	2.7	3.4
Furniture	3.5	5.6	6.0
Current prices			
Automobiles	2.1	3.3	3.4
Household Equipment	2.8	2.4	2.3
Furniture	4.0	5.4	5.8

Source: INSEE.

budget coefficients for these products in constant prices are practically two times greater. On the other hand, in current prices, the increases are much smaller. For household goods, the decline in relative prices is such that it more than compensates for the increase by volume and the share of products with declining consumption by value. Overall, there is a negative correlation between prices and growth of consumption by volume, a correlation that directly reflects the interaction between the transformation of production conditions and the development of a new consumption standard. There are certain significant exceptions, however, notably housing and health expenditures, which increase rapidly in spite of the rise in their relative prices. In the case of housing, the presence of real estate capital and the limited nature of the industrialization process in the construction industry explain why the logic of Fordism hardly penetrated this sector. In the case of health expenditures, the particularities of their financing and the fact that it is assumed by the government are partly responsible for this kind of development. It should be noted, moreover, that with regard to medications, there is the same negative correlation between the decline of relative prices and rapid growth of consumption. In fact, health services (hospital expenditures) show an especially rapid increase in consumption and costs.

❖

The new laws of wage formation emerging after the 1929 crisis allowed the rapid rise of mass consumption by guaranteeing an increase in purchasing power that was faster and less dependent on fluctuations in economic activity than before. There was thus a great coherence in the disruptions occurring on the level of production conditions. The sharp productivity gains that resulted permitted in exchange the increase in real wages. New wage relations, with the spread of collective bargaining and a globalization of the social contract, served to hold everything together. Ultimately, the strength of the mode of growth in the postwar period depended on this close link between the transformation of production processes, the radical change in lifestyles, and the emergence of a new wage relation.

CHAPTER THREE

Price, Profit, and Accumulation

The analysis of changes in modes of fixing prices and profits, as well as in the investment dynamic, will extend the previous observations about the gradual transformation of regulation procedures over the long term. The modifications that have occurred since the beginning of the century will be compared to changes in forms of competition and the functioning of the monetary and financial systems.

An econometric analysis will illustrate the modalities of a shift from competitive regulation to a more administered regulation of prices. The study of the explanatory factors of investment will allow us to qualify the nature of the profit–accumulation linkage and situate it in the context of the previously identified accumulation regimes.

In a final section, the analysis of the modes of overall reproduction will thus take into account the common effects of different regulatory mechanisms on income distribution: the maintenance of the wage share in a certain "area of invariance" and the relative stability of the long-term rate of profit will illustrate the capitalist system's ability to ensure its reproduction, whether through regulation procedures endowed with a certain stability in periods of normal growth or through profound transformations in a period of crisis for the accumulation regime.

Inflation, Forms of Competition, and Monetary Regime

The Development of the Inflationary Process

The evolution of the general level of prices since the beginning of the century reveals significant breaks since the Second World War. While

Table 3.1

Consumer Price Index in the Leading Economies (average annual growth rate in %)

	1896–1913	1913–1920	1920–1929	1929–1938	1938–1950	1950–1973	1973–1979	1979–1989
United States	1.0	10.5	−1.7	−2.1	4.5	2.6	7.9	5.4
France	0.5	17.4	6.9	3.0	28[1]	4.2	11.0	7.2
Germany	1.4			−2.3	4.6[1]	2.0	4.6	2.8
United Kingdom	0.8	14.4	−3.8	−0.7	5.8	3.6	15.6	7.0

Sources: 1896–1970, GRESP-Rennes; 1970-1989, OECD.
[1] = 1938–1951 and 1951–1973

there is a general upward trend for prices throughout the period, certain years or periods show a considerable decline until 1938 (Table 3.1). The downward flexibility of prices during periods of slowdown is more pronounced before the Second World War, as Thorning (1975) and Shapiro (1976) have noted, although their analysis has a different framework. The inflation that developed in advanced capitalist countries from the 1950s on differs profoundly from previously observed price rises. The most extreme of these movements were linked to the two world wars, when price increases were sharp but temporary and stemmed from the pathology of the economic system. By contrast, the inflation observed over the last thirty years is relatively moderate but endless, as if it were indispensable to the functioning of the economy, and it depends rather on the physiology of the system. Between the 1970s and the mid-1980s, inflation became more significant and, in certain countries, less controlled.

Concentration and Forms of Competition

Since the 1950s, a trend toward concentration has emerged in European industry, with the largest firms acquiring increased importance. Moreover, a certain homogeneity can be observed in the industrial structures of the different countries because the most capital-intensive and heavy industrial sectors are generally the most concentrated. These similarities, however, do not exclude the existence of significant inequalities from one country to another, notably between Germany and France where, until the end of the 1960s, the situation of the largest plants or firms remained more limited (Table 3.2). A final characteristic of concentration in France is its largely horizontal nature, which differs from the situation in Germany, where vertical concentration and the pursuit of a close upstream–downstream link are greater. One specificity of British industry can also be stressed: the influence of the leading firms is greater than in other European

Table 3.2

The Growth of Concentration in the Leading Economies Since the 1950s

	% of sales of the n first industrial firms		
EEC	1960	1965	1970
First 4	5.8	6.8	8.1
First 50	35.1	35.1	45.7

Source: A. Jacquemin (1979).

	% of employment in economic units of more than 50 employees								
	Germany		France		Italy		United States		Japan	
	1961	1969	1962	1969	1961	1969	1963	1969	1963	1969
Size of employment	265	326	215	250	198	202	263	255	192	195
50–100	11.9	8.0	15.4	11.5	19.0	16.0	11.7	10.4	19.7	19.3
100–500	34.8	30.0	42.5	42.0	40.7	40.0	37.0	37.3	38.0	37.8
500–1000	14.5	14.4	14.9	17.2	17.2	14.0	14.8	14.4	15.3	14.0
+1000	38.7	47.6	27.2	25.8	29.3	30.0	36.5	39.7	27.0	28.9

Source: B. Guibert (1975).

economies, which reflects the opposition between very large multinationals and a domestic industrial base that is in the process of coming apart.

American industry had already undergone two waves of mergers, at the end of the nineteenth century and during the 1920s. The practice of administered prices developed for certain goods. Concentration and financial centralization were quite advanced by the beginning of the 1950s, even if the large American commercial banks had lost their power over industrial companies around 1920. The concentration of the American economy was continually increasing.

Greater emphasis was placed on a strategy of increasing the power of the market than on sectoral rationalization. During the 1960s there was a significant wave of mergers that privileged financial centralization to the advantage of several dominant centers of control, including in particular four groups: Morgan, Mellon, Rockefeller, and Cleveland.

The modes of profit and price formation were considerably modified by the development of more monopolistic structures that included price fixing agreements, the spread of economic calculations within large firms, the practice of accelerated depreciations, and planned obsolescence through special group structures. The pressure of outlets on prices and profits was modified but did not in any way disappear. While the appearance of rampant inflation and perfect stability of profits reflects the gradual affirmation of a monopolistic regulation, the verification of such phenomena is not easy; indeed, the difficulty is twofold.

The first problem lies in the sensitive nature of measuring the impact of these structural transformations. Traditional approaches in terms of sectors with unequal degrees of concentration are often invoked. For the current period, a group of studies seems to show that the profitability of the most concentrated sectors does not significantly exceed that of the other sectors. Likewise, within a single sector, the profitability of companies belonging to industrial groups does not seem greater than that of other companies.

By contrast, there is a positive correlation between the rate of profit and degree of concentration (which is intensified in the case of strong entry barriers) in the context of more complicated relations defining the main determinants of the profit rate. Likewise, it can be shown how traditional structure–performance relations can be identified through the presence of groups in certain sectors. The profit rate is also more stable in the face of fluctuations in economic activity where larger-scale firms are concerned (see in particular Encaoua and Franck 1980, and Jacquemin 1979).

The second difficulty lies in the fact that the existence of monopolistic structures is necessary but not sufficient for the establishment of an administered regulation. The example of the interwar period in France, the United States, and Germany is significant in this respect, as will be demonstrated below. Increased concentration and the strengthening of monopolistic practices from the 1950s on contributed to the assertion of administered regulation in terms of prices and profits, but it could not have flourished without profound changes on the level of more global mechanisms conditioning the overall operation of the economy. The transformations marking the monetary system played an essential role in this area.

Monetary Regime and Financing of Accumulation

The Gold-Based Monetary System

Until the interwar period, with the exception of brief interruptions caused by war or other grave problems, the monetary systems of the leading economies relied on gold, and the banks were constantly required to demonstrate that their currency could be converted into gold. The structure of the banking systems emerged gradually: the creation of a central bank at the top marked a decisive stage, while the second-tier banks attempted to centralize money as much as possible by developing systems of savings collection. In order to ensure the convertibility of their currency into gold at any moment and to avoid the threat of insolvency, the banks had to respect a certain ratio between their short-term liabilities and their gold and silver reserves, which imposed a strict limit on the expansion of credit. In such a system there was no place for inflation— that is, a permanent trend toward rising prices—but this did not exclude phases of increasing prices followed by downward trends.

Indeed, during the periods of expansion, the debt increased, especially in the short term, in order to sustain accumulation. At the same time, interest rates rose, and the growth trend and the emergence of pressures created a propitious climate for rising prices. At the end of a certain time, however, problems of excess capacity could emerge, especially since the trade deficit led to a reduction of the means of payment. The debtor firms then had difficulty in meeting their payment deadlines; the demand for credit and the need for liquid assets increased simultaneously, and certain banks were no longer able to meet their commitments. At that point, the outbreak of the financial crisis led to the destruction of one portion of the debts by bankruptcy and a sharp reduction in credits. There was increasing decline in demand, and prices began to fall as well. Such sequences of cause and effect were to be found in most of the minor crises of the second half of the nineteenth century; the major crisis of 1929 was no exception following the reestablishment of the gold standard in most economies during the 1920s.

The Monetary System with Fiat Currency

An important change occurred in the functioning of the monetary systems after the Second World War. In an intensive accumulation regime, it was necessary for external financing to fulfill its support function to the utmost. Likewise, the regularity of the growth of demand could not be called into question periodically because of problems of solvency that certain banks would face in case of a decline in their activity. The organization of the monetary and financial systems took specific forms in each country. But overall, the central banks were led to play the role of lender of last resort; the acceptance of the currency issued by the central bank was obligatory, regardless of any possibility of conversion into gold (thus the term *fiat*). The resulting slackening of the monetary constraint, which was indispensable for the spread of intensive accumulation, created in turn permissive conditions of inflation by permitting a continuous rise in the general level of prices. It remains to be seen why this movement was in fact produced and why it took the form of moderate inflation in a period of growth while in a crisis period it often led to a more cumulative process. We shall attempt to answer these questions throughout this study.

Financial Systems and Financing of Accumulation

The 1929 crisis led to numerous transformations in the financial systems of all countries. One of the most important of these was the increased role and power conferred on the central banks. The activity of the financial intermediaries was regulated, and the central banks were given responsibility for monitoring them, often in collaboration with public treasury bodies. Relatively compartmentalized circuits were set up to finance specific activities such as housing or agriculture. All of these measures were primarily intended to avoid repeating the financial crisis, with a string of banks and companies going bankrupt.

Another essential change was the decline of the financial markets, and this took place for a number of reasons. The 1929 stock market crash and postwar inflation had brought about serious losses of capital. In the throes of intensive accumulation, households were encouraged to use their savings to acquire consumer durables, especially housing, and not to make financial investments. As production norms continued to undergo radical change, firms were forced to make investment the basic means of competition, and in order to ensure the stability of financing, they had to turn to credit that was arranged through preferential relations with one or several financial intermediaries.

Before the 1929 crisis, in countries such as France and the United Kingdom, commercial banks were specialized in short-term credit to firms. Investment financing was above all provided by the financial market, which was led by private financial intermediaries, while the central bank privileged monetary stability over that of financing. After the Second World War, credit became the main external means of financing the accumulation of the firms and the Fordist consumption standard. The priority of the central banks was to stabilize interest rates at a low level. This led to the creation of an overdraft economy, in which any demand for credit coming from a presumably solvent agent would be met. If the resources collected by the nonbanking financial intermediaries (often in the public or cooperative domain) were insufficient, the demand for credit was met by the banks, in return for the issuing of currency. The subsequent disintermediation of funds out of banking systems was compensated by refinancing from the central bank.

One of the most typical cases of the overdraft economy was the French financial system until the mid-1980s. Another was the extremely regulated Japanese system, with its very rapid rise in bank credits that served to sustain accumulation and compensate for low self-financing rates. Relative to this model, the West German financial system offered several particular features. The banks played an essential role in the financing and managing of firms through the possibility they had to use their clients' voting rights in stockholders' meetings. The accumulation process was even more dependent on the two-way bank-firm relations than in the other countries. But the system was less regulated. There was a single status for the universal bank, which applied to the large majority of the intermediaries, and interest rates on deposits were freely established. However, the central bank imposed strict cautionary rules, and the refinancing granted by the Bundesbank, in the very traditional context of rediscount ceilings and Lombard credit facilities, was less unconditional than in France or Japan. In its desire to ensure the stability of the currency, the Bundesbank, from the 1950s and 1960s on, was capable of imposing sharp fluctuations in the interest rates and strictly controlling the banks' liquid assets through changes in the reserve-requirement ratios.

The American financial system has often been contrasted with the French and characterized as an economy of financial markets, as opposed to the overdraft economy. This analysis was based on two main observations. In the United States, the firms had less recourse to credit and more to self-financing and the financial markets. The commercial banks did not have structural deficits in relation to the central bank and thus the latter was not constantly required to provide them with refinancing; it intervened at its discretion through the open-market policy. However, this contrast should not be taken too far. In the United States, household debt was much greater than in Europe, and credit played a more important role in the spread of the consumption standard (but the social protection system was much less important than in Europe). In addition, the central bank demonstrated in a variety of situations that it systematically assumed the role of lender of last resort, which implied that the financial system was automatically supplied with the monetary base. Given the central bank's objective of stabilizing the interest rate, it had to adjust its open-market policy in function of the pressures on liquid assets.

These transformations had significant consequences on macroeconomic dynamics. With the development of monetary financing, investment was no longer limited by previously available savings. The creation of currency anticipated the future rise in production, incomes, and thus savings, with the result that the rate of investment could exceed the rate of savings from the very beginning. The guarantee that the central bank provided to the financial intermediaries prevented the spread of panics that would interrupt credit. And the growth of the money supply also allowed for rampant inflation.

Price, Profit, and Investment: An Econometric Study

The Mechanisms of Price Formation: The Shift to Monopolistic Regulation

In terms of price formation, two profound transformations allow us to identify the conditions for the shift from competitive regulation to monopolistic regulation. Many of the results already obtained by Boyer (1977) are confirmed (Table 3.3).

The demand elasticity of prices in France seems to reverse itself over time. In the competitive regime, prices are very dependent on the rhythms of economic activity; during periods of expansion, entrepreneurs profit from increased demand in order to raise their prices. Conversely, the downward flexibility of prices is very marked in a period of slowdown or recession. This competitive regulation predominated until the 1930s (with a demand elasticity of prices in the neighborhood of 0.9), and this is true in spite of the considerable place already occupied by monopolistic structures. After the Second World War, and especially from the 1960s on, a significant change occurs because of a negative relationship that emerges between prices and fluctuations in economic activity. This result may, in part, reflect a new behavior on the part of the entrepreneurs who sought to compensate for flagging growth with price rises in order to preserve a certain profitability of capital. This behavior must be related to a whole group of practices spreading within the large

Table 3.3

Price Elasticities of Demand and Unit Wage Cost in France (all sectors except agriculture)

	a	b	c	R^2	DW
1896–1913	0.87	0.18	−0.76	0.23	1.60
	(1.9)	(0.8)	(−0.6)		
1922–1938	0.91	0.96	−1.07	0.75	1.60
	(4.5)	(5.2)	(−0.6)		
1952–1969	−0.33	0.70	3.4	0.76	1.79
	(−1.8)	(6.2)	(2.9)		
1959–1977	−0.56	0.56	5.56	0.91	2.24
	(−3.8)	(7.3)	(4.6)		

Equation: $p = aY + b\ uwc + c$
p = price index (GNP)
uwc = unit wage cost.
Y = GNP
(annual growth rate)

companies, and it was only further encouraged by the fact that, because of the quasi-indexation of wages to prices, inflation no longer led to a decline in purchasing power and thus in wage demand and outlets.

This transformation in the mode of setting prices, which allowed greater independence relative to fluctuations, is not found in all the economies. Thus, in the United States, the link between prices and growth of production seems more stable in the long term. But the influence of the demand pressure indicator is rather weak over the entire 1892–1978 period. This situation may reflect the less competitive nature of price regulation in the United States since the beginning of the century. On the other hand, there is a very significant break in terms of the influence of the rates of anticipated inflation, which are approximated by the inflation rates of the previous year and the gap between the nominal and potential GNP growth rates. Anticipated inflation played a negative role before 1950 and a positive one after 1950 (see Table 3.4).

A second major transformation emerges with the appearance and subsequent reinforcement over time of the link between prices and unit costs (as seen in Table 3.3). Just as wages were severed from changes in the cost of living at the beginning of the century, businessmen did not yet pass along increases in the unit wage cost in their prices. From the 1920s on—the time when the cost of living figured in wage formation—the unit wage cost was taken into account in the setting of prices. Subsequently, businessmen were more and more inclined to safeguard their profit margins, a behavior that is typical of administered prices: the margin is calculated in relation not only to variable unit costs but also to fixed costs. This last point helps to explain the negative link between price and produc-

Table 3.4

Long-Term Determinants of Inflation Rates in the United States

	a	b	c	d	R^2	DW
1892-1929	0.29	0.18	ns	ns	0.85	2.1
	(3.3)	(1.6)				
1929-1953	0.35	0.07	−0.73	0.15	0.96	1.5
	(9.6)	(3.6)	(−3.0)	(3.2)		
1953-1978	0.34	0.13	0.72		0.96	1.7
	(8.5)	(3.6)	(10.0)			

Source: Robert J. Gordon (1980).

Equation : $p_t = ay_t + bGAP_t + cp_{et} + dy_{t-1}$

p = price index (GNP)

y = GNP at current prices/potential GNP at constant prices.

pet = inflation expected rate = p_{t-1} (annual growth rate)

GAP = log (GNP at current prices/potential GNP at constant prices).

tion growth that emerged in the 1950s, especially since the relative importance of fixed costs tended to increase with the development of new production methods and growing concentration.

The Determinants of Capital Accumulation: Profits and Outlets

From the time of Kalecki (1954) and Robinson (1962), an entire school of thought has held that the rate of profit is one of the main determinants of accumulation as a variable representing both the possibilities of internal financing and company expectations of profitability and outlets. The existence of these multiple effects, which are summed up in a single variable, poses tricky problems of verification and interpretation, for the same relationship can apply to very different phenomena according to the scope of the financing constraints faced by the firms.

Moreover, the rate of profit cannot be considered as the sole determinant of investment. Three other variables are likely to intervene: expectations concerning outlets, which are directly shaped by past fluctuations in demand (the accelerator effect), the cost of credit or, more generally, the relative cost of the factors, and the firms' financial structure, which can exert a direct influence on the decision to invest in the context of the profit and indebtedness models. Without making an exhaustive analysis, we shall use the French and British cases to examine whether in the long run changes in the determinants of investment can be detected in relation to changes on the level of the accumulation regimes.

An initial observation can be made. The accelerator effect seems to have been very strong in both France and the United Kingdom over the long term. In France, adjustment periods increased during the sharp growth of the 1950s and 1960s. The rapid rise of the new consumption standard and the spread of intensive accumulation led to positive expectations that contributed to more consistent investment decisions. The onset of the crisis period at the beginning of the 1970s reduced reaction time and intensified the accelerator effect, which reflected the increased constraint of the outlets. On the other hand, the investment function appears remarkably more stable in the case of the United Kingdom (see Table 3.5).

During the interwar period, which was marked by the major crisis of the 1930s, investment was much more unstable in France than in the United Kingdom, where the crisis, which had begun in the 1920s, was less intense. The accelerator no longer yielded a significant result in the case of the French economy. Investment reacted immediately to the fluctuations of the outlets, with the exception of 1930 when, curiously, it continued to rise in spite of declining production.

The profit–accumulation connection is more difficult to identify, at least in the case of France. During the phase of extensive accumulation

Table 3.5

The Long-Term Acceleration Effect in France and the United Kingdom

France	a	b	c	d	R^2	DW
1896–1913	0.79	0.12	0.05	0.89	0.88	2.0
	(4.9)	(2.5)	(1.0)	(1.2)		
1952–1969	0.87	0.20	0.07	−0.2	0.97	1.8
	(13.2)	(4.7)	(1.5)	(−0.4)		
1966–1978	0.72	0.34	−0.03	0.02	0.94	2.4
	(4.9)	(7.3)	(−0.4)	(1.2)		

United Kingdom		a	b	c	R^2	DW
1881–1895		0.84	0.039	0.019	0.70	1.6
		(4.9)	(2.6)	(1.6)		
1896–1913		0.93	0.052	0.025	0.89	1.5
		(10.6)	(3.1)	(1.4)		
1922–1938		0.88	0.055	0.031	0.84	2.3
		(−6.6)	(4.9)	(3.3)		
1951–1979		0.90	0.055	0.031	0.91	1.1
		(15.6)	(4.0)	(2.2)		

Source: E. Girardin (1986), GRESP-Rennes, France.
$I/K = a\,(I/K)_{-1} + bY + cY_{-1}$
Y = GDP (growth rate)
I/K = rate of accumulation
France: all sectors except agriculture
United Kingdom: all sectors

Table 3.6

The Long-Term Profit–Accumulation Link in the United Kingdom

	a	b	R^2	DW
1881–1938	0.63	0.21	0.87	1.69
	(−6.5)	(3.0)		
1951–1969	0.73	0.26	0.95	
	(6.7)	(3.9)		

Source: E. Girardin (1986).
$I/K = a\,(I/K)_{-1} + b\pi$
with: I/K = accumulation rate ; π = gross profit rate before tax (all sectors).

and the competitive mode of regulation, the rate of profit depended closely on the outlets and did not seem to exert a significant influence on the accumulation rate. For the interwar period, however, it gives a better idea of the instability of investment, as confirmed by the studies of Villa (1993). From the 1950s on, with the shift to more monopolistic regulation, the rate of profit becomes less sensitive to the situation of the outlets and more representative of internal financing possibilities. From that point on, it intervenes along with the accelerator effect, but its influence declines once difficulties in external financing diminish, as the in-depth studies of Muet (1979) on this issue have emphasized. By contrast, the profit–accumulation connection seems more stable and significant in the case of the United Kingdom, at least through the end of the 1960s (see Table 3.6). Finally, it may be observed that in both France and the United Kingdom, the interest rate, whether in the form of a nominal tax, real tax, or relative cost of factors, seems to have only a limited influence—or none at all—on the investment dynamic, and this is true for most periods.

Wage–Profit Division and Profitability: The Long-Term Dynamic

We have seen how the main regulation procedures were transformed over the long term: with the boom in intensive accumulation, labor productivity underwent a particular acceleration from 1950 on, and the wage relation was profoundly modified between 1930 and 1950. The spread of administered regulation from the 1960s on led to the quasi-indexation of wages to prices and a greater independence of the former relative to fluctuations in economic activity. The formation of prices and profits was characterized by the gradual assertion of an explicit behavior with regard to margins and growing autonomy in relation to the demand situation. These transformations in regulation procedures largely determine the dynamics of the wage–profit division and profit rate, which we shall now examine.

Stability of the Share of Wages over the Long Term

The transformation of the wage relation and the shift to the intensive accumulation regime were accompanied by a significant change in the idea of wages. Until the 1930s, the reproduction of the labor force was basically ensured by the direct wage; social services represented less than 2 percent of the wage bill in France, and collective consumption for workers was limited to primary education. After 1945, social services made up a significant and growing portion of the wage bill—over 30 percent by the end of the 1970s—while collective consumption was growing rapidly. We shall base our analysis on the notion of the gross wage as the sum of the net wage and social security contributions. The regulation of the wage–profit division will be examined first in the short and medium term and then over the long term.

Short and Medium Term

The share of gross wages in the GDP, following correction for increasing salaried wages, can be studied on the basis of the usual accounting breakdown:

Figure 3.1 **Long-Term Share of Wages in the GDP in Leading Countries**

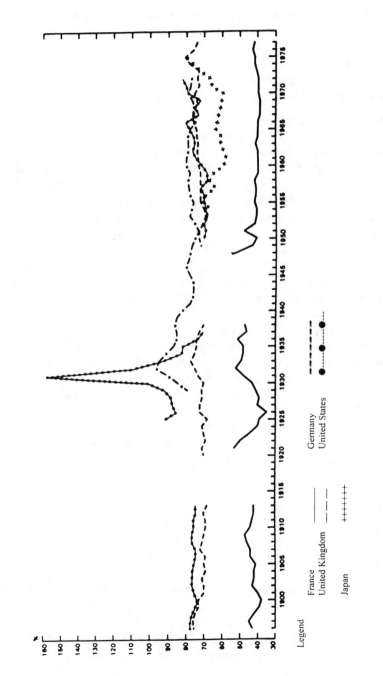

Legend

France ⎯⎯⎯

United Kingdom ⎯ ⎯ ⎯

Japan ++++++

Germany

United States

Source: GRESP-Rennes, France.

$wN/pY = (w/p_c) \cdot (p_c/p) / (Y/N)$
with:
wN/pY = share of gross wages (after correction for increasing
       salaried wages),
w = wages per capita,
Y/N = labor productivity
P_c = consumer price index
p = price of value added.

A first contrast emerges between the 1886–1950 period, characterized by a fairly large variability in the share of wages, and the 1950–70 period, during which the share of wages is more stable (see Figure 3.1). During the first period, the decline in the share of wages is associated with the phases of growth during which prices and labor productivity tend to rise. Conversely, the share of wages increases during the recessions because of the decline in productivity, the trend toward falling prices, and the rigidity of real wages. The cyclical change in prices played a considerable regulatory role in the wage–profit distribution until the end of the 1940s. During the interwar period, significant differences between countries emerged. The share of wages was very unstable in Germany. The fluctuations are all the more considerable in Germany because calculations are based on value added without provision for depreciation. Already sizable during the 1920s, it rose sharply between 1929 and 1931, then quickly declined. These shifts were the result of the intense contradictions that enveloped the German economy after the First World War. In the United Kingdom, by contrast, the share of wages was much more stable during this period, which can be related to the fact that the crisis of the 1930s was less intense there.

From the 1950s on, the growing indexation of wages to prices and the increase in the real wage were compatible with greater stability of the wage share because of the productivity gains permitted by intensive accumulation. The beginning of the 1970s marked a turning point, notably in Germany, where increases in real wages accelerated, and in the United States, where productivity gains declined. The first oil crisis and that of the intensive accumulation regime were to lead to a rise in the wage share, to which we shall return.

Long Term

The share of gross wages (i.e., including social security contributions since the 1930s) in the GDP is stable over the long term. This phenomenon has been discussed at length by growth theorists. It should be noted that it is very difficult to conceive of a clearly rising or falling trend for the wage share. In the first case, profits become insufficient to ensure the simple reproduction of existing capital; in the second, wages are ultimately incapable of ensuring the reproduction of the labor force. Maintaining the wage share in a "range of stability" appears to be a necessary condition for overall reproduction.

Under competitive regulation, a wage share that is too low leads to a recession, which reduces profits because of the lack of outlets; on the other hand, an exaggerated wage share can be corrected by accelerating inflation if market conditions lend themselves to a price rise.

Under monopolistic regulation, changes in the general price level have much less influence on income distribution; the regulation of the wage share depends more on the productivity dynamic and the rapid transformation of production conditions. In certain cases, the regulatory mechanisms reveal themselves to be incapable of bringing the wage share within the "range of stability": this would be considered a crisis of regulation, or a "structural crisis," which could only be resolved through profound transformations of the accumulation regime. A better understanding of these long-term developments requires going beyond the simple wage–profits division and considering the dynamic of the profit rate.

The Long-Term Dynamic of the Rate of Profit

In statistical terms, the profit rate is undoubtedly a more difficult notion to establish than that of the share of profits in the value added, because the latter indicator is determined on the basis of flows while the former implies measuring the stock of capital. There is no need to dwell on the many theoretical debates about the difficulties of defining and quantifying capital. It is useful, however, to stress an empirical difficulty that seems just as important to us: the stock of capital by volume is generally calculated by adding together the different generations of equipment on the basis of a hypothesis of a constant or uniformly variable lifespan, while decisions to downgrade vary in function of the economic situation. The fact that destruction of capital is rarely taken into account distorts the profit-rate indicator during periods of crisis. The rate of profitability of capital (π) can be broken down, very classically, into three components: the share of profits in value added (P/pY), the "productivity of capital" (Y/K), and the relative price of capital goods (pk/p). The first is the complement of the wage share; the second has been discussed in the first chapter; and the third depends on the efficiency and market position of the sectors supplying capital goods.

$$\pi = P/p_kK = (P/pY) . (Y/K) . (p/p_k)$$
with $P/pY = 1 - (wN/pY)$.

Figure 3.2 recapitulates the profit rates in the four leading economies. After a phase of relative stability from 1906 to 1913, the profit rate showed sharp fluctuations during the interwar period. It recovered in Great Britain and France between 1921 and 1926 without any major upheaval in production methods but with diametrically opposed short-term dynamics for ensuring the reestablishment of the share of profits: deflation in the first case and inflation in the second. In Germany, by contrast, profits did not resume, especially since German firms underwent a development crisis well before 1929. After the general collapse of 1929–32, the profit rate evolved quite differently from one economy to another. It increased rapidly in Germany after 1933 through a very clear increase in the share of profits and an improvement in capital efficiency: in 1938, Germany's rate of profit was higher than the levels at the beginning of the century.

There was also a considerable resumption of profitability in Great Britain, but this took place more gradually and in a very different context from that of Germany. In the United States, it was only in 1941 that the rate of profit again reached the 1929 level. In France, profitability remained very low until the 1930s, because of both the low share of profits and the failure to reestablish the production–capital ratio.

From the 1950s on, the profit rate appears to have been more stable, because of the articulation between productivity gains, rise in real wages, and increased outlets that permitted the creation of the intensive accumulation regime. In the United States, Germany, and the United Kingdom, the profit rate reached its highest point at the beginning of the 1960s, which probably represented the peak of Fordism, at least in the first two of these countries. In France, the profit rate remained at about the same level between 1960 and 1973, but in the other countries, a decline began to manifest itself at the end of the 1960s. It was very sharp in Germany, although it must be stressed that this particular series was established on the basis of net profit, which fluctuates more than the gross profit used to determine the profitability series for the three other countries. On the other hand, it illustrates the role played by depreciation in the stabilization of profits. In the United Kingdom, the United States, and Germany, a decline in capital productivity can be observed in the course of the 1960s. The share of profits showed a sharp decline in Germany before 1973; this was less pronounced in the United Kingdom and the United States. In the latter country, the rise in the relative price of capital goods accelerated the decline in profitability. A profitability crisis began to emerge in most of the leading economies at the end of the 1960s, although France was to escape in part.

It is difficult to bring out a very long-term trend for the rate of profit. According to our statistics, it diminishes in France, but this is tied to the long-term rise in the relative price of capital goods, which in fact cannot

Figure 3.2 **Rate of Profit in the Four Leading Economies**

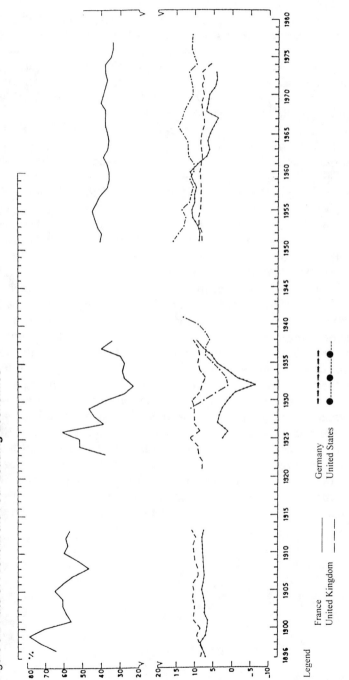

Legend

France	———	Germany	
United Kingdom	– – –	United States	

Source: GRESP-Rennes, France.

be established with any certainty because of the flimsiness of the data prior to 1938. Overall, the profit rate is affected by cyclical movements associated with phases of expansion, slowdown, or crisis.

The expansion phases, which permitted a more intensive use of labor and capital goods, brought with them, especially in the beginning, greater profitability. Conversely, the slowdown phases, manifested by a stagnation or decline in productivity and underutilization of capacities, generally led to a decline in the rate of profit.

In the case of a slowdown, the recession rarely ensures the reestablishment of profits in the short term: even if nominal wages decline, which is the case with competitive regulation but not with monopolistic regulation, the drop in prices or the slowdown in productivity gains brought on by the recession tend to aggravate the situation still further. Under the administered regulation regime, inflation scarcely modifies the wage–profit distribution. In the case of a structural crisis, profitability can only be reestablished in the short term if the growth of productivity gains is sufficient both to exceed that of real wages and to ensure that "capital efficiency" is restored. For the extensive accumulation regime, this implies seeking new outlets (new consumption standards, public expenditures, rearmament, exports, and the conquest of foreign outlets, as in Germany after 1933). But high productivity gains in the medium run can also be obtained through a transformation of the accumulation regime, which is always a slow, contradictory process. In the medium-long term, the rate of profit is affected by the powerful trends involving accumulation, productivity gains, and its own impact on "capital efficiency."

Beyond potentially wide fluctuations that may include profound transformations, no long-term trend can really be singled out. Such stability of the profitability indicators over the long term illustrates the system's ability to ensure its own reproduction, either in the short term through regulation procedures endowed with a certain permanence, or in the longer term, in the case of a severe crisis, through wide-ranging structural transformations. These phenomena are simply the reflection of the short- and medium-term play of tendencies and countertendencies on the rate of profit.

CHAPTER FOUR

International Economic Relations and the Internal Dynamic

It is impossible to study the dynamic of the major powers without taking into account changes in the international economy. For one thing, long-term movements of growth and stagnation always affect a large number of countries. The study of crises requires a precise knowledge of the international economy in order to determine whether they result from an accumulation of internal crises among the major powers, the transmission of difficulties within the leading economy, or imbalances within international relations. For another thing, a country's wealth and growth depend on its rank among national economies and its ability to adapt to changes in the international economy.

The first part of this chapter deals with the main transformations in the world economy since the end of the nineteenth century. The second part studies the factors that have contributed to fluctuations in the competitiveness of the major powers.

Long-Term Changes in the International Economy

The general introduction outlined the ways in which the main concepts of the Regulation School can be developed and adapted in order to explain changes in international economic relations. The international growth regime results from disparities between the dynamics of supply and demand in the most advanced economies; these determine the development of exchanges by product, the configuration of bilateral relations, and the conditions under which national economies adapt to external constraint. International regulation thus consists of all the institutional arrangements, mainly monetary, financial, and commercial, that guarantee the stability of international growth.

The International Growth Regime and Its Transformations

The decades prior to the First World War saw the establishment of modern transportation and telecommunications networks permitting the rapid growth of international exchanges of goods and capital. In 1913, foreign trade already accounted for a large share of production in Europe and certain developing countries; capital exports in France and especially in the United Kingdom represented a significant proportion of their domestic investment. Internationalization was already well under way, but it developed with a very different dynamic and different regulatory procedures from those of today.

During the 1870–1913 period, foreign trade of primary commodities represented a large, stable share of world trade (over 60 percent). By volume, the growth of primary commodities trade was almost as great as that of manufactured goods, while the relative price of primary commodities was, until 1913, affected only by moderate cyclical trends (see Tables 4.1 and 4.2).

European imports of basic materials were the driving force behind foreign trade. Rapid demographic growth (except in France), as well as the slow improvement in buying power, led to a sharp increase in Western Europe's food needs. Europe bought wheat from Russia, India, Argentina, the United States, and Canada and imported meat from Argentina, Uruguay, and Australia. The spread of extensive accumulation and the expansion of new sectors led to a massive increase in imports of raw materials for industry, with North America, South America, and Australia providing growing quantities of wool, cotton, and metals. The new primary commodities exporting countries used their export revenues to buy manufactured goods from Western Europe. A significant share of exports from the advanced capitalist countries was directed toward the periphery and semi-periphery (see Tables 4.3 and 4.4). The data in Table 4.5 illustrate these conclusions: during the period from 1896–1900 to 1913, world imports of primary commodities increased much more than world imports of manufactured goods. The increase in the former was largely the result of purchases by the British Isles and northwest Europe.

Great Britain's capital exports were largely directed toward the new nations and a few tropical countries such as Brazil or the West Indies. They were mainly invested in transportation infrastructures, which encouraged these countries' integration in world trade, and the develop-

Table 4.1

Long-Term Data on International Exchanges (average annual growth rate in %)

	1890– 1913	1913– 1929	1929– 1938	1938– 1950	1953– 1960	1960– 1972	1972– 1977
Manufactured goods	3.4	1.5	−2.5	3.2	9.0	9.6	7.2
Primary commodities	3.2	1.8	−1.2	1.9	5.3	5.3	2.0

Source: 1890 to 1950: W.A. Lewis (1952).
Tableau I et II, Manchester School of Economics and Social Studies, vol. 20, 1952.
1953–1977; GATT, "Le commerce international en 1965," "Le commerce international en 1977–1978."

Table 4.2

International Exchanges: Unit Value of Primary Commodities/Unit Value of Manufactured Goods

1890	1913	1929	1938	1950	1953	1960	1963	1972	1977
95.6	100	88.9	74.7	102	113.6	100.5	100	100.4	157

Source: See Table 4.1.
1890–1950 = 100 in 1913.
1953–1977 = 100 in 1963.

Table 4.3

Distribution of Manufactured Goods Exports from Advanced Capitalist Countries (by destination, current prices, prices, in %, 1899-1955)

	1899	1913	1929	1937	1955
Advanced capitalist countries[1]	54.3	50.1	47.4	41.2	47.7
Other countries	46.7	49.9	52.6	58.8	52.3

Source: Maizels (1971), table A3.
[1]Japan included.

ment of complementarities since the loans ultimately served to import manufactured goods coming from Great Britain. These flows took the form of bonds issued by the large banks. In the case of France, capital exports were less consistent with the international growth process; some were influenced by international policy goals. Until 1913, the world economy was organized according to a vertical division of labor: the advanced capitalist countries mainly exported manufactured goods and

Table 4.4

Distribution of Manufactured Goods Exports from Advanced Capitalist Countries (by destination, current prices, in %, 1953-1977)

	1953	1960	1973	1977
Advanced capitalist countries	55.1	61.3	74.0	67.4
Developing countries	35.7	28.9	18.4	24.9
Central planned countries	2.0	3.9	4.5	5.1

Source: GATT, "Le commerce international en 1961" and "Le commerce international en 1977–1978."

Note: Advanced capitalist countries = North America, Western Europe, Japan; developing countries = other except Australia, New Zealand, and South Africa.

Table 4.5

Development of International Demand–Regional Shares in the Variation in World Imports (current prices, in %); 1896–1900, 1900–1938

	Imports			Primary goods imports			Manufactured goods, imports		
	1896–1913	1913–1928	1928–1937	1896–1913	1913–1928	1928–1937	1896–1913	1913–1928	1928–1937
U.S. and Canada	13.8	20.8	20.0	13.7	26.1	20.6	14.2	13.6	19.3
U.K. and Ireland	10.6	16.7	8.2	12.9	21.5	6.5	6.3	10.3	10.2
Western Europe	36.6	14.6	28.0	41.2	19.0	36.7	27.8	9.1	17.5
Europe (others)	15.3	11.1	20.9	14.0	7.2	19.2	18.1	16.1	23.0
Latin America, Oceany, Africa, Asia	23.7	36.8	22.9	18.2	26.2	17.0	33.6	50.9	30.0
Imports absolute change in millions of dollars	11,312	13,812	–7,274	7,260	7,914	–3,982	3,997	5,953	–3,292

Source: P.L. Yates (1959), Table A18–A21–A22.

imported primary commodities. The other countries experienced different forms of development: the new countries, privileged by the flow of capital and immigrant labor coming from Europe, enjoyed more rapid growth than the industrialized countries because of a rapid expansion of supply, while the tropical countries showed a variety of results, notably with poor performances in Asia. These circumstances have been extensively described by Kenwood and Lougheed (1971) and Rybczynski (1978).

This coherent international growth regime was destabilized by the shock of the First World War. The weakening of the European countries allowed India and Japan to create or reinforce their own industries. But above all, the war led to a very sustained demand for primary materials at a time when production was declining in Europe because of the lack of manpower. The rise in prices allowed developing countries to increase their production capacities considerably in agriculture and mining. European production took off again in the early 1920s, with the result that by 1925 there were increasing surpluses of primary materials. This led to an inflation of supplies and a slow decrease in prices until 1929; with the financial crisis, there was total collapse. Subsequently, the change in the accumulation regime of the industrialized economies led to the creation of a new growth regime.

During the 1950–73 period, there was a general acceleration in the growth of trade (see Table 4.1), but this was much more pronounced for manufactured goods than primary materials. The growth of trade in primary materials, relative to that of manufactured goods, was limited by several factors. The consumption of food products showed only a slight increase in the industrialized countries and did not advance adequately in many Third World countries for lack of sufficient creditworthy demand. The industrialized countries reduced their food dependency by modernizing their agriculture. Outlets for the raw materials used in the textile and leather industries were limited by the unfavorable development of the downstream branches and the growing use of synthetic products that were often derived from hydrocarbons.

The considerable acceleration in the growth of manufactured goods trade varied greatly, with the sharpest increases registered by production equipment, transportation materials, chemical products, and, to a lesser extent, consumer durables. Trade of semi-finished goods and textile products increased less rapidly. These trends as a whole correspond to the dynamic of social demand in the intensive accumulation regime, which is characterized by a constant overturning of production and consumption standards. The differential increase in volumes and the decline in the relative prices of primary materials led to a clear decrease in the share of primary commodities (including combustibles) in foreign trade. According to Rybczynski, this proportion went from 54 percent in 1913 to 49 percent in 1953 to 35 percent in 1973, while there was a symmetrical rise in the share of manufactured goods.

The need to sell off production that was growing rapidly because of the reversal of production standards and the pursuit of increasing return to scale led the firms in the advanced capitalist countries to seek foreign outlets. Following the Linder schema (1961), these outlets were sought in countries where the demand structure was closest to that of the exporting country, with the result that trade tended to concentrate on exchanges between advanced capitalist countries. This dynamic implied the lowering of customs barriers, which was gradually achieved through various international agreements. The imports of most advanced capitalist countries included a growing and soon predominant proportion of manufactured goods. While in the extensive accumulation regime manufactured goods exports are the counterpart of primary materials imports, in the intensive accumulation regime manufactured goods imports are the counterparts of manufactured goods exports, because the penetration of foreign markets generally has to be accompanied by a reciprocal opening up of the domestic market. This type of exchange gradually spread after the period of reconstruction. It was much more common among European countries, notably Germany and Great Britain, than in the United States and Japan.

Although certain advanced capitalist countries were major importers of primary commodities, the uneven development of foreign trade by goods considerably modified the shares of the different regions between 1950 and 1973. The share of advanced capitalist countries in total world exports went from 65.4 to 74 percent. That of the countries of the South went from 24.1 to 17.3 percent. The trend is similar for imports: over the same period, the share of advanced capitalist countries went from 63.4 to 72.9 percent and that of the countries of the South from 26.2 to 17.9 percent. The latter thus underwent a veritable marginalization, as Destanne de Bernis (1977) has emphasized.

As a result, the countries of the periphery and the semi-periphery played a diminishing role as outlets for the industry of the advanced capitalist countries (see Tables 4.3 and 4.4). Thus, from 1899 to 1937, the advanced capitalist countries sold an increasingly large share of their manufactured goods exports to nonindustrialized or little industrialized countries; the trend was completely reversed between 1953 and 1973. From 1958 to 1972, manufactured goods trade between advanced capitalist countries went from 29.3 to 48.1 percent of total world trade. These phenomena were largely accentuated by the decline in the relative price of primary materials from 1952 until 1965.

Among advanced capitalist countries, the trade of similar goods increased rapidly: even when the analyses are carried out with very detailed classifications, it seems that many countries had exports and imports of an equivalent magnitude for the same goods, and that this kind of trade increased considerably in the 1960s, especially in Europe. This was less true for the United States because of its size, and for Japan, which maintained tight control over its domestic market. However, trade between industrialized countries also reflected a growing hierarchy of productive systems. The United States maintained a dominant position for many goods with heavy technological content, such as aeronautics products, computers, and scientific instruments. Likewise, West Germany dominated in chemical goods manufacture and machine tools. In 1973, Japan, West Germany, and the United States were the countries with the largest surpluses in productive capital equipment.

In the long term, there were thus profound changes in the way that the international division of labor determined foreign trade. Before 1913, the main factor was the vertical division of labor between industrialized countries and new countries exporting primary materials. From 1950 to 1973, the horizontal division of labor gradually took over, and trade of goods between advanced capitalist countries came to predominate.

After the Second World War, the United States became the main investor. But the behavior of American capital was completely different: it invested more and more in the manufacturing sector and in Europe and less and less in the mining sector and in the countries of the periphery. The foreign investments of European countries that developed subsequently followed the same evolution. Among American foreign investments, direct investments predominated. It was typical for international capital to withdraw from regions producing raw materials in order to establish itself in regions where Fordism was developing. Vernon's schemas correspond to a phase of the international economy characterized by the expansion of the intensive accumulation regime outside the United States. These developments confirm the idea that from 1950 on foreign trade was reorganized around the pursuit of outlets for the manufacturing sectors of the advanced capitalist countries. In the long term, the internal dynamic of the center, the trade of goods, international investment flows, and even population migrations are all consistent with one another.

The international growth regime set up after the Second World War was weakened by several factors during the 1970s and 1980s. The oil price shocks abruptly increased the relative price of energy, which had already undergone a rapid increase in demand with the spread of the Fordist consumption standard. Since one part of the oil-producing countries had a limited absorption capacity, their surpluses suddenly rose. Faced with tapering growth, the major powers limited their deficits; on the contrary, the developing countries, which sought to maintain their growth, became heavily indebted.

The crisis of Fordism led to an intense restructuring of the capital goods and intermediate products sectors; the new dynamic increased the growth differentials between sectors, with the decline of traditional metallurgy and the rapid rise of electronics. Japan was better able to adapt to these changes and enjoyed increasing foreign trade surpluses, a large part of which served to finance the Untied States' deficit. The rapid industrialization of several Southeast Asian countries contributed to weakening the production of manufactured consumer goods in the countries that had long been industrialized. The disequilibria of the international growth regime played a considerable role in the rise of the international debt and encouraged the industrialized countries to maintain or increase nontariff barriers (see chapter 10).

Changes in International Regulation

The historical analysis of the way the international economy is organized shows its close ties with the dynamic and internal regulation of the leading economies. The end of the nineteenth century saw the emergence of an international regulation guaranteeing the stability of interdependencies. Weakened by the First World War, this regulation collapsed during the crisis of 1929. The Second World War led to the establishment of a new international order on bases that were very different from the preceding one.

International Regulation Before 1914

Before 1914, international regulation was based on the gold standard, the international mobility of capital, and protectionism. The gold standard is a principle of both national and international regulation. Domestically, it implies the automatic regulation of monetary stability: the function of money as the repository of value is privileged, if necessary, to the detriment of its transaction function. Monetary stability is ensured at the price of financial crises that lead to a reduction of trade. The goal of these adjustments is to encourage savings, which appears, in a period when per capita income is fairly low, as the main prerequisite for capital accumulation. The mechanisms of the gold standard are also aimed at reducing government intervention as much as possible, because they prohibit discretionary monetary policies and impose a limit on public deficits. Internationally, the gold standard guarantees the absolute stability of the parity of the major currencies and implies a strict adjustment of the balance of payments.

According to the most popular theories of that period, international equilibrium was explained by the mechanism of gold movements. When a country showed a gap between supply and overall demand, this was followed by a surplus (or a deficit) in the current balance, which led to inflows (or outflows) of gold, which increased (or decreased) the money supply and led to a rise (fall) in prices, which reabsorbed the foreign-trade surplus (deficit). Combined, to be sure, with the mechanisms of pure, perfect competition, this would permit the stabilization of the balance of payments and full employment in all countries. This theory has often been contested. Without going into all the details of the debates, we shall recall the two most important points. For one thing, the empirical data show that gold movements were very limited and the gold reserves of the major powers remarkably stable. For another, this theory implied a comparison of national situations, since the country with a deficit, which was losing gold, underwent deflation, while its partners, which were benefiting from the inflow of gold, were undergoing inflation. In reality, the economic situations of a growing number of countries were synchronized, and the crises associated with the Juglar intermediate cycle spread on the international level. In fact, this kind of reasoning ignored the fact that the period was characterized by a very high international mobility of capital, which constituted an essential component of international regulation (Vidal 1989).

Transfers of capital mainly took two directions: two-way exchanges of short-term capital between the main financial centers, and exports of capital from the major powers toward the less advanced countries. When an industrialized country experienced a sharp expansion, this led to a spontaneous or voluntary rise in its interest rate, which was likely to impose a slight restriction on demand, but above all attracted capital and compensated for the trade deficit. The fluctuation of the interest rate was intended precisely to stabilize the relation between gold reserves and the domestic money supply. Exchange rate and reserves were instantaneously stabilized. On the other hand, countries undergoing outflows of capital were required to raise their interest rates somewhat. International capital was more sensitive to fluctuations in the English rate than in that of other countries: the English rate played a leading role on the international level. As long as there was expansion in all countries, the rise in the interest rate continued, ultimately leading to a financial crisis that reduced the inflationary gap on the world level (Juglar cycle). This regulation process was fairly harsh and entailed bankruptcies as well as a reduction of international operations.

Long-term capital exports allowed the less advanced countries to have lasting current balance deficits, because the interest rates were relatively low. In addition, for Great Britain, which was by far the leading capital exporter, domestic and foreign investment had contrasting phases in the medium and long run (Kuznets cycle). During the phases where English accumulation was stagnating, foreign investments rose rapidly, which mainly permitted increased exports of primary materials coming from nonindustrialized countries through the creation of transportation networks. This infrastructural effort benefited English industry, which was able to compensate for the weakness of domestic accumulation through increased exports. The dynamic and orientation of international capital contributed to the stability and cohesion of international growth.

The essential role played by international capital movements was reinforced by the international monetary system. On the one hand, the stability of parities limited speculative tendencies, and moderate fluctuations in the interest rate set off short-term transfers of capital that balanced the trade markets. On the other hand, the spread of the gold standard throughout almost all countries encouraged the rapid growth of international finance. A prime example is the Russian adoption of the gold standard, with the deliberate intention of gaining the confidence of capital holders and obtaining massive loans in the international markets.

In the years before the First World War, all but two countries (United Kingdom and Netherlands) resorted to protectionism. This remained moderate in France and Germany, but the United States and Russia, which were undergoing rapid industrialization, imposed prohibitive tariffs averaging 40 percent, while Japan, which was initially required to maintain low tariffs by the major powers, managed to increase them as it grew stronger. The colonies, obviously, were required to open their markets to products from the metropolis. Protectionism had a double function. First, it maintained political balances between social categories. In Germany and France, the rise in tariffs at the end of the nineteenth century mainly affected agricultural products, with the aim of avoiding simultaneous worker and peasant discontent. Second, it compensated for the constraints imposed by the gold standard and encouraged the rapid rise of a national industry in the face of the power of English industry. It is significant that Italy and Russia accompanied the stabilization of their gold parity with a rise in tariffs.

Between 1875 and 1913, the European powers were engaged in a veritable race for the colonial conquests that were to add some 25 million square kilometers to their empires. This led Marxist authors, but also such liberals as Hobson, to argue that imperialism was an essential element of regulation at the end of the nineteenth century, notably because the colonial outlets compensated for the inadequacy of worker consumption. This form of expansion is said to have led to the First World War by aggravating conflicts among the powers. In reality, the importance of the colonies from one metropolis to another varied greatly before 1914 (see Table 4.6). It is true that a very large share of the United Kingdom's trade was carried out with its colonies, but essentially with those that had been conquered before 1870. In the case of France, the contribution of the colonies was minor until the First World War, and in the case of Germany, practically nonexistent. These two powers mainly traded with other European countries, and it was only during the 1930s that France massively drew on its colonial empire. The late nineteenth-century colonial expansion was also motivated by diplomatic considerations concerning the balance of power between European countries. Furthermore, the

Table 4.6

Contribution of the Colonies to the Trade of the European Powers (in %)

		1870	1890	1910	1925	1935
United Kingdom	Exports	26	33	37	43	48
	Imports	21	23	25	29	39
France	Exports		8	13	15	32
	Imports		7	11	11	29
Germany	Exports		0.2	0.7	0	0
	Imports		0.1	0.5	0	0

Source: J.L. Miege (1977).

First World War broke out following an attack in Bosnia (rather than Africa or Asia), the area of confrontation between the Austro-Hungarian Empire and Russia, both of whose semi-industrialized economies had not reached the highest stage of capitalism.

Between 1913 and 1938, trade continued to be determined by the vertical division of labor between industrialized and "primary exporting" countries. During the 1920s, loans were once again floated by the nonindustrialized countries, but trade resumed in a context of growing overproduction of primary materials. Trade stabilized in the 1925–26 period. The official adoption of the gold exchange standard by several countries did not basically change the international monetary system; it only gave official sanction to the inclusion of key currencies in the central bank reserves, a practice already existing before 1914. However, relations between major powers underwent changes: New York's role as a financial center came to rival that of London, and the Bank of France, whose policy was sharply tinged with nationalism, frequently obstructed international cooperation, notably with the bankruptcy of Credit Anstalt.

The Crisis in International Regulation, 1914–1915

In the conclusion of his work on the 1929 crisis, Kindleberger (1988) argues that this was the result of a crisis in hegemony: during the interwar period, the United Kingdom was no longer able to function as the dominant economy, but the United States did not wish to take over the role. A detailed chronological examination of the data concerning long-term capital and trade reserves leads to a more tempered view: a crisis in hegemony would first of all create disturbances in international financial and monetary relations, which would then have repercussions on the different national economies. The United States' long-term capital exports showed normal development until mid-1930, moving in the opposite direction from the short-term American economic situation. They declined with the boom of 1928–29 and remained steady at the beginning of 1930, in the first months of the crisis. The stability of the major currency parities continued until autumn 1931, and the collapse of the international monetary system and the escalation of European protectionism only occurred during the second phase of the crisis. Two factors should be noted. First, the collapse of international prices, with unprecedented scope and speed (the prices of raw materials, which had begun to decline in 1925, collapsed in the days following the stock market crash), left debtors insolvent and led to a wave of industrial and banking bankruptcies. Developing countries were driven to repudiate their debts and were denied access to international financial markets for decades. In the United States, this process was accompanied by the withdrawal of deposits, but, in the beginning at least, it did not involve the flight of short-term capital; this was only to take on major proportions in summer 1932. In Europe, by contrast, the bankruptcy of the Credit Anstalt in spring 1931 immediately set off violent movements of international capital, with depositors fearing monetary depreciations like those at the beginning of the 1920s. The First World War had weakened orthodox monetary policies; in order to finance military expenditures, the warring parties had abandoned the gold standard. After the war, several of them allowed inflation to develop in order to balance their debts. The gold parity religion suffered a decisive blow. In order to halve inflation, English and, especially, American authorities definitively abandoned the gold standard at the beginning of the 1930s. Changing attitudes toward the role of currency in the leading economies played a major role in the abandoning of traditional regulations.

International Regulation After the Second World War

The international regulation in effect after the Second World War was based on different, indeed opposite, principles—fixed but adjustable parities, the control of international capital movements, and free trade. It was set up by the United States, whose supremacy went unchallenged.

The Bretton Woods system reestablished the stability of trade, but the automatic imposition of monetary stability disappeared. A country was authorized to devaluate in order to restore the balance of its foreign payments, and it became acceptable to practice a discretionary monetary policy with the goal of stabilizing prices, guaranteeing full employment and foreign equilibrium, and favoring strong, stable growth. In practice, growth would be buttressed by the expansion of credit, and the issuing of bank currency validated by the central banks. A country that accustomed itself to an inflation higher than the average would adjust its parity, with broad autonomy granted to national economic policies. Moreover, the parity grid at the beginning of the system corresponded to potential disparities in growth. In 1949, practically all of the European currencies, including the mark, had been sharply devalued relative to the dollar. This contributed to reducing international disequilibria, since the war had revived American industry while its destruction had weakened the European economies. In the same way, Japan benefited from the undervaluation of currency during the 1950s and 1960s.

In addition, the transfers from the United States to Europe were massive. During the discussions that had preceded the Bretton Woods Agreement, the English estimated that Europe would need some $30 billion after the war, while the United States envisioned a loan of no more than $5 billion. At the time of the agreement, the American point of view won out, with the result that the credit of the International Monetary Fund was severely limited. However, in the years that followed, Europe's economic difficulties, the social agitation, and above all the growing rivalry with the Soviet Union led the United States to grant several tens of billions of dollars in foreign aid, notably within the framework of the Marshall Plan.

The principles of stable exchange and autonomous monetary policies are only compatible if international capital mobility is limited. During the 1950s and 1960s, nearly all countries monitored trade. When the United States became concerned about the disequilibrium of its balance of payments, the authorities took measures to limit capital outflows (Interest Equalization Tax of 1963 and Voluntary Restraint Program of 1965). In addition, the rise in investment taxes that accompanied the growth of intensive accumulation limited the industrialized countries' capacities to export capital. Financial assistance to developing countries took the form of loans and government aid, albeit of minimal scope. Private international capital was mainly invested in the developed countries, notably in Europe, where the perspectives for growth were good.

The principles of exchange-rate stability and monetary-policy autonomy can only operate to the extent that the global mobility of capital is limited. In all countries where foreign trade is weak, central bank holdings in hard currency constitute a significant indicator of economic policy. In the Bretton Woods system, international liquid assets depended above all on the American balance of payments. Many writers, notably in France, have thus concluded that the issuing of international liquidity was arbitrary. But this thesis neglects the fact that until around 1965, international liquidities showed a slow but steady increase, and it is implicitly at odds with the observation that the 1950s and 1960s saw an exceptionally strong and relatively steady rise in foreign trade. In fact, the system included two mechanisms for regulating international liquidity.

The first was that exports of American capital fluctuated in inverse proportion to the trade balance: a period of steady growth in the United States led to a decline in its trade balance, but the capital balance improved because domestic growth perspectives encouraged American multinationals to reduce their foreign investments in favor of domestic ones. This limited fluctuations in the liquid assets balance. Furthermore, gold played an active role: between 1950 and 1970, American gold reserves were practically divided in half. When the liquid assets deficit increased, the rest of the world converted part of the increased dollar reserves into gold, which resulted in a destruction of international liquid assets. The Bretton Woods system was thus initially a coherent mechanism for international regulation (Vidal 1989).

During the 1950s and 1960s, the industrialized countries reduced their customs tariffs to insignificant levels, and free trade among the OECD countries became a basic principle of international regulation. As we have seen, the growth of mass production resulted from the pursuit of greater returns and, consequently, from the increasing size of the markets.

The role of the gold problem in the weakening of international regulation should not be overestimated. Many writers insist on the fact that the total amount of international dollars greatly exceeded American gold reserves, which called into question the dollar's parity relative to gold. But empirical studies have shown that before 1914, the sterling balance clearly exceeded the United Kingdom's gold reserves, which were, moreover, considerably below those of France, the United States, or even Russia before 1905. After the 1929 crisis, the rules of monetary policy changed; no one could be certain that the United States would impose an austerity program to guarantee the stability of the dollar. Two other facts should be noted. First, and notably in the wake of the internationalization of industrial firms and banks, international capital mobility showed a considerable increase. In a context where parities are not irrevocably determined, international capital becomes "feverish," and central bank interventions through the manipulation of the interest rates or foreign-exchange transactions lose their effectiveness when they are faced with increasingly large speculation crises. Second, the major powers adopted different policies in response to the crisis of Fordism. During the 1970s, the United States implemented policies of accommodation resulting in negative interest rates, while West Germany made the fight against inflation its absolute priority. The dollar–mark parity, which played a central role at the end of the 1960s and the beginning of the 1970s, could not be stabilized. The floating of the main currencies, which became imperative in spring 1973, coincided with the assertion of the German model of crisis management in international relations and reflected the weakening of American hegemony.

Analysis of the Main Determinants of Competitiveness

The term *competitiveness* is used here in the broad sense, to indicate an economy's ability to ensure its external equilibrium and avoid external constraint. The latter is defined as the ability to make the potential growth rate defined on the basis of domestic factors coincide with the growth rate that is compatible with external equilibrium. A country under constraint is one that is forced to slow down its growth, and thus accept high unemployment, because of payment problems. This definition of competitiveness is broader than that of price competitiveness, and it does not coincide with the neomercantilist conception according to which competitiveness means maximizing the foreign surplus, because such an objective, if it is achieved, necessarily results in deficits for the client countries and disturbances in the international economy.

Many factors are likely to determine competitiveness—quality of the goods, efficiency of the commercial circuits, flexibility of the production apparatus, efforts at innovation, level of relative prices and costs—and the list could go on indefinitely. For our purposes, the most important factors are the mastery of the domestic market, the exchange rate, and nonprice competitiveness.

Mastery of the Domestic Market

Many analyses stress the role of exports in competitiveness. But the development of imports plays an equally important role, even outside of a strict accounting logic in terms of foreign balance. Firms produce for a specific demand and they have better knowledge of the national market. In general, it is easier and less expensive to conquer nearby markets, while the penetration of distant ones is often difficult and unpredictable. It is rational for an industry to begin by imposing itself on a national market and then, when the latter starts to become saturated, to conquer foreign markets. This has been Japan's strategy for a century.

Nonetheless, analyses asserting the national market's primary role in competitiveness have to be qualified, for they are addressed above all to national firms in large, developed countries. When the country is small, the national market may, from the very outset, be inadequate for certain industries that will very quickly be led to export in great quantity and for whom the conquest of the domestic market does not play a major role. Technical progress tends to increase the minimum market size in many sectors. This can vary considerably according to the products; indeed, a country's market may seem "small" or "large" according to the branch involved. In addition, if an industry is created through the implantation of foreign firms, these can immediately develop exports toward the home

Table 4.7

Germany's Import Elasticity Relative to Net Domestic Production

	1850–1870	1870–1890	1890–1913
Intermediate products	1.7	1.5	1.0
Final goods	2.7	1.0	0.8
Net domestic production (average annual growth rate in %)	2.0	2.6	3.2

Source: Hoffmann (1965), Table 103-129-131 (op. cit.).

country. In other words, the mastery of the domestic market is imperative if industrial development depends on national capital. Among the examples of such a process, the case of Germany before 1913 and that of Japan in recent years are particularly noteworthy.

Germany underwent a first phase of industrial development from 1850 to 1870, during which time the creation of a national market played a major role. However, this development remained quite dependent on imports of manufactured goods (see Table 4.7). Around 1870, the creation of the national market was wrapped up with political unification and the establishment of a central bank. Germany's dependency for manufactured goods was reduced, while domestic growth accelerated. Beginning around 1890, exports of manufactured goods showed a rapid increase and guaranteed Germany a top-ranking position in foreign trade. Greater protectionism around 1880 contributed to accelerating the reconquest of the domestic market. Although customs barriers had checked the flight from the land, the dynamism of German industry hardly suffered, to say the least, from protectionism. Similarly, protectionism did not prevent the United States from becoming the world's leading industrial power during the same period. On the contrary, it was probably because they were sheltered from powerful customs barriers that these two countries were able to weaken the power of English industry.

Obviously, it could be countered that the import-substitution process in Germany before 1913 occurred at a time when protectionism was the rule (except in Great Britain). But since the end of the 1950s and the spread of free trade, Japan clearly shows the greatest improvement in competitiveness among the advanced economies, and it also shows the smallest increase in the rate of penetration of the domestic market (see Table 4.8). For the 1960–70 period, Great Britain, West Germany, France, and Japan are countries with a similar level of development and size, which allows a comparison of their integration in foreign trade. Not only are the rates of penetration in Japan much lower than those of the other

Table 4.8

Domestic Market Penetration Rates (ratio of imports on internal demand, current prices, in %)

	1960				1970			
	A	C	I	E	A	C	I	E
United Kingdom	—	—	—	—	19.0	15.0	14.8	19.1
France	5.9	5.2	13.7	8.9	7.8	12.3	22.3	19.1
Germany	6.1	9.2	16.1	5.3	8.6	14.8	21.7	11.3
Japan	3.6	5.2	10.0	5.2	3.6	5.2	8.6	3.3

Source: Japan: Y. Barou (1979), annexe statistique.

France, Germany, United Kingdom: Y. Barou, M. Dolle, C. Gabet, E. Wartenberg (1979), Table T83.

A = Agroindustry, C = Consumer goods, I = Intermediate goods, E = Capital goods.

three countries, but they decline for capital goods and intermediate products between 1960 and 1970, while they increase sharply in the other countries. The rates of penetration in capital goods in 1970 provide a good indication of the relative competitiveness of the four countries. Japan's rate is much lower than that of West Germany, which is in turn much lower than that of Great Britain and France. These observations confirm the analyses of Mistral (1978), who maintains that the market-share positions in this sector play a decisive role in a country's competitiveness. This is probably due to the fact that production and consumption norms are mainly transmitted by capital goods. A country with significant surpluses for these goods imposes its own growth norms on its partners, which gives it a decisive advantage insofar as it can thus influence the development of worldwide demand.

Exports, Devaluation, Regulation

Cost and price disparities between countries are often cited to explain the development of exports. Relative export prices, which are important variables for explaining macroeconomic export functions, depend on the one hand on the domestic inflation rate compared to that of competitors, and on the other, on the exchange rate. Apart from cases of hyperinflation, which are exceptional in industrialized countries, parity varies more in the short run than does the inflation gap, owing to the fact that financial markets are generally flexible, while product markets are sluggish. But in the medium run, devaluation pushes domestic prices upward, and may increase the inflation gap relative to other countries, which is likely to cancel out the price-competitiveness margin acquired through a devaluation. This extremely important mechanism is largely tied to regulation

Table 4.9

Variation in Exports by Volume in the 1930s and 1970s

	Relative volume of exports (in comparison with U.K.), 1930 = 100			Relative volume of exports (in comparison with Germany), 1973 = 100		
	1931	1933	1935	1975	1977	1979
France	112	86	71	106	105	110
Belgium	134	106	107	93	95	92
Italy	133	110	89	112	115	123
Sweden	107	114	120	97	87	90
U.K.	100	100	100	103	105	98
Japan	136	178	233	121	137	123
U.S.	108	82	73	108	96	107

Source: J.F. Vidal (1989).

procedures, which thus play an essential role in the effectiveness of depreciations, as is shown by a comparison of devaluations in the 1930s and the 1970s.

During the 1930s, countries opting for devaluation often achieved better performances than those that remained tied to the gold bloc. During the 1950s and 1960s, several devaluations were successful, notably those of the franc in 1958 and 1969 and that of the pound in 1967, which allowed English exports to increase considerably. By contrast, during the 1970s, most of the devaluations—those of the franc, the pound, or the Swedish crown—led to only limited gains. Relations between the success of a depreciation and the domestic and international contexts in which it occurs (deflationary or inflationary) are decisive.

During the structural crisis, Japan undertook depreciations on an exceptional scale. In 1931, the United Kingdom and Sweden modified the parity of their currencies, while France, Italy, and Belgium remained attached to gold (Belgium was to devaluate in 1935). A few years later, the volumes of exports in these countries showed considerable disparities, especially with regard to France, the United Kingdom, Sweden, and Japan, as Table 4.9 demonstrates.

In 1973 the central banks of the major powers stopped stabilizing currency rates, and growth underwent a sustained slowdown. West German and Belgian currencies gained in value, while those of Italy, France, the United Kingdom and the United States declined. After 1976–77, the yen showed a sharp gain, while the Swedish crown was devaluated. But as the preceding table shows, differences in the growth of exports by volume were much more limited than during the 1930s. France and the

United States showed only limited gains, and the United Kingdom and Sweden none at all. To be sure, these diachronic, international differences cannot be explained solely in terms of prices and costs. It must be recalled that the 1930s saw the creation of protectionist trade blocs, notably in the colonial empires, which helps to explain the drop in American exports despite the depreciation of 1933. On the other hand, market shares also depended on nonprice competitiveness, which we shall address below. However, export performances remained sensitive to price and cost differentials.

The relative ineffectiveness of the post-1973 devaluations can be explained either by a weakening of the sensitivity of export and import volumes to changes in price levels or by the domestic effects of the devaluations. The price elasticities of foreign trade depend in part on the composition of the exchanges by goods. Until 1938, the industrialized countries mainly imported supplementary raw materials, and they also protected their domestic markets with customs tariffs. There was thus a strong possibility that the price elasticity of imports would have been slight. After 1945, the shift from the vertical to the horizontal division of labor and the lowering of customs barriers sharply decreased the proportion of raw materials in the total imports of the industrialized countries (except for Japan) to such an extent that manufactured goods constituted two-thirds of purchases abroad. These two developments probably increased the price elasticity of imports. The consequences of these changes in world trade as far as exports are concerned remain more ambiguous: the elimination of customs tariffs left the field wide open for price competition, but the rise in the share of capital goods, which can be diversified ad infinitum, increased the role of quality competition. For lack of a clear-cut conclusion, it is necessary to examine the statistical estimates of the price elasticity of exports.

For the interwar period, systematic econometric estimates for a large number of countries have been obtained by Polak (1954) and Neisser and Modigliani (1953) with their multinational models. The functions used are typical and explain the volume of exports by world demand and relative prices. In most cases, the effect of the latter is weak and of little significance, which justified the "elasticity skepticism." But during this period, such specification often yields biased results, notably because the explanatory variables, relative prices, and worldwide demand are subject to multicollinearities. Haberger (1957) sought to improve the estimates of price elasticities over the interwar period by using MacDougall's regressions concerning English and American exports and Zelder's estimates for disaggregated time series. His conclusion is that the price elasticity of exports in the majority of industrialized countries was between −1 and −2.

For the 1960s and 1970s, the numerous estimates studied by Goldstein and Kahn (1985) led them to propose a consensual value between −1.25 and −2.5, which, as they point out, is close to the conclusions of Haberger (1957). Empirical studies on import and export functions do not permit the conclusion that price elasticities have decreased since the Second World War.

The limited effectiveness of devaluations during the 1970s should rather be explained by the fact that the economic situation in the 1930s was deflationary, while in the 1970s it was inflationary. The idea that currency depreciation can lead to a vicious circle of inflation that may eliminate competitivity gains had already been advanced by observers in the early 1920s. The data in Table 4.10 indicate that at the beginning of the 1930s, there were severe disparities in export prices between Belgium and France on the one hand and between the United Kingdom, Sweden, and Japan on the other. Conversely, during the 1970s, the countries that opted for devaluation were unable to obtain massive price advantages.

The sequence of cause and effect is as follows: depreciation leads to a rise in the price of imported goods; in the most advanced economies, imports are in large part consumer goods, so there is also a rise in wages, the extent of which depends on the kind of regulation. The firms transfer the cost increase to the production price and may profit from the price rise of competing imports to increase their margins. Obviously, these behaviors depend on the kind of regulation (i.e., the institutional givens), but also on anticipations: a firm will be that much less hesitant about raising its prices if its competitors are likely to do the same. The 1930s and 1970s differ with regard not only to their institutions but also to the fact that raw materials prices underwent radically different changes, generating expectations of deflation in 1930 and inflation in 1974.

Table 4.10

Relative Price of Exports

	(in comparison with U.K.) 1930 = 100			(in comparison with Germany), 1973 = 100		
	1931	1933	1935	1975	1977	1979
France	100	114	114	101	95	97
Belgium	105	116	98	100	98	104
Italy	99	101	101	105	100	103
Sweden	100	100	100	103	103	116
U.K.	100	89	88	114	110	108
Japan	64	68	64	93	91	89
U.S.	93	95	97	104	100	94
Germany				100	100	100

Source: J.F. Vidal (1989).

Table 4.11

Devaluation and Inflation, 1921–1938 and 1965–1979, Estimate of Parameters

1921-1938	Ratio M/Y	elasticities			
		W/Pc	P/CS	P/Pm	P/E
U.S.	0.05	0.8	0.6	0.1	0.23
U.K.	0.25	0.8	0.3	0.2	0.32
France	0.16	0.7	0.5	0.2	0.36
Japan	0.2	0.3	1.1	0.15	0.29
1965-1979					
U.S.	0.07	0.5	0.9	0.1	0.23
U.K.	0.27	0.9	0.8	0.15	0.72
France	0.18	1	0.8	0.15	0.85
Japan	0.1	0.8	0.6	0.1	0.26
Germany	0.2	1	0.6	0.1	0.42

M = Imports, Y = GDP, W = wage rate, Pc = consumer price index, P = producer price index, CS = unit wage cost, Pm = import price index in national currency, E = exchange rate.

The inflationary impact of a depreciation depends on the following parameters: the share of imports on the domestic market, the elasticity of wages in response to living costs, the elasticity of production prices in response to labor costs, and the elasticity of production prices in response to exchange rates. The regulation methodology presented in chapters 2 and 3 allow us to provide rough estimates of these parameters and, on the basis of a simple model, to deduce the exchange rate elasticity of producer prices (see Table 4.11).

In Europe, the intensification of monopolistic regulation, combined with the rise in import rates, greatly diminished the effectiveness of devaluations by increasing the wage–price spiral. By contrast, the United States showed little vulnerability to imported inflation because of its low import rates and indexation coefficient. Furthermore, it appears that its exports, mainly composed of high-tech goods, were relatively impervious to prices, while imports including few supplementary raw materials and many manufactured consumer goods had a relatively high price elasticity in relation to other countries.

The reaction of domestic prices to fluctuations in the exchange rate also affects domestic demand. At the beginning of the 1930s, the fall in prices contributed to serial bankruptcies and pushed real interest rates to very high ex post levels. By raising the price of foreign goods on the domestic market and allowing the central banks to pursue expansive policies, devaluation helped to halt deflation. By contrast, during the 1970s, the vicious circles of devaluation forced authorities to adopt restrictive policies. In the medium run, devaluation can be a useful weapon against international recession in a context of stable or falling prices, but it may aggravate difficulties tied to stagflation; in this context, the depreciation of the exchange rate becomes an additional constraint.

At the beginning of the 1980s, wages were de-indexed; inflation was brought down to very low levels, while primary materials prices were directed downward. This new context was more favorable to the success of exchange-rate depreciations. The devaluation of the Swedish crown in 1982 and the depreciation of the pound sterling in 1984–85 considerably accelerated the growth of exports.

Nonprice Competitiveness

The long-term development of a country's trade cannot be explained solely by relative prices and costs. But the nonprice factors in competitiveness cannot be directly measured. As Mathis, Mazier, and Rivaud-Danset (1988) show, the importance of nonprice competitiveness can be approached by studying the different volume and price elasticities of foreign trade. As indicated above, a country that is competitive in the quality of its goods or its specialization will show a low price elasticity of its trade volume, but estimates of these parameters are subject to frequent biases. The parameters of export-price equations are generally more significant. Indeed, at least for the monopolistic regulation regime, firms seek to transfer domestic price rises to the prices of their exports, while taking into account, if need be, the prices of their competitors. A country enjoys qualitatively strong competitiveness if its export prices respond in elastic fashion to domestic costs and are not strongly affected by the prices of its competitors: the country will thus be a "price maker," as is the case for the United States and West Germany. A country showing the opposite features will be a "price taker"; Italy is one of the most frequently cited cases.

The analyses drawn from the price equations reflect the level a country's "monopoly power" attains on its foreign markets—in other words, its ability to make its exports profitable. But this is not the same thing as its ability to increase sales. This can be studied with equations describing the changes in import and export volumes, which mainly depend on prices, domestic demand, and foreign demand. A country that has a high foreign demand elasticity of its exports and a low domestic demand elasticity of its imports (estimated with price elasticities taken into account) can maintain its foreign trade balance while showing greater growth than its competitors. The ratio between these two elasticities allows us to evaluate a country's ability to maintain its foreign equilibrium by volume, given its growth differential relative to the others.

Table 4.12

Indicators of Nonprice Competitiveness Drawn from Macroeconomic Functions

	Domestic cost elasticity of export price[1]	Income elasticity of export/ income elasticity of import[2]
U.S.	0.8	0.55
Germany	0.7	1.2
U.K.	0.64	0.52
France	0.53	1.3
Japan	0.49	3.2
Italy	0.18	1.1

Sources: [1]Mathis, Mazier, Rivaud-Danset (1988); [2]Goldstein and Kahn (1985).

The econometric equations indicate that Japan faces such a situation, while the United Kingdom faces the opposite one. Table 4.12 gives the evaluations of competitiveness drawn from price equations on one hand and demand elasticities of volume on the other. It shows that these two conceptions of nonprice competitiveness are very different: the United States is clearly a "price maker," while it has an unfavorable ratio of volume elasticities of demand; conversely, Japan has a vast capacity for enjoying greater growth than its competitors while maintaining the external balance, but overall, it does not set prices on the world markets.

Nonprice competitiveness is often related to the quality of specialization. There are two methods for translating this into quantitative terms. The first involves a purely mechanical breakdown of export growth (or the fluctuation of market share), as carried out by Maizels (1971) or Tyszynski (1951) and more recently in a study by the National Statistics Institute (INSEE). A second method, proposed by G. Lafay (1979) and the CEPII, is also quite common. Before examining the specialization of the French economy and its dynamic, it is useful to compare the two approaches.

Maizels's method consists of breaking down export growth in terms of three factors: (1) the momentum effect of the different markets on the basis of the positions acquired at the outset; (2) the adaptation effect, when a country withdraws from the less dynamic markets or increases its share of the most dynamic ones; (3) the competitiveness effect resulting from the gains or losses on each market. The nature of the specialization appears twice: that which is acquired enters into the first term, while its development determines the second. Maizels has used this breakdown for five subperiods between 1899 and 1959. His calculations show that for each subperiod, the adaptation effect (2) is fairly limited. By contrast, the effect of pure competitiveness (3) plays an important role when a country's market share undergoes heavy growth. Since 1913, Great Britain's losses have largely resulted from the effect of pure competitiveness, namely losses on practically the whole of the markets taken individually. At the opposite extreme, Japan's gains essentially resulted from gains in pure competitiveness. Until 1937, Japan's specialization remained negligible, or negative, because the most significant gains took place in the textile industry.

For the 1961–74 period, the calculations of Barou, Dolle, Gabet, and Wartenberg (1979) show that most of Great Britain's losses resulted from the effect of pure competitiveness, with the adaptation effect playing a much less important role. In the case of Germany, a slight increase in the market share resulted solely from the specialization acquired at the outset; the adaptation effect was negative, but not enough so as to reverse the trend resulting from the initial specialization.

The CEPII's method leads to a very different set of conclusions. Since the statistical concepts are not the same as those used in the previous method, it is somewhat difficult to compare them. It seems, however, that the difference in the results can be explained above all by the fact that Maizels's method is descriptive while that of the CEPII is normative. Indeed, it consists of rating each country according to the growth of its foreign trade, and the scale adopted favors the adaptation effect. Losses on a sluggish market earn the same number of points as a gain on a dynamic market; entering an expanding market is rated in the same way as withdrawing from a contracting market. On the other hand, the pure competitiveness effect (gains or losses on each market taken individually) is not always taken into account: a country that starts out with deficits on all markets and increases its deficits on all of them shows an implicit disengagement across the board, which gives it an average of 10/20. Obviously, its position remains constant in terms of adaptation, but more broadly, it declines. This exaggerates the adaptation, which naturally leads to favoring the Japanese growth model since 1960. Nonetheless, the CEPII method has at least one advantage over that of Maizels, insofar as it takes imports into account whereas the other deals only with exports.

Finally, these studies show that when a country undergoes sharp fluctuations in its world market share, these can be explained above all by gains over most of the products and partners, and that these cannot be attributed solely to price and cost competitiveness. This residue can only be analyzed by simultaneously studying domestic growth mechanisms and the country's integration in the international division of labor.

Part II

Structural Crises: Why and How?

CHAPTER FIVE

Origins of the Interwar Crisis

A few basic figures illustrate the considerable differences that can be observed in the way the great powers evolved after the First World War. Beyond the decisive lead taken by the United States, these show that among the three European belligerents, France is the one that best surmounted the consequences of the war, despite the fact that it suffered the most extensive material losses. The contrast with Germany is striking, insofar as the latter's capital stock rose only slightly and its labor productivity remained virtually stagnant (see Table 5.1).

The economic and social consequences of the war differed sharply from one country to another depending on whether they were winners or losers and the way they chose to distribute the sacrifices necessary to pay the economic and financial costs of the conflict. In addition, the development of the crisis also varied significantly. Since it is not possible to apply a uniform frame of analysis to all countries, we have chosen to focus mainly on the origins of the 1929 crisis in the two countries that were hardest hit, the United States and Germany, plus certain developments in France.

United States: Real Factors Often Underestimated

The past ten or twenty years have seen many English-language publications on the 1929 crisis in the United States. As indicated in several recent surveys (Eichengreen 1992; Calomiris 1993; Romer 1993), these are almost exclusively devoted to the role of monetary and financial factors. Discussions have mainly addressed the role of the Federal Reserve System's policy, the imperfection of the financial markets and the rationing of credit, and debt and household goods.

Table 5.1

GDP, Investment and Labor Productivity in 1929 (private sector, at constant prices, 1913 = 100)

	United States	France	United Kingdom	Germany
GDP	162.6	125.5	114.1	119.4
Capital	139.8	123.3	110.8	102.5
Productivity	131.6	126.5	120.0	102.5

Source: United States, Kendrick (1961); France, GRESP (1979); United Kingdom, Feinstein (1976), Germany; Hoffmann (1965).

The Debate on Monetary Policy and Credit

The thesis of Friedman and Schwartz (1963) is well known. In essence, it argues that the main cause of the Great Depression was the contraction of the money supply. This is attributed to the central bank's restrictive monetary policy in 1928 and 1929 and, from late 1930 on, to banking panics that led to a sharp contraction of the credit multiplier. Above all, Friedman and Schwartz criticize the authorities for not having intervened sufficiently to stop bank failures. It was only at the beginning of 1933, with the new government's decision to close the banks, that the panics were halted and the crisis came to an end.

Within this thesis, one point is widely accepted: it is true that from 1928 on, the central bank had set up a restrictive policy to limit speculation on Wall Street, and this led to a considerable increase in nominal interest rates that lasted until August 1929. On the basis of monthly data on industrial production, the beginning of the recession is usually placed in spring 1929, which means before the stock market crash. Construction and the durable goods industries were the first to be affected, which supports the thesis of an initial shock caused by monetary policy.

Another widely accepted point is that currency played a major role in the continuation and aggravation of the American crisis after the end of 1931. Indeed, during the 1920s and until summer 1931, the United States benefited from short-term capital inflows. Since American gold reserves were also considerable, the central bank was hardly subject to the constraints of the gold standard and enjoyed a large margin for lowering its interest rate. This freedom became more limited after the devaluation of the pound sterling. Operators then maintained that the dollar should drop, with the result that it underwent speculative assaults and the short-term rate rose sharply in late 1931 and early 1932. In addition, the devaluation of the pound, followed by that of many other currencies, intensified falling prices in the countries that had maintained their parity.

On the other hand, the idea that the money supply was the ongoing cause of the Great Depression until 1933 has been sharply contested, notably by Temin (1976). In other words, the role of money in 1930 and 1931 has been the main subject of the discussions. It is true that the nominal money supply decreased during each year of the depression, but this contraction can basically be related to an autonomous drop in demand. Indeed, in a neo-Keynesian schema, an exogenous decline in the real demand for goods and services will lead to a decline in the demand for money and credit, and a reduction in the nominal interest rate, while a restriction of the money supply increases the interest rates. Since the latter showed a sharp decrease in 1930 and 1931, the Keynesians would argue that the decline in activity is the cause of the decline in the money supply and not the reverse. Furthermore, in 1930 and 1931, the money supply dropped less than the level of prices, so that real cash balances rose.

The monetarist reply consists of stressing that if the nominal interest rates declined during the depression, the ex post real rates increased. This raises the question of the anticipation of deflation. If deflation is not anticipated (which corresponds to a traditional Keynesian hypothesis), the decline in the nominal rates can only encourage investment and the depression is slowed down. To be sure, the debt burden will increase in the long run, so that the recession will ultimately worsen, but for the moment, it will have been postponed or slowed down. In other terms, if the drop in prices was not anticipated, the 1929 crisis, which was characterized by extremely rapid adjustments, cannot be blamed primarily on money because the nominal interest rates declined during the two years that followed the stock market crash. On the other hand, if deflation was anticipated, the rise in real interest rates may have been an immediate and persistent cause of the crisis, and the drop in the nominal interest rate does not reflect an abundance of money but simply the state of anticipations. It is thus necessary to reconstruct what these were, and they can be indirectly observed. Nelson (1991) has undertaken a detailed study of the economic and financial press of the time and concludes that during the first half of 1930 many commentators largely underestimated the deflation and even predicted a fairly rapid recovery. Awareness of the seriousness of the crisis probably took hold around the middle of 1930. Nelson interprets his findings as rather favorable to the monetarist theses, because the monetary illusion would have quickly vanished. However, his data is purely qualitative because it is drawn not from statistical series but from assertions and conjectures advanced in the press. A more rigorous method would be that of Hamilton (1992), which consists of analyzing price series on the futures markets because futures buying and selling orders depend on anticipated spot prices. His conclusion is that in 1930, deflation had practically not been anticipated; in 1931, the operators had foreseen it but underestimated its consequences.

Another objection to the monetarist thesis is that since monetary policy in 1928–29 was not very restrictive, it cannot explain the cataclysm that followed. In other words, the presumed cause would not be proportional to its effects. This argument is worth examining more closely, notably in terms of the factors or elements that underwent an exceptionally sharp fluctuation during the 1929 crisis. This can be done by comparing the 1929–33 period with earlier developments. More specifically, it is possible to calculate the average values of the aggregate growth rates or the interest-rate levels between 1891 and 1916, along with their standard deviations. By evaluating the location of the values observed during the crisis in relation to this distribution, the distance between the economic situation for one year and the average situation for the 1891–1916 period can be measured in standard deviations. The years 1916–22 are excluded from the base sample because of the undue influences of the war. By standard usage, a distance equal to or greater than two standard deviations is held to be considerable. These calculations (see Table 5.2) show that in 1929 and 1930, the monetary variables (real cash balances, nominal interest rate, real ex post interest rate) do not show exceptionally large variations, although the contraction of activity was already considerable. In 1931, the real interest rate was starting to be quite high, but real cash reserves were only moderately checked. It was only in 1932 that the monetary variables took on extreme values. It must also be stressed that in 1930, the decrease in the GNP deflator remained moderate. In other words, the first half of the crisis was absolutely not characterized by an exceptional deflation, while the decline in activity was already quite significant.

The traditional monetary factors—cash reserves and interest rate—only explain the onset of the recession before the crash of the stock market and, in part, the aggravation of the crisis in 1932. But monetary dynamics do not depend on the central banks alone; they also result from behaviors of the commercial banks. It has been argued, notably by Bernanke (1983), that the commercial banks had rationed credit. According to this hypothesis, the banks used their resources to acquire sure assets, namely government securities, which lowered the interest rate on the money market. At the same time, they reduced their credit supply, which forced firms and households to limit their expenditures. To be sure, the observed decrease in net credit flows cannot be invoked to validate this thesis because this could result from an autonomous decline in investment. The main indicator is the gap between the interest rate on bonds issued by corporations rated Baa and government bonds, insofar as this reflects a distrust of borrowers held to be less certain. The charts presented by Kindleberger (1986) indicate that this gap began to widen at the end of 1930 and became sizable by summer 1931. As with the traditional monetary variables, credit rationing would also seem to have played a limited role during the first half of the crisis.

Table 5.2

United States, Depression of 1929–32 Compared with the 1891-1916 Period
(monetary factors)

	Fluctuations 1891–1916				
	annual growth rates			annual levels	
	GNP	GNP deflator	real money	nominal interest rate	real interest rate
Average	3.67	1.47	5.31	5.55	4.08
Standard deviation	5.74	3.54	4.36	0.86	3.87

Great Depression Compared With the Fluctuations of the 1891–1916 Period
(value in t minus average value in 1896–1916/standard deviation in 1891–1916)

1929	–	−0.41	−1.17	0.35	0.46
1930	−2.3	−1.28	−1.03	−2.29	0.66
1931	−1.98	−2.99	−0.9	−3.4	1.98
1932	−3.05	−3.5	−2.46	−3.29	2.51

Source: Balke and Gordon (1986).

From Financial Variables to Real Variables: Household Expenditures

The limits of attempts to explain the crisis in terms of monetary and credit factors leads us to consider the role of real variables. Temin (1976) had brought out the fact that household consumption declined to an unexplained degree in 1930, as demonstrated by the presence of negative remainders in the consumption function. Indeed, data on the components of overall expenditure bring out the major role of consumption in the Great Depression (see Tables 5.3 and 5.4). At the beginning of the recession, the decline in investment preceded that in consumption. But in 1930 and 1932, the years when the crisis was at its worst, the role of consumption was considerably greater than that of investment. This observation is largely accepted by English-speaking authors, who propose an explanation linking real and financial factors. This idea was developed notably by Mishkin (1978), who reconstituted net household property by evaluating debts and financial assets. During the 1920s, households increased their debts in order to acquire housing and consumer durables; during the crisis, their financial holdings were severely depreciated. They reacted to the deterioration of their balance sheet by reducing their durable goods purchases. Romer (1993) defends a similar argument: the stock market crash in October 1929 increased the uncertainties of consumers and pushed them to reduce their durable goods purchases. Olney (1989)

Table 5.3

United States, Depression of 1929–1932 Compared with the Fluctuations of the 1891–1916 period (real factors)

(value in t minus average value in 1891–1916)/standard deviation in 1891–1916

	Contribution of the expenditures to the GNP change				Average growth rates	
	Consumption	Investment	External balance	Public expenditure	Real wage	Employment
1929	0.34	−0.26	−0.45	0.14	0.63	0.69
1930	−1.92	−1.5	−0.41	1.56	−1.42	−3.79
1931	−1.42	−1.67	−0.57	0.73	0.48	−4.4
1932	−2.77	−1.69	−0.40	−1.95	−2.34	−5.1

Source: Expenditures, Kendrick (1961); real wages, "Historical Statistics..."; employment Weir (1992).

The contribution of an expenditure (C) to the GNP (Y) change is $(C_t - C_{t-1})/Y_{t-1}$

takes the argument further: in response to the deterioration of their net wealth and an increased risk of illiquidity, households reduce the whole of their expenditures, including the consumption of nondurables.

These arguments are supported by econometric tests explaining consumption in terms of income and net wealth. But estimates of the effects of wealth remain very imprecise. Furthermore, according to Mishkin's evaluations, household debts accumulated in the purchase of consumer durables and housing constituted only 10.2 percent of their financial assets in 1929 and 15.2 percent in 1932. The low level of these percentages does not seem to imply massive adjustments in consumption.

The majority of the English-speaking authors who link indebtedness, the fall of stocks, and household expenditures insist on the importance of consumer durables, the demand for which began to rise mainly after 1910. As a result, most of them underestimate the role of nondurable consumer goods, which was much more important during the depression. This fact emerges quite clearly in the quarterly data reconstituted by Balke and Gordon (1986). This series suggests that the Great Depression can be broken down into three phases: an initial collapse from summer 1929 to autumn 1930, stabilization from autumn 1930 to spring 1931, and a second collapse from spring 1931 to winter 1933 (see Table 5.4). Table 5.4 shows an essential fact: it is clearly the drop in consumption of nondurable goods that played the most important role in the two collapses. The debts incurred by the households to acquire durable goods and the drop in their portfolio probably do not suffice to explain this decrease. Another more simple and widespread factor may be cited: layoffs and the rapid rise in unemployment. Indeed, the calculations presented in Table

Table 5.4

United States: Contribution of the Expenditures to the GNP Change (%)

	Producers residential		Consumption		Public	Exports	GNP change (%)
	Investment	Construction	Durables	Non durables			
1929 III to 1930 IV	−3.9	−2.0	−1.7	−5.6	+1.4	−1.1	−17.2
1930 IV to 1931 II	−1.7	+0.4	−0.3	+1.1	+0.3	−0.4	+1.9
1931 II to 1933 I	−4.7	−2.0	−1.9	−10.2	−1.4	−1.3	−24.4

Source: Balke and Gordon (1986). Roman figures are quarters.

5.3 indicate that in 1930, 1931, and 1932, the decline in employment was exceptionally violent, and these results coincide with the study of employment adjustment functions presented in chapter 2: the interwar period is characterized by a very rapid adjustment of employment.

Figure 5.1 shows the quarterly growth rates for consumption of nondurables and real money as evaluated by Balke and Gordon, for real earnings from manufacturing employment, and from stock prices given by the Federal Reserve Board. It shows that consumption of nondurable goods is much more closely tied to real money from manufacturing employment than to the quantity of money or financial wealth. Fluctuations in stock prices are too irregular to be correlated with consumption. Real cash balances increased between late 1929 and spring 1931 and thus cannot explain the drop in consumption. Industry's wage bill and employment level dropped sharply between late 1929 and summer 1930, and again in summer 1931 and summer 1932; these contributed a great deal to the two main phases of aggravating the crisis. Layoffs led to a decline in the wage bill, mechanically and through the downward pressure of unemployment on the average wage. The decline in the wage bill quickly led to a drop in consumption, which quickly led to the drop in production and employment. With such a dynamic, the effects of the Keynesian multiplier were quite powerful.

It must be stressed that a circular link between employment and production was reinforced over time. Indeed, as Joshua (1994) emphasizes, American agriculture employed nearly half of the labor force at the end of the nineteenth century but only one-fifth in 1929. Agricultural employment is rigid, while nonagricultural employment in the private sector is extremely flexible; this profound transformation of productive structures considerably increased the instability of employment. During the 1970s and 1980s, American economists focused on the monetary and financial factors of the crisis and forgot that real factors also have real effects. In the America of 1929, wage-earners represented a majority of the workforce; their consumption, which was an essential outlet for manufacturing, was very sensitive to changes in the wage bill. Increasing flexibility of employment and wages played an important role in the cumulative collapse of the American economy.

Household Expenditure and Income: Long-Term Evolution

Beyond the short-term economic aspects, which have just been considered, it must be asked whether the Great Depression was also the result of long-term structural imbalances in growth. During the 1920s, the American economy did not undergo an exceptional boom; in reality, growth was slightly more moderate than before the First World War, and

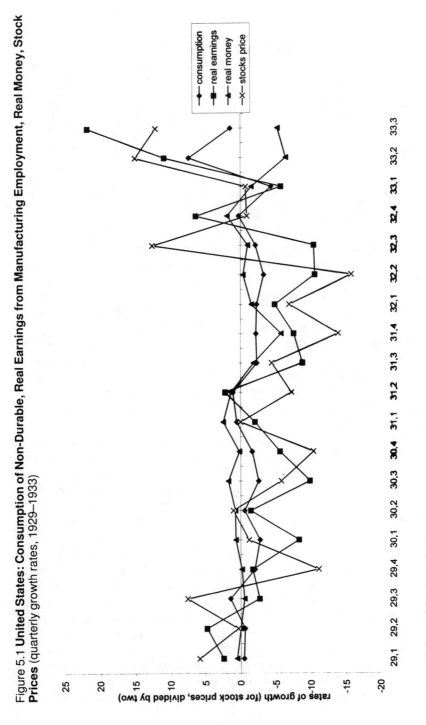

Figure 5.1 **United States: Consumption of Non-Durable, Real Earnings from Manufacturing Employment, Real Money, Stock Prices** (quarterly growth rates, 1929–1933)

Source: Balke and Gordon (1986).

Table 5.5

United States: Long-Term Growth (average annual growth rate in %)

	1901–1919	1919–1926	1926–1929
GNB (private sector)	2.9	4.2	2.7
Employment (private sector)	2.0	1.5	1.2
Labor productivity (private sector)	0.9	2.7	1.5
Real wages	1.4	2.0	3.2
Non-durable consumption	–	3.4	2.3
Durable goods consumption	–	3.7	1.6
Housing construction	–	6.5	–6.1

Source: Product, productivity, employment, Kendrick (1961); wages, "Historical Statistics. . . "; households, Balke and Gordon (1986).

the investment rate was lower. However, growth underwent a qualitative change. It became more intensive, as seen in the evolution of productivity gains (see Table 5.5). This change in rhythm was particularly marked in the hourly productivity of industry, thus reflecting the profound transformations of production conditions that characterized the first burst of Taylorism. The comparison between the growth of productivity and that of real wages is difficult because these are very irregular between 1917 and 1922. However, a close examination of the average real wage/productivity ratio shows that over the whole of the 1920s in the private sector, labor productivity did not significantly outdistance wages. Dumenil and Lévy (1993) have insisted on this point in order to criticize regulation theory.

At the same time, a new consumption standard was developing; the automobile industry emerged as a growth sector that, in particular, favored the spread of suburban areas. Housing construction developed rapidly until 1926 and stimulated the purchase of consumer durables. However, from 1926 on, the growth of durable goods consumption underwent a clear slowdown, while housing construction also declined considerably. The emerging phenomenon of demand saturation has been analyzed by several writers. Hickman (1961) has shown that over the 1920s, new construction projects for housing largely surpassed the number of occupied housing units. Bolch, Fels, and MacMahon (1971) have demonstrated that the increased supply of housing exceeded the needs resulting from population growth and the demand for better quality housing. This surplus supply resulted in part from speculation and an excessive distribution of credit. In the automobile sector, Mercer and Morgan (1972) have shown that as of 1926 demand began to slow down and unused production capacities increased, although consumption credit grew rapidly. In other words, during the years before the 1929 crisis, a disequilibrium began to emerge because of the slowdown in household durables consumption. In relation to long-term changes, the growth of the Fordist consumption standard slowed down at the end of the 1920s, when it was still far from being widespread among the wage-earning class.

However, as Dumenil and Lévy stress, it is impossible to speak of underconsumption in the traditional sense of the term: during the 1920s, the consumption–GNP ratio did not decline; for the private sector as a whole, profits occupied a smaller share of added value than before the war and did not increase. There was thus no lack of consumption as a whole. But the forms of monetary and wage regulations were not suited to the growth of the Fordist consumption standard, namely the acquisition of housing and durable consumer goods by the majority of wage-earners: the instability of employment and the fragility of the financial system severely limited the households' recourse to credit.

This analysis of the main causes of the 1929 crisis in the United States shows that it largely resulted from the persistence of competitive regulation in a very different context from that of the years before the First World War. The average wage remained highly sensitive to the short-term situation; the production elasticity of nonagricultural private-sector employment remained high. On the other hand, the financial system remained unstable, notably because of the small size of the banks. In 1913, a central bank was created, but the experience of the crisis showed that the banking system had not been strengthened. This was largely due to the federal structure of the U.S. central bank system, whose individual components had different conceptions of monetary policy; as a result, the Federal Reserve System hesitated between combating the depression and stabilizing the gold parity.

This strongly competitive regulation became increasingly unsuitable in the face of four basic changes in the economic structures. The first two relate specifically to the American economy. The drop in agriculture's share in total employment relative to the nonagricultural private sector strongly increased employment instability. Demand, meanwhile, was increasingly dependent on wage-earners' incomes; the consumption of durable goods increased, notably through indebtedness, so that the demand of households depended increasingly on their solvency, which was in turn linked to their incomes and, for a small minority of them, the value of their financial assets. Two other changes resulted from the international consequences of the First World War. As Kindleberger (1988) shows, the war led to the massive growth of raw materials production in the Third World. After the war, the revival of European production led to a situation of world overproduction, which culminated in the collapse of world prices and thus worsened the debt burden everywhere. On the other hand, monetary and financial disequilibria reduced the confidence of capital holders in the stability of the currency. During the interwar period, there was massive capital speculation, which constituted an additional factor of deflation in the countries that had maintained the parity of their currency.

Germany: The Impossible Compromise

The 1929 depression in Germany cannot be analyzed as a consequence of the forms of its prior growth. Indeed, the 1920s were already crisis years: the hyperinflation of 1922–23 was followed by a period of stagnation marked by numerous disequilibria. However, the methods of regulation theory bring out the fragility of the Germany economy, even if this is very different in nature from that of the United States. As we shall demonstrate, this fragility resulted from the impossibility of coming to a reasonable agreement with the other powers on the question of reparations and the difficulty of finding an internal compromise on the sharing of sacrifices linked to the war. In other words, the disequilibria cannot be understood in a purely economic context in the neoclassical sense, but in an institutional approach that would take into account internal and external conflicts. These features of the German economy emerge quite clearly in the study of the beginnings of the depression and in that of the economic policies pursued during it.

Premature Recession

The particularity of the German depression is that it began, according to the quarterly data on industrial production, in summer 1927, and, according to the annual national accounts, in 1928. The traditional explanation is that the German economy, dependent on external financing, suffered from the drop in capital inflows from the United States. Temin (1971) has criticized this thesis by comparing data on the United States capital balance, the German capital balance, and the sources of investment financing in Germany. Table 5.6 illustrates his argument on the basis of slightly different data.

It is true that American capital exports and German capital imports decreased in 1929, because the rise in the discount rate and stock prices in New York, checked the outflow of funds. But in Germany, capital formation decreased from 1928 on, in spite of considerable inflows of funds. Since the balance of payments data suffer from significant margins of error, it is useful to complement them with statistics on the exchange reserves of the Reichsbank and the difference in interest rates between Berlin and New York which, when they undergo brutal fluctuations, re-

Table 5.6

Germany: International Finance and Evolution of the Economy

	1927	1928	1929	1930	1931
Net exports of capital from U.S. (billions of $)	0.4	1.1	0.3	0.3	−0.2
Net imports of capital from Germany (billions of marks)	3.5	3.1	1.5	1.2	0.7
Variation of currency reserves of Germany (billions of marks)	0.11	0.37	0.1	0.3	−0.9
Short term interest rate differences Berlin–New York	2.04	2.45	1.83	1.95	5.2
Variation of investment in Germany (billions of marks)	4.8	−1.2	−3.3	−0.8	−4.1
External balance of Germany (billions of marks)	−0.3	−0.14	0	+0.14	+0.24

Sources: Line 1, "Historical Statistics"; Line 2, Keese (1966); Lines 3, 4, 6, Statistiches Handbuch der Weltwirtschaft; Line 5, Hoffmann (1965).

flect heavy capital movements. According to the annual data, the Reichbank's reserves increased between 1927 and 1930; the variation in the interest rate was fairly stable during this period: it was only in 1931 that the reserves declined and the gap between the rates expanded. The monthly data provide a more precise, nuanced view (although this cannot be provided here for reasons of space): Germany suffered capital outflows in spring 1929 with the emergence of the difficulties over reparations, in winter 1930–31, with the first electoral victories of the Nazi Party, and, to be sure, in summer 1931, with the banking crisis. The fact that the flights of capital in 1929 lasted only briefly confirms that between 1927 and 1930, the German economy, which was highly dependent on foreign capital, did not really lack a foreign supply of financial resources: the drop in capital inflows in 1929 and 1930 took place when domestic investment had already greatly declined.

The beginning of the German recession cannot be explained by a deterioration in its international context. Balderston (1983) provides a much more convincing explanation, according to which the German economy underwent a strong recovery in 1926, and this considerably aggravated the foreign trade deficit (see Table 5.6) at a time when there were already severe constraints from the balance of payments. The government thus decided to halt growth, notably by rationing credit.

According to the yearly data, the recession was serious by 1929, as can be seen in Table 5.7, which is structured like Table 5.3 comparing the 1929 crisis in the United States with the economic situation during the 1891–1913 period. Unlike the situation in the United States, business invest-

Table 5.7

Germany: Great Depression Compared with the 1897–1913 Period (observed value in t minus average value in 1897–1913/standard deviation in 1891–1913)

	Rate of growth of national income	Contributions to national income variations				
		Private consumption	Housing construction	Investment	Public expenditures	External balance
1928	−0.4	−0.5	0.24	−1.2	0.59	2.61
1929	−2.24	−1.6	−0.98	−3.0	−1.71	3.66
1930	−2.39	−3.3	−3.9	−3.3	−3.8	0.29
1931	−4.38	−2.9	−4.1	−3.3	−6.3	0.69
1932	−2.47	−2.4	−0.6	1.7	−2.8	5.9
1933	3.37	0.93	1.6	1.9	11.8	−0.97

Source: Hoffmann (1965)

ment played a major role in the beginnings of the German depression. The significant influence of public expenditures can also be observed between 1930 and 1932, and we shall come back to this below.

The low level of capital accumulation illustrates the structural weaknesses of the German economy—which had not really recovered from the war—during the 1920s. The firms were still in a difficult state: while net profits represented 28.5 percent of value added in 1913, they accounted for only 8.7 percent in 1925; between these two dates, the rate of profit had gone from 6.7 to 2.2 percent. Labor productivity was stagnating while real wages were on the rise. This increase was sharply aggravated by a considerable increase in the relative price of consumer goods, resulting in part from the rise in prices in the textile–garment industry, a sector whose productivity had sharply diminished. The result of the drop in profits was to increase the role of bank financing. In 1913, financial intermediaries had financed 51.8 percent of all net investments; between 1925 and 1929, their share reached 68.3 percent (all of these ratios are calculated on the basis of Hoffmann's series).

In addition to this internal constraint on profits there was obviously an external one. In 1913, Germany's foreign trade suffered a slight deficit. This became much greater after the war, basically because of the imports of agricultural products and raw materials, insofar as foreign dependency increased with the territorial losses in the East and the West. In addition, trade balances in services declined owing to the confiscation of a large part of the merchant marine and interest on the foreign debt, as well as reparations.

The hyperinflation of 1922–23 added a monetary constraint as well:

stabilization was sanctioned by a 1924 banking law that required the central bank to cover 40 percent of the money issued by gold and hard-currency reserves, and the monetary financing of the budget deficit was prohibited. Because the contribution of foreign capital was indispensable to maintaining the balance of payments, the central bank almost always wound up implementing a restrictive policy; between 1925 and 1929, the interest rates, both long- and short-term, were established at a level almost double that of the prewar period.

Role of Economic Policy

The economic policy pursued by the Brüning government during the depression is traditionally denounced as having considerably aggravated the crisis. Indeed, it consisted of reducing public expenditures (see Table 5.7) and imposing decreases in prices and income; it was explicitly deflationary. However, Borchardt (1982) has defended the thesis that Brüning's policy was not an error, but rather the only possibility given the constraints weighing on monetary and budgetary decisions. Borchardt insists on the idea that from the 1920s on, the German economy was structurally weakened by the reduction of profits. In his view, the Weimar Republic was a fragile government, violently contested by nationalist elements. The authorities were driven to make systematic concessions to the unions, notably when they were called on to arbitrate labor–management disputes (as provided for by the Constitution). Furthermore, the margins of macroeconomic policy were practically nonexistent: on the one hand, it was impossible to implement a policy of budgetary stimulation because of the 1924 law; the stability of the mark was part of the international agreements to which Germany had subscribed. For Borchardt, the depression only became very serious with the banking crisis of summer 1931. At that point, it was already late for revival measures, and in order to get the economy going again, it would have been necessary to assume a massive deficit. The central bank was prohibited by law from financing such a deficit, and the commercial banks, on the verge of bankruptcy, were incapable of doing so. It would thus have been necessary to seek a foreign loan, but in 1931, France was the only country able to provide such support, and it would have imposed political conditions that were unacceptable to German public opinion. A revival through the depreciation of the mark was also impossible because it ran counter to Germany's international commitments. Moreover, according to Borchardt, German public opinion, traumatized by the memory of hyperinflation, rejected the idea of a devaluation.

As Hau (1994) indicates, this thesis has proven extremely controversial. On the one hand, the scope of the rise in wages during the 1920s has been contested, but as we have already seen, the reduction of profits was also tied to the rise in the relative price of consumer goods. Whatever the cause, it is obvious that profits and investments were inadequate from the 1920s on. On the other hand, several writers have advanced the idea that the crisis had been "instrumentalized" by the Brüning government with the double aim of obtaining a decrease in wages and showing that Germany was in such a state of weakness that the reparations had to be ended. Far from being the result of internal or external constraints, the deflationary policy would thus have been a choice, but this question depends more on the analysis of political motivations than on that of economic dynamics.

However, those who challenge Borchardt have not really shown that it was possible to implement another policy. Indeed, strict respect for the law, notably that of 1924 and the international treaties signed by Germany, required the authorities to amplify the deflation. It was clearly impossible to maintain a policy of effective budgetary stimulation while preserving the stability of parity. Such a policy would have had to be massive in order to stop the depression and would probably have set off violent flights of capital. Floating the mark against all the other currencies represented a considerable risk because Germany had reduced short-term foreign debts and had only limited exchange reserves, so that the floating would have been difficult to manage.

However, with the banking crisis of 1931, the Brüning government had begun to bypass these constraints. It had instituted very strict monitoring of exchanges, with rationing of currencies allocated to importers. At the same time, the Reichsbank had initiated massive issues of notes to compensate for the destruction of banking deposits, with the result that in January 1932, the ratio of reserves to notes had fallen to 10 percent. But it had refused to devalue the mark when the pound was devalued in autumn 1931. At the time, the English authorities had proposed that Germany enter the sterling area, but the German government declined to accept these offers because it was accused by most of the political parties of wanting to encourage inflation(!). The debates that took place in the Reichstag during this period show that only the ultra-Right proposed undertaking a reflation policy and calling into question the international treaties. Borchardt's analysis has the merit of showing that the Germany economy was subject to strong institutional constraints. However, it can be challenged on several points. In our view, the crisis was already quite serious in 1929 and 1930 in comparison with the pre-1914 recessions, which means that a reaction would have had to be envisioned well before the banking crisis of 1931. At the same time, an absolute respect for the law could hardly have been advanced as a categorical imperative when the economic and social situations were rapidly disintegrating and violent confrontations breaking out. It is necessary to look more carefully at the possibilities of devaluing the mark while monitoring all currency exchanges as of 1930 or in relation to the pound sterling in September 1931. As the surveys of Eichengreen (1992) and Temin (1993) indicate, recent studies of the international aspects of the crisis have shown that the countries that undertook a premature devaluation were the first to emerge from the depression.

These debates show that the Weimar Republic was built on a series of institutionalized compromises that added up to anything but coherent economic regulation. At the time it was founded, the positions of employees' organizations had been strengthened, so that wages and social spending were pushed upward. Following the hyperinflation, systematically restrictive monetary policies were instituted. And in its position of weakness, Germany was forced to accept international agreements that considerably reduced its room to maneuver. The seriousness of the crisis in Germany was not tied to the internal contradictions of an accumulation regime, but rather to the tension between institutions created within a logic of internal and external political stabilization and a productive system weakened by the war.

France: A Dynamic Out of Step

There are two generally accepted propositions concerning the French economy in the interwar period. On the one hand, the growth of the 1920s was spectacular, in spite of the monetary disequilibria, or rather, owing to the depreciation of the franc. It is true that public opinion and the leaders of this period held a less positive view of things, but for lack of a coherent statistical system describing changes in real variables, they focused most of their attention on the financial disorders. On the other hand, there is general agreement that the crisis was prolonged in France by the pursuit of a strong franc policy after the devaluations of the pound and the dollar.

By contrast, the causes of the crisis remain a subject of controversy. According to one thesis, maintained notably by Asselain (1984), the crisis began in 1931 and was essentially a result of the deterioration of the international context; according to Marseille (1980), it began around 1927. But the defenders of the second thesis are themselves divided over the nature of the disequilibria that built up in the course of the 1920s: for Boyer (1979b), the first signs of intensive accumulation were stymied by an inadequate advance in wages, and as a result, the crisis assumed a different character from those of the prewar period. For Lorenzi, Pastré, and Toledano (1980), on the contrary, it had the characteristics of the classic late-nineteenth-century crises. Our analysis will focus on these points of controversy.

A first look at the crisis can be obtained by comparing it with the short-term economic situation of the period prior to 1914, as was done for the United States and Germany (see Table 5.8). If we apply the same criteria as for these countries—that is, the crisis is considered serious if the variable departs from its average by at least two standard intervals—the French economy did not undergo a severe depression until 1931, with growth remaining constant until the end of 1930. Subsequently, France was to undergo a long period of stagnation until 1936, but there is a kind of French exception: in comparison with the other countries, the crisis was not violent, but it was long.

The staunch resistance of the French economy in 1930 is not easy to explain. The role of agriculture could be invoked: its share in production was around 15 to 20 percent, which was no longer decisive; in employment, it was around 35 percent, but as indicated in chapter 2, the downward flexibility of employment was strong during the crisis, and this is confirmed by the data in Table 5.8. Contrary to what is sometimes asserted, the export rate was relatively high in 1929, so that the French economy was not isolated. It has often been said that the undervalued franc of President Poincaré had encouraged exports, but in reality, the foreign trade balance began to play a depressive role in 1928, and this effect had become considerable by 1930 (see Table 5.8). In 1927, profits represented 60.9 percent of the value added in nonagricultural firms, as compared to an average of 57.7 percent between 1896 and 1913, but from 1927 on, the proportion declined, and in 1930 it fell slightly under this average value, while the investment rate reached its peak, 13.7 percent as opposed to an average of 10.3 percent between 1896 and 1913. In the financial and monetary area, it is true that France's situation was favorable: after the stabilization of the franc in 1927, capital flowed in, with the result that the short-term interest rate was low until 1934. But the long-term interest rate remained higher than it had been between 1896 and 1913. In fact, the good performance in 1930 can essentially be explained by the continued boom in business investment. For Villa (1993), the econometrics of the investment function does not provide a direct explanation because 1930 was characterized by a large positive residue that he attributes to an error in anticipation on the firms' part. It would be interesting to establish the causes of such an error: did the firms think that the lively growth of the 1920s would continue even though it was no longer fed by the depreciation of the franc? Were they overly influenced by the renewed confidence of the capital bearers, which was reflected by capital inflows at the beginning of the 1930s? In any case, these exaggeratedly optimistic expectations were followed in 1931 by an abrupt correction that affected not only investment but employment.

Table 5.8

France: Great Depression Compared with the 1897–1913 Period (observed value in t minus average value in 1897–1913/standard deviation 1897–1913)

	Rate of growth		Contributions to GDP variations				
	GDP	Employment	Private consumption	Housing construction	Investment	Public expenditures	External balance
1928	0.8	−2.2	−0.4	6.3	4.7	3.7	−0.6
1929	0.7	6.3	0.7	0	4.3	0.7	−1.8
1930	0	−1.9	−0.7	7.7	3.7	1.7	−2.2
1931	−2.0	−13.8	−0.1	−8.9	−8.8	3.5	−1.3
1932	−1.7	−16	−0.3	−3.0	−10.5	1.4	0.3
1933	−1.1	−0.8	−1.3	0	−3.5	−2.6	2.2
1934	−1.1	−5.6	−1.3	0	−3.5	−2.6	2.2
1935	−0.2	−5.2	0	−0.5	−1.2	5	−0.4

Source: P. Villa (1994).

Table 5.9

Labor Productivity and Real Wage (average annual growth rate, nonagricultural private sector, in %)

	1896–1913	1913–1930	1921–1930
Labor productivity (GRESP)	1.4	1.1	5.1
Labor productivity (Villa, 1994)	1.6	0.7	5.1
Real wage (GRESP)	2.2	0.8	0

The length of the depression is often explained by the loss of competitiveness resulting from the maintenance of the gold parity and by restrictive economic policies. But the impact of the trade balance would seem to have been exaggerated because in reality it played an expansive role from 1932 to 1934 (see Table 5.8). Indeed, in spite of declining market shares, the recovery of world trade had nonetheless permitted a slight expansion of exports; in addition, imports continued to decrease, which left a margin for domestic production to grow. It is true that on the whole, economic policy was restrictive. But the budgetary policy often varied in the course of the crisis, and real changes in the budget diverged from declared intentions. In reality, the need for financing the public service increased sharply from 1931 to 1935, which brought the mechanisms of automatic stabilization into play. The strong franc policy, maintained in a context where many competing countries had devalued their currency, increased downward pressures on domestic prices. Between 1932 and 1935 French prices dropped while those in the United States and Germany rose. But in France, employment continued to plunge, with the result that the share of profits leveled off in 1932 (see chapter 4) while the investment rate continued to decline until 1935.

Since it has not really been demonstrated that the prolonged depression in France can be exclusively attributed to economic policies, we shall reexamine the possible imbalances in growth during the 1920s. As already indicated in chapter 1, it does not appear that, on the macroeconomic level, France had actually entered an intensive accumulation regime before the Second World War. Indeed, the high labor productivity gains noted during the 1920s can be attributed above all to a kind of making up for lost time. It is true that average real wages were stagnating, but in 1921 they were still ahead of productivity, which had been weakened by the war. The new series published by Villa (1994) confirms that over the whole of the 1913–29 period, productivity gains remained limited (Table 5.9).

On the other hand, the imbalances in the growth of the different sectors, which had begun to emerge before the First World War, were mag-

Table 5.10

Average Annual Growth Rate of Capital Stocks by Sectors

	1896–1913	1913–1930	1930–1955	1955–1972
Group 1	3.1	3.2	1.7	5.6
Group 2	1.4	0.8	0	4.0

Source: GRESP.

Group 1:Intermediate goods, capital goods, energy, and transportation.
Group 2:Agriculture, agroindustry, consumer goods, housing, services.

nified in the course of the 1920s (Table 5.10). The capital-goods, interme-
diate-products, transportation, and energy sectors accentuated their
growth differential relative to the others. Until 1929, the producer-goods
sector underwent a process of vigorous (and extensive) accumulation
while the consumer-goods sector showed only slight growth. This imbalance had many causes. The traditional sectors depending on precapitalist
modes of production occupied an important position and often had conservative, Malthusian behaviors. The influence of the rural world and the
structure of large cities that had been built for another era did not lend
themselves to a radical change in behaviors. The lag in social legislation
also contributed to blocking the modernization of a considerable portion
of the French economy.

These data reinforce the thesis of Lorenzi, Pastre, and Toledano
(1980), according to whom the stagnation of the 1930s was tied to an
excess of self-expansion in the producer-goods sector. But this conclusion must be supplemented and qualified by adding that the consequences of these imbalances were considerably magnified by the
deterioration of the international context after 1929 and prolonged by
the maintenance of the gold parity after 1931. Intersectoral growth differentials began to develop before 1914 and widened considerably during the 1920s. The modern sectors, located upstream in the productive
system, could not develop their capital and production indefinitely in a
context where the investment and production of the traditional sectors
showed only slight growth. This kind of disequilibrium was frequent at
the end of the nineteenth century but limited by the mechanisms of
competitive regulation. When an excessive accumulation boom developed, it wound up being blocked by the limits that the gold standard
imposed on the creation of money. Between 1920 and 1926, the inflationary monetary policies that had permitted the liquidation of war-related
domestic debts and the return of firms' profitability stimulated investment in the most modern sectors, but the obstacles that weighed on the
growth of accumulation in the traditional sectors remained.

Table 5.11

International Exchanges

	1929	1930	1931	1932
Imports variation (1913 prices, in millions of $)				
North America	361	−782	−608	−512
Europe	632	−608	−519	−1,903
Least advanced countries	304	−989	−1,036	−400
World price variation (in %)				
Manufactured goods	−0.5	−7.6	−16.8	−24.3
Primary goods	−3.6	−13.5	−26.5	−23.0
External resources of least advanced countries				
(1913 prices, in millions of $)	121	−1,174	−254	−476
Exports (volume)	−118	−258	−421	−96
Terms of trade	−482	−555	−818	−504
Flows of capital				
Total	−479	−1,992	−1,493	−1,076

Source: J.F. Vidal (1989).

The Role of Prices and World Trade

In recent years, English-speaking economists have insisted on the role of the gold standard and short-term capital movements in the international transmission of business cycles, as Temin (1993) has indicated. We have discussed these factors in the analyses of the crisis in Germany and France. However, other mechanisms of transmission relating to the situation of developing countries in international trade must also be cited (see Table 5.11).

The data for world imports shows that in 1930 and 1931, the imports of developing countries declined more than those of Europe and North America; the countries of the Third World were an important factor in the transmission of the depression during those two years. In 1932, the decline in European imports became very pronounced, at the moment when the United Kingdom abandoned its traditional free-exchange policy, which led the other European countries to raise their customs tariffs. But at the time, the consequences for the countries of the Third World were limited by the creation of a monetary and customs bloc around the United Kingdom.

Three factors explain the sharp drop in imports by developing countries. To be sure, following the drop in North African and European imports, the volume of exports from the Third World was reduced. But in addition, the terms of trade of the raw materials exporting countries took a serious turn for the worse following the collapse of raw materials prices. Kindleberger (1988) has shown that this was due to a situation of structural deflation resulting from the First World War, during which developing countries had improved their production capacities in order to compensate for the drop in production in Europe and to meet military expenditures. It must also be emphasized that this drop in basic materials prices reduced farmers' incomes in the developed countries. Capital inflows declined, in 1929 because of the boom, which attracted capital to Wall Street, and from 1930 on because of the payment defaults that were to become widespread in 1931.

CHAPTER SIX

The Crisis of Intensive Accumulation

The crisis that began in 1974 in the leading economies was profoundly different from those of the 1930s because the economic situation was more homogeneous—intensive accumulation was widespread, as were Fordism and mass consumption; the markets were interdependent in terms of both suppliers and consumers. However, each economy retained the imprint of its path-dependency and encountered genuinely national factors of crisis that were to combine with the play of international economic relations to bring lasting change to earlier growth mechanisms.

National Factors in the Accumulation Crisis

The most spectacular aspect of the crisis that emerged in the 1970s was the decline in the overall profitability of capital. This resulted from the slowdown in spending and the simultaneous disincentive for future investment. The drop can be examined as the consequence of a deterioration in the physical conditions of growth but also as a result of tensions over the distribution of income and the rise in the relative price of investments. It differs according to country, and ad hoc compensations were sought through recourse to public assistance to businesses or increased indebtedness on the one hand and inflation on the other.

Declining Productivity

The end of the 1960s marked a turning point for investment in certain countries. The rate of investment relative to the GDP declined in Germany, Italy, and Japan, while it remained stable in the United Kingdom and the United States between 1965 and 1970. The 1960s saw the continuation of this development, with investment in France slowing down after 1973. Movements of decelerating investment become even more apparent when the manufacturing sector alone is considered. (Figure 6.1)

At the same time, productivity gains were winding down. Per capita production showed less growth, especially in Germany and the United States. It seems that the significant advantage that the United States enjoyed, in terms of productivity level, was eroded in the early 1970s, at least in relation to Germany and France, with Japan still attempting to catch up and Italy and the United Kingdom lagging behind. This situation is demonstrated by the international comparisons of productivity levels that have been made in purchasing power parities (see Kravis, Heston, and Summers 1978). The analyses in terms of hourly productivity of labor also tend to confirm the declining trend from the late 1960s on.

At that point, the radical change in production conditions and the intensification of growth became increasingly expensive in terms of capital (Figure 6.2). After an initial rise, the output–capital ratio leveled off and resumed its decline, which was only a reflection of trends that had been at work for years on the margin. The slowdown in growth was in fact one of the essential features of the intensive accumulation regime, and it was particularly pronounced in the consumer-goods sector, the site of the most significant transformations in conjunction with the growth of mass consumption. Along with the usual aggregates of the national accounts system, this analysis of the links between the decline of growth, productivity gains, and renewed decrease in the output–capital ratio can be shown to reveal the traditional mechanisms related to the "downward trend of the rate of profit."

However, these trends had neither the same intensity nor the same scope in the different leading economies. In most cases, the reversion to a declining ratio emerged fairly early, notably at the beginning of the 1960s in Japan and the United States. In France, on the level of the economy as a whole, what appears to be only a simple leveling of the output–capital ratio is observed between 1969 and 1973. The downward trend appears more clearly in the traditional sectors (services, commerce, construction), where the capitalist division of labor rapidly came up against limitations.

These differences from one economy to another, concerning both labor productivity and capital efficiency, go back to the structural features of each productive system. An initial argument can be eliminated immediately: the transfers of labor power between sectors does not seem to have played a significant role in the slowdown of productivity gains. This slowdown hit the large majority of industrial and service sectors. In addition, the role of intersectoral transfers can be precisely analyzed with the help of a mechanical calculation, in which the change in productivity

in all the branches is broken down into two terms isolating the fluctuations in productivity proper to each branch and the effects of intersectoral transfers of labor power. The calculations carried out by the OECD show that these intersectoral transfers only explain a small portion of the productivity gains recorded at the peak of Fordism (see Table 6.1). While the positive effect of these transfers disappeared in several countries between 1969 and 1973, it played a minor role in the changes in productivity gains observed after 1965 in the United States, during the 1960s in West Germany, and from 1973 on in France and Japan.

The slowdown in productivity gains and the renewed decline in the productivity–capital ratio resulted above all from an erosion in the Fordist organization of work and the technologies associated with it—this being more or less pronounced according to the country. The United States was thus very representative of the crisis in Taylorist production methods, which had been developed very early. The growth of labor productivity, which had remained inferior to the other major economies, showed a notable upturn in industry and the economy as a whole in 1966, at the very time that there was accelerated growth in capital per worker.

By contrast, France showed a relative delay in the introduction and spread of Fordism, notably because of the initial importance of traditional activities. It would seem that there was more room for maneuvering until the end of the 1960s. An identical phenomenon can be observed in Italian industry. Among the major European countries, only Great Britain was farther behind, with a smaller number of salaried employees working in shifts in industry (see Table 6.2). This situation may be explained in part by the resistance of the British unions in the face of new production methods. This union control can also be related to the difficulties encountered by British industrialists in their attempts to intensify growth and undertake new investments.

The case of the Japanese economy calls for several additional explanations (Barou 1979). The sharp acceleration in the growth of capital per worker from the 1960s on, for industry and overall, barely permitted the maintenance of the productivity gains generated during the phase of catching up and extensive accumulation. New production methods imported from the United States took hold, and shift work spread until the middle of the 1960s. But a very clear stabilization appeared because of certain social rigidities (union resistance, considerable travel time in the big cities). The Japanese productive system had to use more specific methods in order to improve its efficiency. Rather paradoxically, shift work showed a smaller increase in Japanese industry than in France in 1974. Beyond this explanation, the relative inefficiency in the creation of investments (as reflected by the drop in the output–capital ratio from the mid-1960s on) seems directly related to the extent of overaccumulation phenomena in Japan.

Table 6.1

The Role of Intersectoral Transfers in the Evolution of Labor Productivity (1965–1977)

	United States			Japan			Germany			France		
	1965–1969	1969–1973	1973–1977	1965–1969	1969–1973	1973–1977	1965–1969	1969–1973	1973–1977	1965–1969	1969–1973	1973–1977
Average annual rate of growth of the productivity of labor	1.1	1.7	0.2	8.6	8.4	3.3	4.8	4.0	3.2	4.9	4.9	2.8
Effects of intersectoral transfers	0.3	0	-0.1	1.3	0.8	0.0	0.3	0.2	-0.1	0.5	0.4	0.1

Source: OECD, in J.C. Milleron and Y. Younes (1980).

Table 6.2

Shift Work in the EEC Countries in 1975 (% employees working in shifts)

	France	Germany	Italy	United Kingdom	Belgium
Industry	19.6	21.9	22.3	18.4	24.1
All activities	14.6	18.5		16.0	18.7

Source: Eurostat (1977).

Wage–Profit Division and the Profitability of Capital: Growing Tensions in the Early 1970s

The changing rate of profit over the medium term can be analyzed with the classic accounting breakdown that has already been used in chapter 3. Two factors must be taken into account: the ways in which the division between wages and profits was carried out, and the role of price relative to investments.

In terms of the share of wages, first of all, a turnaround took place at the end of the 1960s in most of the leading economies. The intensification of capital related to the implementation of new production methods had initially generated sufficient productivity gains to compensate both the rise in real per capita income and social contributions (see chapter 2). Two countries were to some extent exceptional because of more limited productivity gains. These were the United States and, especially, Great Britain, where the share of wages tended to rise, with short-term fluctuations tied to the employment cycle. In the latter country, there were also a new expression of the resistance of British workers and obstacles to the spread of Fordism.

At the beginning of the 1970s, the rise in the share of wages that emerged in certain economies marked a significant change (see Figure 6.3). This change was not uniform, however. The rise was most pronounced in Germany, Japan, and Italy from 1970 on. In Great Britain and, especially, in the United States, the smaller rise in purchasing power permitted the leveling off or even reversal of previous changes after 1970 without leading to any real recovery in terms of profits. In France, productivity gains permitted the increase in the share of wages to be limited until 1973.

This change in the wage–profit division demonstrates in another way the constraints faced by the intensive accumulation regime from the early 1970s on. The calling into question of working conditions, the rise in absenteeism, the decline in productivity, the social conflicts, and, in cer-

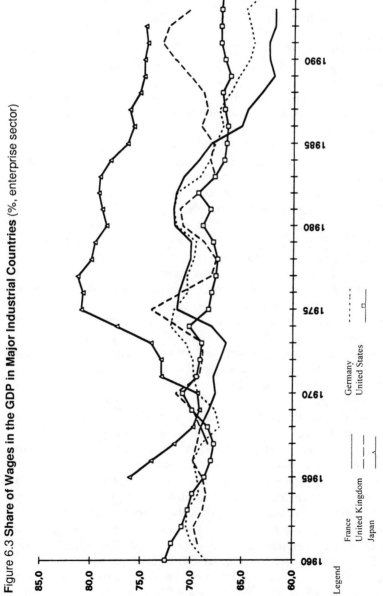

Figure 6.3 **Share of Wages in the GDP in Major Industrial Countries** (%, enterprise sector)

Legend

France	Germany
United Kingdom	United States
Japan	

Source: OECD, 1995.

tain cases, the rise in per capital wages were all symptoms of this development. Likewise, the recourse to immigrant and female labor, and the use of the labor reserves existing in the rural world (France, Italy, Japan), reached certain limits. In the case of the United States, the more rapid growth of cost prices relative to output prices accounts for most of the decline in the share of profits after 1966, especially in the industrial sector (Weisskopf 1979). In many countries, a rise in social contributions also accentuated the pressure on profits.

A second factor, related to the role of relative prices, must also be taken into account. During the 1950s and 1960s, a number of countries showed a downward trend in the relative price of investments. This played a limited but not insignificant role in favor of the profitability of capital. However, its impact must not be overestimated because, on the one hand, it did not intervene in all the economies and, on the other hand, it was only compensating for a sharp upturn following the Korean War. Nonetheless, the reversal that occurred in several countries at the beginning of the 1970s reinforced pressures on the profitability of capital.

Overall, a trend toward a decline in the rate of profit emerged in most of the leading economies well before the onset of the crisis of 1974 (see Figure 6.4). This decline was pronounced in Germany and Great Britain because it had in practice gotten under way in 1960. It can also be observed in the United States after 1966 (i.e., after the end of the "Kennedy–Johnson boom"). The years 1971–73 were marked by a clear recovery, but this did not compensate for the previous deterioration. In Japan, after a sustained period of growth from 1950 to 1970, which was interrupted only by phases of overaccumulation, the profitability of capital only began to decline after 1970. The situation of the French economy seems more particular because no downward trend is observed; on the level of the branches as a whole, the rate of profit continued to increase until 1969 and then remained stable until 1973.

This very general preliminary observation must be qualified in several respects. First of all, the notion of rate of profit that is used divides gross income by a productive capital measured at recovery prices. In other words, this is the broadest possible concept of the rate of profit, before direct taxes and before distribution. Other statistical indicators might be imagined, such as gross or net profitability of capital, before or after taxes, measured in relation to fixed capital alone or to the whole of the capital advanced. More detailed studies show, however, that beyond the differences that emerge according to the conventions that are used, the results obtained are fairly divergent (INSEE 1975 and 1980; Hill 1979; Barou, Dollé, Gabet, and Wartenberg 1979). The initial situations must also be taken into account. In spite of the difficulties of international comparisons, it seems clear that the initial level of the rate of profit in

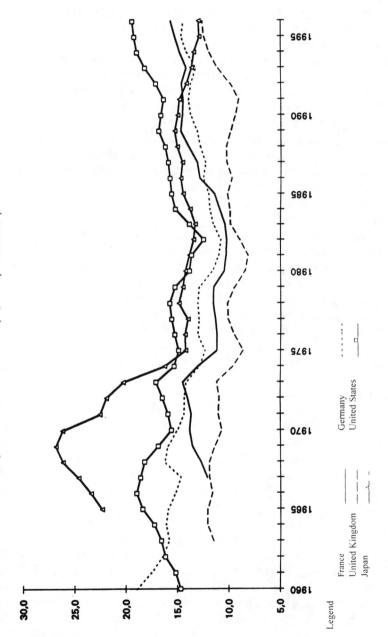

Figure 6.4 **Rate of Profit in Major Industrial Countries** (%, enterprise sector)

Legend

France	———	Germany	·······
United Kingdom	— — —	United States	—□—
Japan	—△—		

Source: OECD, 1996.

Germany at the end of the 1950s was higher than that in the other European countries. From that point on, the decline of profitability in Germany could have been just a return toward more normal levels. Similarly, it is likely that the profitability levels reached by Japan at the end of the 1960s were high. On the contrary, the English and Italian rates of profit seem to be situated on much lower levels.

If industry alone is taken into account, the preceding results are reinforced, although there are certain nuances. Thus, the profitability of Germany industry during the 1960s would be constantly higher than that of French industry, and the decline in the rate of profit would be more limited than on the overall level. German industry would profit from both its clear superiority in the utilization of fixed capital and the maintenance of relative industrial prices, which show a less appreciable decline than in France. On the other hand, the British manufacturing sector would be in a more critical situation because its decrease in the rate of profit would be more pronounced than on the overall level and in the nonindustrial sectors. The same is true for the United States, where the rate of profit in the manufacturing sector declines much more than that of nonmanufacturing societies under the effect of a very unfavorable change in relative prices.

Beyond these nuances, it is possible to speak of a profitability crisis throughout the leading economies at the beginning of the 1970s, since the rates of profit could no longer be maintained at the previous levels. This deterioration of the profitability of capital contributed in turn to blocking the accumulation dynamic, both because it reduced the available means of internal financing and because it made the expectations nurtured by the capitalists even more unfavorable. Accumulation tended to be blocked all the more because of a relative erosion of the factors of postwar growth.

Relative Erosion of Growth Factors

In the postwar mode of growth, a crucial role was played by the rapid rise of mass consumption and, by extension, accumulation in the consumer-goods sector. But on both levels, a certain slowdown can be observed by the beginning of the 1970s. Although our data are mainly French, similar phenomena, albeit of a different scope, can be observed in the other leading economies.

In relation to mass consumption, several authors have taken pains to show that the limits of growth had already been reached in 1973 (Lorenzi, Pastré, and Toledano 1980). In fact, most of the durable consumer goods that had structured the household consumption norm during the 1950s and 1960s were in a phase of "maturity" at the beginning of the 1970s. In France, the rates of households equipped with durable goods in 1973 (85 percent for refrigerators, 78 percent for televisions, 61 percent for automobiles, 65 percent for washing machines) were high, as were the rates for housing comforts (indoor toilets, bathroom plumbing). Similar observations may be made in the other leading economies.

The leading role played by mass consumption would be weakened because of a relative saturation for certain goods, and this would lead to a diminished growth dynamic. This argument must not be overestimated, because it is obviously not possible to speak of a "saturation" of needs at the beginning of the 1970s. Significant needs remained to be satisfied and sharp inequalities existed from one social category to another. Moreover, new consumer durables made their appearance in the early 1970s (freezers, dishwashers, color televisions) or more recently (VCRs).

It is clear, however, that the driving role of durable consumer goods could no longer be what it had been earlier on. Furthermore, overall expenditures, related to the construction of infrastructures and urbanization, which made up another essential component of Fordism, underwent a certain decline. From a strictly demographic point of view, a clear downward trend can be observed in many countries. All of these elements came together to diminish the dynamic of demand, whether or not it was related directly to mass consumption, even though it is not possible to attribute a major role to them.

A second factor also contributed to halting growth at the end of the 1960s. Accumulation in the consumer-goods sector, which had been at the heart of the postwar growth regime, also began to show signs of decline. The consumer-goods sector remained subject to significant transformations that incorporated technological innovation, but transitions from forms of craft production to new, more capitalistic and more encumbering forms were less frequent. This explains the lower investment levels in the consumer-goods sectors or, more precisely, a slowdown in the substitution of indirect labor for direct labor.

Thus, two of the basic motors of the postwar mode of growth, the rapid rise of mass consumption and the transformations of production conditions in the consumer-goods sector, underwent significant shifts after the beginning of the 1970s, thus contributing to a slowdown in the rhythm of growth. The erosion of the intensive accumulation regime, which was already considerable with the slowdown in productivity gains, the renewed decline of capital efficiency, and tensions over profitability, was thus accentuated. However, counter-trends were implemented to confront the decline in the rate of profit and avoid a halt in accumulation.

Indebtedness, Assistance to Firms, and Inflation: Counter-Trends at Work

An Overdraft Economy

The practically uninterrupted deterioration of businesses' financial structure in all of the leading economies from the middle of the 1960s is a strikingly widespread phenomenon. In France, first of all, the ratio between amounts of indebtedness to the stock of productive capital (measured at the replacement price) doubled between 1954 and 1973 (Goldet, Nicolas, and Séruzier 1975). The accounting data for firms confirm these results: for taxable businesses as a whole, the overdraft rate (ratio of total debt to equity capital) went from 1.66 in 1967 to 2.46 in 1974 (INSEE 1981).

A similar trend can be observed in the other European economies, even Great Britain, where the recourse to bank credit was traditionally limited but where the drop in self-financing rates forced firms to go into debt under difficult circumstances from the 1970s on. The decline of the financial structure of Japanese firms during the 1960s has long been emphasized (Sautter 1973). The cumulative debt process of American businesses lies at the heart of Aglietta's analyses: from 1964 to 1974, the ratio of permanent capital to amounts of debt dropped from 3.95 to 2.15 for the whole of nonfinancial businesses.

The recourse to external financing obviously had a different significance from one country to another according to the nature of the relations between industrial and banking capital. Thus, the ties between banks and firms are traditionally less close in France than in Germany, and especially Japan, where the large industrial groups in fact have their own banks. Moreover, significant institutional transformations—in terms of both the law and the structure of capital—occurred in many of the countries and thus mitigated the effects of an overly large break between banks and firms. This was notably the case in France where, beginning in the 1960s, the banking apparatus began to wake up, and there was a whole series of "major maneuvers" in which finance capital coming largely from the banks played an active role. In any case, the indebtedness of firms was used as a means of compensating and attempting to redress the decline in the profitability of capital. Through the leverage effect (i.e., the difference between the cost of indebtedness and the return rates of the capital invested), the profitability of firms' equity capital could be improved. More basically, given limited possibilities of internal financing, credit played a major role in sustaining accumulation. The preservation of a sufficiently sustained rhythm of investment was in fact necessary to free new productivity gains, intensify labor, and redress the share of profits.

To a considerable extent, these efforts proved fruitless, and the blockages encountered by the intensive accumulation regime could not be surmounted at the price of increased indebtedness. In some respects the difficulties were even aggravated. The increase in financing costs, tied to the rapid increase in amounts of indebtedness and the rise in the interest rate, reduced the margins for self-financing and accentuated the pressures on the profitability of capital.

Aid to Businesses and "Public Financing"

This issue arose in all the leading economies and not without considerable controversy: on the one hand, some denounced "gifts to business," while on the other, firms themselves complained of ever-increasing costs. On the macroeconomic level, a rapid increase in social security contributions compensated in part by a slight reduction in direct taxes can be observed in France over the short term. A detailed analysis of the formation of the rate of profit in France confirms the preceding results (Mairesse and Delestré 1978). For private businesses taken as a whole, the impact of direct taxation (excluding subsidies) does not modify the development of profitability. Similar studies carried out in Great Britain and the United States show, on the other hand, that fiscal policy was used more aggressively to improve firms' self-financing capabilities (Weisskopf 1979).

Beyond these observations largely based on accounting, "government aid to industry" in its most varied forms (subsidies, preferential interest rates, tax write-offs, loans, procurement contracts) has given rise to specific studies. In the industrialized countries, these forms of benefits were significant and assumed a structural nature. Thus, in France and Germany between 1972 and 1977, they represented about 25 percent of manufacturing firms' productive investment, including research and development expenditures.

In practice, the complexity of the system of government aid to industry makes it difficult to study. There have been a number of reports in France but they remain little known. One of them shows that in 1976, 50 percent of all government aid went to seven major industrial groups that represented less than 10 percent of industrial employment and added value, while the SMEs (small and medium enterprises) received only a very limited fraction.

Le Pors (1976) has attempted to analyze government aid to firms in their most varied forms, including the advantages resulting from procurement contracts and transfers linked to the depreciation of public capital. The total thus obtained, 64 billion francs in 1974, seems considerable because it represented 28 percent of the firms' investment and 43 percent of their gross savings. Furthermore, this government aid was mainly channeled toward a few sectors (aeronautics, nuclear energy, and computers, but also the iron and steel industry and shipbuilding).

Whatever the difficulties of analysis and the uncertainties of the results, transfers to the firms seem to constitute a structural phenomenon that reinforced the accumulation process well beyond the preliminary estimates we had presented. Overall, these transfers also favored the largest and most internationalized firms. And a final factor, the acceleration of inflation, played an active role in maintaining the profitability of capital.

Inflation of Distribution and Monopolistic Regulation

At this point our analysis takes a more post-Keynesian or Cambridge turn. We rule out the thesis advanced by some that the acceleration of inflation originates in the rapid growth of credit and the increasing instability of firms' debt structure that would result. To be sure, it is not impossible that the growth portion of the short-term debts poses a problem in case of a slowdown of growth in volume, and that a solution might be found in inflation, which would then permit the depreciation of old debts (Aglietta 1976; Mandel 1978). But it seems to us that the root of the acceleration of inflation at the end of the 1960s lies rather in the growing tensions that emerged on the level of income formation and the distribution of wages and profits. Boyer and Mistral (1978) have offered solid proof of the existence of an inflation of distribution and profit. Their studies show that all attempts on the part of the different economic agents (firms, banks, wage-earners, government, individual entrepreneurs) to increase their share in the distribution of income leads to an acceleration of inflation.

The 1960s were characterized by the emergence of increasingly sharp tensions over the distribution of income. This included a greater share for wages resulting from the limits encountered by the growth of Fordism and worker resistance, a defensive behavior on the part of individual entrepreneurs and craftsmen who strove to maintain their incomes in the face of the setbacks they encountered, a rise in European agricultural prices following various institutional maneuvers, a rise in financing costs because of firms' growing indebtedness, and the defense of the markup rate by firms that had to develop the major investments they had previously undertaken. This search for a minimum rate of profitability was made all the more difficult insofar as efficiency in the implementation of production conditions declined in the whole of the leading economies from the mid-1960s onward. Only the government, through tax exemptions and subsidies, lessened the constraint arising from the distribution of income and thus contributed to diminishing inflationist tensions. Boyer and Mistral's simulations, carried out within the framework of the French economy to describe the acceleration of inflation over the 1968–73 period, should be extended to the other leading economies (see Table 6.3).

At this stage in the analysis, however, this explanation does not allow us to understand why such a permanent contradiction in the capitalist system, the conflict on the level of the distribution of income, only manifested itself in the form of an acceleration of inflation from the end of the 1960s, while phases of deflation were frequent in the earlier periods. This can only be understood if we recall that the 1960s saw a new form of "monopolistic or administered" regulation, which marked a break rela-

Table 6.3

Acceleration of Inflation in the Early 1970s (price of private
consumption, average annual rate of growth in %)

	1950–1960	1960–1970	1970–1973	1973–1980
France	6.5	4.2	6.0	10.8
Germany	2.2	2.8	6.0	4.8
United Kingdom	3.5	4.0	7.9	15.7
Italy	2.3	4.0	8.2	17.6
U.S.	2.3	2.5	4.5	7.9
Japan	2.6(*)	5.8	6.9	9.0

Source: OECD, national accounts.
Note: (*) 1952–1980

tive to the predominant mode of competitive regulation during the earlier stages of capitalism (see chapters 2 and 3). Nominal prices were
hardly more sensitive to the appearance of surplus production capacities
and depended much more on firms' markup behavior. Nominal wages
were indexed to the general level of prices and appeared to be partly
induced by the productivity gains observed in certain leading sectors.
The growing share of the indirect wage also contributed to making wage
income relatively independent of the "labor market." And to a large extent, the need for accumulation dictated the distribution of credit, while
the monetary constraint was unable to function because of the imposition
of a monetary system with fiat money and the central bank's role as
lender of last resort. Accelerated inflation thus appears to have been the
result of exacerbated tensions around the distribution of income in the
context of a regulation that had become monopolistic. From this point of
view, the inflationary trend can be interpreted in part as an attempt to
restore the profitability of capital.

Internationalization and Crisis

International economic relations played a significant role in the maturing
of the crisis and aggravated the specific national factors at work. In the
most general terms, the growing questioning of American hegemony led
to the disappearance of one of the essential factors of cohesion in the
world capitalist system. In addition, the strengthening of foreign constraint limited the internal dynamic of each economy and the effectiveness of national economic policies; with increased internationalization,
the whole prior logic of growth was called into question. And the rise in
oil prices also played a decisive role in triggering the crisis. All of these
points must be examined.

The Questioning of American Hegemony and the Crisis of the International Monetary System

The unprecedented growth of international exchanges of manufactured goods from the 1950s on led to increased international competition. Under the circumstances, the American economy suffered a sharp setback, with a major loss of export market shares. This sanction came with a reduction of the American trade surplus leading to a growing disequilibrium in the balance of payments accompanied by a rapid growth of floating capital. At the same time, the internationalization of production continued to increase from the late 1960s on, but this was not due solely to American firms. Through significant restructuring in their home economies, European and Japanese firms increasingly developed their activities abroad.

All of these factors together called into question the hegemony of the American economy and that of the dollar. At that point, the Bretton Woods system could only be confronted with a crisis, especially since the periodic adjustments of parity, which became more frequent with the monopolistic regulation of prices, posed a problem within a fixed-exchange regime. The spread of the flexible exchanges that came into effect in February 1973 deprived the world capitalist economy of a real international monetary system while giving international financial capital a disproportionate role. However, if the perverse effects of the floating exchanges were to manifest themselves most clearly after the onset of the crisis, they were nonetheless a significant factor of destabilization from 1973 on.

Internationalization and the Questioning of the Prior Logic of Growth

The postwar growth model in all of the leading economies was based on two largely contradictory principles. The first, going back to the intensive accumulation regime, relied on an essentially national base, whether in terms of actual regulation procedures or underlying institutional forms (wage negotiations, forms of government intervention, or money management). The second, by contrast, relied on the choice of free exchange of merchandise and free circulation of capital, which implied growing internationalization. Furthermore, such a choice marked a break with the dominant practice of capitalism, which had almost always opted for protectionism (except for the 1860s and 1870 in the case of Western Europe). This choice largely resulted from pressures exerted by the leading firms, for whom national markets constituted spaces that were too limited in face of the potentialities of the new production methods.

During the 1950s and 1960s, this basic contradiction between national regulation and the logic of internationalization remained latent in most countries. As the previous chapters have shown, the fairly self-centered nature of growth at that time had allowed the coherence of the intensive accumulation regime to be maintained in countries such as France, but also the United States and Japan. On the contrary, the United Kingdom, which was quite open to the outside from the very beginning, had to limit its growth from time to time because of the weight of the foreign constraint, which contributed to imprisoning it in a vicious circle that is well known (Barou 1978). Only Germany was able to rely with impunity on a more extroverted growth because of the excellent specialization that it enjoyed from the outset and which lay at the origin of its famous virtuous circle (Keiser 1979).

This contradiction was considerably aggravated from the end of the 1960s because of the continued trend toward internationalization. Several factors were involved. First of all, international competition increased, as did the weight of the foreign constraint with the rise of German and Japanese trade surpluses. The world market's sanction on deviations from production norms in effect became stricter. Exports from certain rapidly industrializing countries that had opted for an extroversion strategy also began to show rapid growth. But competition from this kind of country remained fairly limited at the beginning of the 1970s and applied only to very common products. Major industrial restructuring was undertaken at this time in many national economies, and particularly in France with the "industrial imperative," so as to bring them into the international division of labor. This led to a more intensive specialization of productive systems already tending to call into question the overall coherence of certain production tracks, and led simultaneously to greater dependence on imports and more extroverted growth. The contradictions thus became more apparent between this increasingly marked internationalization and the national character of regulation procedures.

Beginning at the end of the 1960s, or even earlier in countries such as West Germany or Italy, international exchanges assumed increasing importance, and in France, this culminated in the essential role played by the export sector. The devaluation of 1969, the policy of support for exports, and the declining opportunities for investment on the domestic market all contributed to such a development in France. The earlier growth scheme based on a national logic was thus gradually abandoned and a new phase undertaken. But the pursuit of new outlets abroad could not be entirely substituted for the "internal motor." The relative weakness of the export sector and the exacerbation of international competition, related to the fact that similar developments were taking place throughout the leading economies, meant that the "external motor" could only constitute a limited, stopgap measure.

More essentially, the substitution of foreign markets for domestic demand, and of investments in export production capabilities for those that were revolutionizing the production of national consumer goods, completely transformed the functioning of the entire economy. The fairly well accepted necessity of continually expanding domestic outlets in order to increase and realize production was replaced by the famous "foreign constraint" of competitiveness, which seemed conversely to imply a permanent moderation of demand and wage costs. There was no place left for the overall coherence among the transformation of production conditions, productivity gains, increasing purchasing power, and expansion of outlets. The de facto and ex post solidarity of wages and profits seemed to be giving way, in part at least, to out-and-out antagonism.

The reduction of wages is favorable to competitiveness in the short run because in principle it permits decreasing cost prices or increasing the profits necessary for accumulation. Reducing domestic demand, meanwhile, permits exportable surpluses in the short run. In the long run, obviously, another growth strategy more oriented to the domestic market, more skilled jobs, and high wages would be conceivable and might give favorable results in terms of foreign trade. But in the short run, such a strategy might have negative effects on the trade balance. This is one reason why governments seeking a rapid improvement in their foreign balance opt instead for blocking wages and reducing demand. When a majority of countries make this choice, the result is a gradual freeze in accumulation.

The new growth scheme contradicted the preceding regime. It did not invoke the same institutional forms, whether in terms of income and wage policy, forms of money management, or new forms of work to be implemented. A growing imbalance thus appeared between the state of institutional and structural forms and the current regulation procedures. Independent of the national factors of accumulation crisis, the problems posed by the interaction between national regulation and internationalization established the conditions for a "major crisis." The oil crisis was to emerge as its catalyst and symptom.

Effects of the Rise in Oil Prices

The trend toward declining terms of exchange for developing countries that had begun after the Korean War reversed itself at the end of the 1960s. This rise accentuated the problems of capital development in the leading economies but its scope remained limited. It reflected a certain political empowerment among Third World countries, but these underdeveloped raw-materials producers did not have the means to organize themselves in order to impose a real reversal of the trend.

The situation of the oil-producing countries appears very different insofar as, independent of the balance of power favorable to the OPEC countries, the early 1970s saw a shift from decreasing to increasing costs.

Table 6.4

Base Prices of Raw Materials and Raw Petroleum per Barrel

	1973	1974	1975	1976	1977	1978
Raw materials 1970 = 100	166	212	174	196	236	226
Annual rate of growth (%)	54.9	27.9	−17.9	12.3	20.5	-4.2
Petroleum (in $)	2.7	9.8	10.7	11.5	12.4	12.7
Annual rate of growth (%)		261.5	9.8	7.4	7.7	2.4

Source: IMF, international financial statistics, 1979.

The rise in oil prices at the end of 1973 cannot be compared with that of other raw materials (see Table 6.4). The effects of this increase have given rise to very contradictory explanations. For some, it was the sole cause of all subsequent disturbances; for others, it had no effect. In fact, its role cannot be overlooked, because 1974 unquestionably marked a break in the dynamic of the advanced capitalist countries. But the oil crisis was mainly a catalyst for the larger crisis in a system that had undergone major disequilibria on both the national and international scales since the beginning of the 1970s.

For a better understanding of the results of the rise in oil prices, it is useful to distinguish between mechanical and induced effects. The first mechanical effect concerns the acceleration of inflation directly related to the rise in imported petroleum product prices. Calculations made with the help of input–output tables show that even in 1974 the rise in oil prices only offers a mechanical explanation for a limited share of the acceleration of inflation (in France, 3.2 percent for a total rise of 13.4 percent in household consumer prices).

The other mechanical effect was an increase in the OPEC surplus of current payments, since their imports rose less quickly than their exports. This surplus, which averaged $3.5 billion between 1971 and 1973, reached $68 billion in 1974. It then declined until 1978, but rose sharply in 1979 and was more than $100 billion in 1980. By accounting balance, all of the non-OPEC countries showed equivalent deficits. What made international regulation more difficult was not the rise in oil prices per se but these OPEC surpluses. A revealing calculation has been carried out by Artus and Debonneuil (1979) with the help of the Metric model. On the basis of a central account established by assuming the stability of the relative price of oil, the authors calculated the consequences of a 10 percent annual rise in that relative price. When OPEC showed a foreign surplus, domestic growth was slowed down, the foreign deficit rose, and unemployment increased. Conversely, when OPEC spent all of the additional oil revenues, the rise in the GDP accelerated sharply relative to the central account. Three years later, the number of job seekers was 116,000 below the base level, but the foreign balance declined because the recovery led to an overall rise in imports. Ultimately there is nothing surprising about these results—a rise in the price of raw materials that was entirely spent by the exporting countries would probably give a boost to the advanced capitalist countries. Conversely, OPEC's foreign surplus contributed to aggravating the crisis because it was in part an "income drain" within the international circuit.

Beyond these mechanical effects, the oil crisis had significant induced effects by triggering a recessionary process: the drastic reduction in domestic purchasing power resulting from the rise in oil prices, often aggravated by the restrictive nature of economic policies, led to a contraction of real demand and thus of production. The scale of the subsequent destocking accentuated the recessionary sequence. Thus, the rise in petroleum product prices at the end of 1973 was not at the origin of the crisis, but it played an essential role as a triggering factor that helped to reveal the extent of the tensions that had been incubating since the early 1970s.

❖

The crisis that began in 1974 originated in the conjunction of two different crises:

- There was an accumulation crisis in the national economies that went back to the limits encountered by the postwar mode of growth: decline in the physical conditions of growth; questioning of the work organization characteristic of Fordism; growing tensions on the level of income distribution; relative erosion of growth stimuli in terms of both mass consumption and transformations in production conditions. In the face of these changes, counter-trends were implemented to thwart the declining profitability of capital through increased company debt, a policy of government aid, and above all an acceleration of inflation. The inflationary thrust at the end of the 1960s was thus a result of increased tensions around income distribution within a monopolistic-type regime.
- There was a multifaceted crisis on an international scale: the questioning of American hegemony and the crisis of the Bretton Woods system deprived the world economy of any structured form and notably an effective international monetary system. More fundamentally, the growing internationalization of the economies in the late 1960s and the growing weight of the foreign constraint increasingly called into question the postwar mode of growth and contributed to a gradual freeze of accumulation. The rise in petroleum product prices at the end of 1973 then served as a catalyst to trigger the crisis, while the OPEC

countries' surplus of current payments directly aggravated the recession on a world scale.

Until about 1970, increasing exchanges favored economic growth. The opening of borders multiplied export outlets and permitted economies of scale that encouraged productivity gains; in return, growth generated increasing quantities of imports. The play of foreign-trade multipliers was a precious aid for capital accumulation. However, between 1969 and 1974, this virtuous circle of free exchange became a vicious circle of economic warfare. The growth slowdown in the leading economies tied to the crisis of the intensive accumulation regime halted the expansion of international demand for many industrial products.

The origins of the crisis of the 1970s thus appear profoundly different from those of the 1930s. In the first case, it is possible to speak of a crisis of the intensive accumulation regime compounded by an international crisis, and this for all of the leading economies. By contrast, the crises of the 1930s differ from one economy to another: a crisis in the introduction of intensive accumulation in the United States, a crisis of extensive accumulation in France, foreign constraint and freezing of accumulation in Germany and Great Britain.

Nonetheless, the specific features of each economy at the beginning of the 1970s should not be underestimated. France was less affected by the profitability crisis, but this is where the effects of growing internationalization most directly called into question the logic of postwar growth. Foreign constraint played a determining role from 1974 on. While Great Britain was less marked by Fordism, it was subject to foreign constraint very early on because of its greater openness. West Germany also experienced a less self-centered growth in the 1960s but profited from its excellent specialization. On the other hand, the deterioration of the physical conditions of growth and the profitability crisis played a more important role. Japan relied heavily on its domestic market but was more sensitive to successive waves of overaccumulation. As in France, the increasingly extroverted nature of its growth at the beginning of the 1970s marked an essential turning point. It was probably in the United States, where the economy was basically closed and exempt from foreign constraint because of the role of the dollar, that the crisis of Fordism could be observed in its purest state, with the erosion of productivity gains and the manufacturing sector's profitability crisis.

CHAPTER SEVEN

The 1930s: Fascism or Fordism?

During the 1930s, the gravity of the economic crisis forced governments to question competitive regulation procedures. The Democrats in the United States, the National Socialists in Germany, and the Conservatives in the United Kingdom all remained in power from 1933 until the war, with the result that, notwithstanding certain hesitations, their respective economic policies maintained the same orientations. France was an exception, however, insofar as traditional forms for managing the economy were preserved until 1936 and subsequent changes were largely burdened with debts from war preparations. It was probably in Germany that economic policy underwent the greatest change, as the ruthless Nazi dictatorship imposed authoritarian methods for managing the economy and the pursuit of autarky. In the United States, the New Deal modified the equilibrium between labor unions and management on the one hand and between the federal government and the private sector on the other. In the United Kingdom, there were fewer changes on the domestic level, but foreign economic policy was radically altered by both the devaluation of the pound and the abandoning of free trade that had been practiced since the middle of the nineteenth century. These varied choices led to significant differences in the short-term dynamics of the major powers.

Table 7.1 gives an initial overview of the results obtained, which must, however, be interpreted with caution. In macroeconomic terms, Germany showed the sharpest recovery, but this was obtained through methods that were ethically unacceptable. The United Kingdom obtained better results than the United States and France, but this was due not to the expansion of the 1932–38 period but to a less severe depression between 1930 and 1932. The United States showed frankly disappointing results.

Table 7.1

Comparative Rates of Growth (1921–1938)

	United States	United Kingdom	Germany	France
Production (annual rate of growth)				
1921–1929	4.8	3.2	4.1	5.7
1929–1932	−10.4	−1.7	−5.6	−3.8
1932–1938	4.6	3.8	8.8	1.3
GNP per capita (evolution)				
1938 (100 in 1929)	88	114	132	94

Source: A. Maddison (1982), statistical annex

Given the fact that the depression had left many production capabilities unemployed, the recovery of the 1930s lacked force. It is true that the New Deal came up against sharp resistance at home, with the result that it was applied with some hesitation. Indeed, the emergence of new forms of regulation is a slow process in countries with democratic governments. For a variety of reasons, the creation of new economic institutions in such countries is accompanied by debates and conflicts: because it implies a questioning of economic orthodoxy, because the result of major innovations is always uncertain, and because the changes lead to a modification of the distribution of wealth and power among social groups. During the 1930s, three major issues dominated the choice of economic policy: the form of parity, the growth of government intervention and public spending, and the search for a new wage relation.

Exchange Rate and the Response to External Constraint

Recent research on the 1929 crisis, notably that of Eichengreen (1992), Temin (1993), and Romer (1993), yields one prevailing judgment: devaluation was indispensable for halting the crisis, and the countries that devalued first were those that enjoyed the strongest recovery. This observation is supported by the comparison of the four major powers (see Table 7.2), since the United Kingdom, the United States, and France devaluated in 1931, 1933, and 1936, respectively, and while Germany did not carry out an official devaluation, it instituted a system of multiple exchange rates. The devaluating countries were able to benefit from three expansive effects: the revival of exports through the improvement of price competitiveness, greater liquidity through the increased value of national currency reserves and especially inflows of capital stimulated by the devaluation, and finally, the renewed rise of international prices in domestic currency, which put a halt to the fall in domestic prices. The relative importance of these three effects depended on the international situation of the countries that devalued.

It is obvious that the devaluation of the pound sterling first affected the English economy by halting the decline of exports, while those of the other countries continued to fall in 1932; in addition, the contribution of the foreign trade balance to the expansion of overall English demand was clearly positive in 1932. But at that time, exchange rates were not the sole determinants of exports, because there were emerging protectionist blocs during the 1930s. Germany was, in this context, the least favored nation, because it had no colonial empire, and this led it to conclude bilateral exchange agreements with its smaller neighbors in Southern and Eastern Europe. Furthermore, its foreign reserves were extremely weak (see chapter 5), which led in 1931 to the establishment of a system for rationing currency, and this was reinforced from 1933 on. France had its own colonial empire, with which it had intensified its ties during the depression, but the French colonies were not well developed, and above all, the overvaluing of the franc until 1936 led to considerable losses of market shares elsewhere in the world. The United Kingdom was the country in principle able to draw the most benefits from a bloc policy because of the size and diversity of its empire, which included both developed countries and poor ones. A preferential system was set up in 1932; however, over the next six years, the expansion of exports remained limited. Many British colonies had high levels of indebtedness, which was further aggravated by the fall in prices, and, as Maddison (1985) indicates, the metropolis did not accept defaults in payment; rather, it imposed deflationary policies on them. By contrast, most Latin American countries unilaterally reduced their debt burdens, and the United States did not react with harsh retaliatory measures. During the 1932–40 period, Latin America enjoyed a vigorous recovery stimulated by interventionist policies and facilitated by the reduction of the debt following payment defaults. Maddison stresses that the Latin American countries were better able to surmount the crisis of the 1930s than that of the 1980s. Exports from the United States, their main supplier, were facilitated; however, given the fact that the latter was little open to the rest of the world, foreign trade played only a limited role.

The devaluations allowed a very sharp lowering of the interest rate, first of all in the United Kingdom and then in the United States, notably through the inflows of capital that they set off. Indeed, capital was repatriated for speculative gains, and also out of fear of a depreciation of currencies that remained attached to their former parity and were thus overvalued. It is not certain, however, that this movement played a decisive role in halting the crisis. Indeed, the lowering of the interest rates undertaken in 1930 in the United States and France (see Table 7.2) did not suffice to end the depres-

Table 7.2

Conjuncture in Crises (1929–1938) for the Four Leading Countries

	United States	United Kingdom	Germany	France
Volume of exports				
1929	1,000	1,000	1,000	1,000
1931	669	624	862	762
1932	515	624	595	585
1935	588	738	537	558
1938	794	705	621	619
Short-term rate of interest				
1929	5.9	5.3	6.9	3.5
1931	2.6	3.6	6.8	1.6
1932	2.7	0.7	5.0	1.3
1935	0.8	0.6	3.1	3.2
1938	0.6	0.6	2.9	2.8
Price index (private sector)				
1929	1,000	1,000	1,000	1,000
1931	827	961	849	911
1932	709	928	517	849
1935	744	891	781	726
1938	773	987	862	1,159
Employment (private sector)				
1929	1,000	1,000	1,000	1,000
1931	884	954	825	967
1932	810	959	759	943
1935	884	1,026	884	875
1938	908	1,090	1,002	899
GNP (private sector)				
1929	1,000	1,000	1,000	1,000
1931	848	940	809	927
1932	719	942	715	852
1935	853	1,092	992	882
1938	958	1,175	1,296	926
Profit share in % of GNP (private sector)				
1929	20.7	30.9	9.8*	59.8
1931	10.9	29.6	−4.5	53.2
1932	3.5	28.3	−47	50.9
1935	12.9	29.6	15.5	51.2
1938	13.8	31.1	27.3	52.9

Source: Exports: Madison (1982). Rate of interest: Homer (1968). GNP, index price, employment and profit share in the private sector: GRESP (1984).

* Germany: GNP and profits are nets.

sion. In the United States in particular, the lowering of the rates resulted in part from the financial panic, which led capital bearers and financial intermediaries to acquire government loans; in reality they reflected a preference for sure financial assets at the expense of consumption and investment. The improvement of the monetary situation depended first of all on putting a stop to bank failures. This was initially attained by closing down the banks, enlarging the central bank's possibilities for intervention, and setting up regulations for the financial system. In Germany also, the stabilization of the banks was obtained through direct government intervention in the financial system.

The third effect of the devaluations was to slow down or halt the fall of domestic prices by raising the level of international prices in national currency. Indeed, the decline of prices was so violent that it blocked the adjustments proper to competitive regulation. In case of depression, bankruptcies and reduced numbers of employees were supposed to eliminate the least efficient activities, exert downward pressure on wages, and allow the surviving firms to improve their profitability, all of which was to lay the groundwork for the recovery. This was the curative virtue of the crisis in the neoconservative logic, which was placed in the wrong during the 1929 depression. The fall in prices was sharp, especially in Germany and the United States, which underwent a grave financial crisis. Nominal wages and employee numbers declined, but less so than prices; furthermore, in companies where an increasing share of the employees were salaried, the drop in the wage bill massively reduced outlets. The firms were unable to stabilize their profits, and bankruptcies followed. The devaluations allowed this vicious circle to be broken by slowing down or interrupting the drop in prices; this was the case by 1932 in the United Kingdom, 1934 in the United States, and 1936 in France, although in this last instance, the abandoning of the gold parity took place in a very particular context, as we shall see below.

In the short run, abandoning the old gold parities was decisive. On the one hand, this was not for the most part a government choice but a result of international capital movements. On the other hand, devaluation was a means of recovery, but most of its effects took place at the expense of countries that refuse to devalue, since the latter faced a decline in their price competitiveness and outflows of capital caused by the overvaluing of their parity, while on the domestic market, the decline in the prices of their foreign competitors aggravated the deflation. The only effect of international recovery generated by the devaluations was the rising value of exchange reserves in national currency. In addition, this allowed the destruction of international liquid assets in hard currency in 1931 and 1932 to be compensated, but the consequences were limited because the decrease in money supplies was not the most important cause of the crisis (see chapter 5, notably the analysis of the crisis in the United States). The devaluations were not a real remedy for the world crisis; they modified the distribution of the deflationary burden between countries, and they were that much more effective on the national level insofar as the other countries were slow in devaluating. From this point of view, the recovery through increasing public spending or the rise in wage consumption had very different effects because it also benefited the partners in business who could increase their exports as long as the country taking the initiative of recovery through domestic demand did not opt for a policy of autarky.

Increased Government Intervention and Public Spending

Increased government intervention was a general trend during the 1930s; one of its primary objectives was to control prices, and this was reflected nearly everywhere by the creation or reinforcement of mechanisms for stabilizing farm prices and subsidizing farmers. But beyond this point in common, the increase in the government's field of activity varied greatly from one country to another. Leaving aside the management of the labor force, we can begin by comparing the cases of England and Germany. In the first country, very few sectors or firms had been placed under government control—mainly the coal mines, London's transportation system, and one airline. By contrast, in the Third Reich, firms were required to belong to a cartel that had the power to forbid the creation of new firms and control the growth of existing ones; it negotiated prices with the government and was able to distribute certain primary goods. In addition, the firms were divided into seven large groups whose government-appointed leaders were supposed to rationalize production. This was a typically interventionist system, clearly inspired by the methods of a war economy.

The first New Deal, from 1933 to 1935, was an intermediate case. The National Industrial Recovery Act (NIRA) of 1933 allowed for creation of fair trade codes by firms belonging to the same branch; to the extent that these codes led to agreements on prices and production, they constituted a legal framework for the creation of cartels. The president could require all the firms in a given branch to respect it. The Agricultural Adjustment Act (AAA) organized a freeze on land financed by a specific tax, the reduction of farmers' debts, and the creation of a price stabilization system. These two laws came up against sharp opposition and were overturned by the Supreme Court in 1935 and 1936 on the grounds that they constituted an infringement by the executive branch on the powers of the legislative, the states, and the freedom of the private sector. This invalidation of the main mechanisms of the first New Deal show just how much the establishment of centralized instruments for intervention ran counter to the American traditions of decentralization and economic liberalism. This reversal pushed the federal government to set up a second New Deal based on the development of social legislation.

The governments also used the policy of public works. With the exception of France, the growth of public spending accelerated after 1932–33 (see Table 7.3). It was massive in Germany, first in order to build civilian infrastructures and then to prepare for the war. During the 1930s, public finances showed a deficit in most countries, with the exception of the United Kingdom. Public spending played an important role in putting an end to the crisis. Indeed, other tools for boosting the economy have limits that require the use of the budgetary weapon. Devaluation cannot be used indefinitely because competitors ultimately devalue as well. It was practically impossible, in the middle of the 1930s, to lower interest rates to any great extent because they were already quite low (see Table 7.2). A massive increase in wages was difficult to envision in countries where the firms' profitability had been weakened. In Germany, the rapid increase in public spending was the prime mover behind the recovery. In the United States, on the other hand, budgetary policy was subject to hesitations. Indeed, in 1936 and 1937, the American authorities feared the return of inflation, which led them to increase taxes in order to reduce the budget deficit and sharply increase compulsory bank reserves in order to sterilize capital inflows, as Kindleberger (1988) has indicated. This reversal of economic policy largely contributed to the 1938 recession, at the end of which the American government switched over to a policy of repeated budget deficits in order to put an end to the crisis.

Transformations of the Wage Relation

The wage policy carried out in Germany was very different from that in other countries. The unions were prohibited and their leaders prosecuted. Workers were required to join the Labor Front, which included employers and employees. The 1934 law on the organization of labor reaffirmed the authority of the company manager and set up government-appointed labor mediators whose role was to deliver binding arbitration in labor disputes. The labor market also came under authoritarian measures. The creation of a compulsory labor service allowed young people to be assigned to activities determined by the State. Women were discouraged from carrying out professional activities. The statistical data show that in Germany, the growth of real wages remained very limited (see Table 7.3).

In the United States, the second New Deal had the opposite effect. The political and legal failure of the first New Deal had led President Roosevelt to seek the support of the unions in a context of increasing labor–

Table 7.3

Public Expenditures and Real Rate of Wages (annual rate of growth)

	United States	United Kingdom	Germany	France
Public expenses				
1921–1929	3.3	0.2	–	1.9
1929–1932	3.8	2.1	–7.0	14.8
1932–1938	6.7	8.2	25.4	3.8
Real Rate of Wages				
1921–1929	2.4	–0.4	–	0.0
1929–1932	–1.4	1.6	0.6	–2.2
1932–1938	2.5	1.1	0.8	1.8

management disputes that was marked notably by a vast wave of strikes in 1934. The main measure enacted was the 1935 Wagner Law instituting electoral procedures for designating the most representative union, with which company heads were required to negotiate. In addition, the administration protected union delegates from retaliatory measures on the part of management and discouraged the creation of management-controlled unions. From 1932 to 1941, the number of union members rose from 2.1 to 10.5 million. A system of unemployment insurance and old-age pensions was also created, but social services remained limited. In spite of the persistence of high unemployment throughout the 1930s, real wages rose and the recovery was, for the most part, bolstered by increased consumption, while firm investment remained hesitant.

The evolution of labor–management relations in France stands out because of the drastic changes with the election of the Popular Front government in 1936. Wages were increased between 7 and 15 percent; the workweek was strictly limited to forty hours, without reduction of weekly wages; and a two-week paid vacation was instituted. The principle of legally binding collective agreements negotiated between unions and company heads was adopted. At the time, the economic consequences of this turnabout were very controversial. Today, with hindsight and the growing research in quantitative economic history, the conclusions are more nuanced. For Asselain (1984) and Villa (1993), the massive rise in wages led to a moderate recovery in production and sharp inflation. The latter led to three devaluations of the franc between 1936 and 1938. Paradoxically, consumption showed little increase in 1937, while investment enjoyed a considerable recovery. The devaluations hardly allowed the volume of exports to increase because the strict application of the forty-hour week had reduced the time the equipment was in use, while the high customs tariffs imposed by business closed the foreign markets. Nonetheless, the devaluations permitted a massive rise in export prices much greater than that in the general level of prices and wage costs, and this increased the profitability of the industrial sector.

❖

The 1929 crisis had led to a profound break in the organization and dynamic of capitalism. The institutional framework for the intensive growth of the 1950s and 1960s had been shaped by the lessons that government leaders and economists felt they should draw from the 1929–38 period. During the 1920s, governments believed that the transformations that had affected economies during the First World War were accidental or transitory and that it was necessary to return as quickly as possible to the pre-1914 traditional economic order. By contrast, the 1929 crisis greatly contributed to the weakening of traditional neoconservatism—the fact that the excesses of stock market speculation had apparently led to a very serious international depression cast doubt on the idea that markets should be left to themselves, and the limits of the recovery of the 1930s were also perceived.

It was in the area of money and finance that the transformations were most drastic. Prior to 1929, bank regulation was practically inexistent. During the 1930s, many industrial countries saw the introduction of measures that, at the least, imposed precautionary rules on commercial banks and reinforced the central banks' ability to intervene. In addition, the domestic conversion of gold currencies was definitively abolished, which created the possibility of implementing monetary policies that were not solely aimed at stabilizing currency but might also be used to stimulate growth and encourage full employment.

In the area of the wage relation, the reforms of 1933–47 prolonged and amplified changes that had begun to emerge in the late nineteenth and early twentieth centuries. Indeed, the first social security system based on compulsory contributions was set up by Germany during the 1880s. The other industrialized countries were to follow with considerable delay, and these systems did not become widespread in Europe until the 1940s. Labor unions began to be recognized during the First World War because they had participated in the "holy union" and agreed to contribute to the introduction of mass production methods in the weapons industries. Their role in wage negotiations was officially confirmed in Germany during the 1920s, in the United States and France during the 1930s, and in the United Kingdom in the 1940s.

In the area of international economic relations, government leaders recognized the need to prevent overly strict constraints from inhibiting domestic stabilization policies, and trade-bloc or autarkic policies from slowing down foreign trade and limiting returns on scale. The lessons of the difficulties and tensions of the 1930s had been well learned. The Bretton Woods Agreement of 1944 and that of the GATT in 1947 confirmed a compromise between the autonomy of national economic policies and the growth of trade: the rates of exchange were to be stabilized by the central banks but the adjustments of official parities were authorized under certain conditions; customs barriers were to be lowered, but protective clauses, as well as exceptions, for services or agricultural products were allowed.

CHAPTER EIGHT

The 1970s: The End of Growth and the Persistence of Regulation Modes

With the 1970s, the leading economies entered a major crisis, marked above all by rising unemployment, stagnating investment, the crisis in industry, aggravated economic warfare, and increased domestic and foreign debt. While changes in volume ultimately remained fairly similar from one economy to another, trends in prices and foreign trade showed considerable differences. External constraint exerted very different pressures depending upon the countries, and in the economic war, the industrialized nations manifested varying strengths. Rather paradoxically, seen from Europe with a certain hindsight, the 1970s appear almost prosperous: the postwar growth model was indeed brought to a halt, but after the first oil crisis, most of the major industrialized countries maintained a rhythm of growth in volume of roughly 2 to 3 percent.

The turning point was to come in 1980. The second oil crisis had led to a new breakdown, but above all, the strengthening of deflationary policies, the rise of real interest rates, and the questioning of previous modes of regulation brought the general crisis into a second phase.

The End of Growth

The first oil crisis served as a catalyst in setting off a crisis that had been brewing since the early 1970s. The drastic reduction in domestic purchasing power tied to the oil levy (which was aggravated by the restrictive policies implemented and the play on external constraint in many countries) had led to a decline in real demand and set off a recessionary trend.

But this trend did not degenerate into a cumulative decline, and by 1976 most economies showed signs of moderate recovery.

Freeze in Accumulation and Profitability Crisis

The two driving forces behind the growth of the previous years, the rapid rise in mass consumption and the steady rhythm of accumulation, were blocked from 1974 on (see Table 8.1). The growth of private consumption by volume slowed down (and even became negative in the United Kingdom), mainly owing to a decline in the growth of real income, but it did not collapse entirely and did not really change the structure of consumption. It was above all investments that dropped sharply in 1974–75, with only a moderate recovery afterward. This drop occurred in the context of a significant downward trend that had been felt in many countries since 1970. The oil crisis only accentuated the crisis of the accumulation regime. In the face of increasingly unfavorable expectations with regard to profitability and outlets, businesses limited their investment programs.

This observation about investment must, however, be qualified in two respects. First of all, an analysis of the rate of investment shows that in fact, while its average levels for 1976–80 did not reach those of the early 1970s, the decline remained limited. Japan probably experienced the sharpest decline, but the Japanese investment rates remained at levels that were clearly higher than those of the other leading economies. Rather than a drop in investment, we can thus speak of adaptation to a regime of slower growth.

Second, investment developments varied greatly from one branch to another. The decline was much more significant in industry than in the tertiary, which maintained its growth to a larger extent. Similarly, government investment often played a major support role through large infrastructural programs, as was the case in France with nuclear power, telecommunications, and transportation. Even within industry, the developments were also quite different, and a vast redeployment effort manifested itself in varying degrees from one country to another. Disengagements or modernization investments were alternately carried out in heavy industry and traditional consumer goods; capital equipment generally showed more stable growth in its investments with increasing involvement in new technology sectors.

In most of the leading economies, the first oil crisis was followed by major efforts to reestablish external equilibrium by limiting growth to reduce imports and undertaking programs aimed at economizing on energy, but also by increasing exports and opting for a redeployment strategy. Exports remained fairly steady because of the emergence of new markets in the OPEC and developing countries and also because of rising international debt. Growth became increasingly extroverted. But the abil-

144

Table 8.1

The Rate of Growth in Five Leading Economies (1973–1980)

	France		United States		Japan		Germany		United Kingdom	
	1	2	1	2	1	2	1	2	1	2
GNP	1.7	3.3	-0.7	3.6	0.6	5.0	-0.6	3.6	-0.8	1.6
Consumption	3.1	3.7	0.4	3.7	1.7	3.7	1.7	3.2	-1.2	2.6
Investment	-3.5	5.6	-6.0	4.7	-8.6	8.3	-4.9	7.0	-2.6	5.1

Source: OECD, national accounts
1 = 1973–1975; 2 = 1975–1980

Table 8.2

The Evolution of Exports and Imports in Five Leading Economies (1973–80)

Annual rates of growth 1973–80	France	United States	Germany	Japan	United Kingdom
Export of goods and services	6.4	5.5	11.2	5.2	3.4
Import of goods and services	6.3	2.7	2.6	6.5	1.3

Source: OECD, national accounts.

ity to maintain it by improving the foreign trade balance in volume varied greatly by country (see Table 8.2). Japan showed the greatest recourse to this mechanism, which grew over time. Germany's dynamic was different because of much greater reliance on improvement of the terms of trade. In France, the upturn of the foreign trade balance in volume remained limited with the exception of 1975, which marked the peak of the recession. Overall, the balance of trade was readjusted to different extents from one country to another. The external constraint varied in its impact, but in most cases it constituted an important factor in spreading the crisis within each country's economy. We shall return to this question in greater detail.

From 1973 on, the decline in growth went hand in hand with a very pronounced slowdown in productivity gains, which was quite widespread even if its scope varied from one economy to another. The origins of this slowdown have given rise to many controversies. In the short term, it was due above all to inertia in the adjustments that were more or less rapid depending on the nature of the social relations in each country. In the medium term, a more structural explanation is needed to describe the lasting slowdown in labor productivity.

Several explanatory factors may be ruled out immediately. With the exception of the United States, for example, a decline in capital intensiveness cannot be evoked because there was often at least a partial adjustment of workforce numbers. The same is true for the consequences of tertiarization because, as we have seen, such intersectoral transfers from manufacturing to services had fairly limited effects. Here, too, the exception of the United States must be noted, however, insofar as intersectoral workforce transfers toward the tertiary played a greater role in stabilizing productivity (i.e., the development of low-productivity jobs in the services). Similarly, the slowdown in productivity cannot be described in terms of the exhaustion of technical progress incorporated into facilities or advances in the organization of work. On this level, we find fairly contradictory phenomena because a major technological transformation was already under way with the growth of automation and microelectronics applications.

The most likely explanation for the slowdown in labor productivity gains must be sought in the mechanical effect of the slowdown in growth. The Kaldor–Verdoorn law applies here. As a reduced form of a system of complex relations, it indicates that the growth of an economy leads to increasing returns to scale that are static, learning effects, and mutually enhancing performances. A short-term slowdown generates the opposite phenomena plus the consequences of weakening the dynamism of demand on product innovations and related research-and-development expenditures (Boyer and Petit 1981).

The freeze in accumulation can be explained by two main factors—dim prospects for outlets and declining profitability of capital. In most countries apart from the United States, the share of wages showed a sharp increase between 1973 and 1975 because real wages continued to rise, while labor productivity stagnated because of the recession and the phenomenon of retaining workers rather than laying them off. With the slow recovery from 1976 to 1979, patterns of change showed greater divergences (see Figure 6.3, chapter 6, p. 125). In West Germany, the share of wages was brought back to its 1970 level through control over the rise of real wages and relative maintenance of productivity gains, while in France and Japan it remained at a high level. In Great Britain, the share of profits also increased, in spite of stagnant productivity, but at the cost of a process of adjustment from the bottom up.

In all countries, the deterioration of firms' financial situation was aggravated by two other phenomena (Table 8.3). On the one hand, the rise in social security contributions intended to finance social budgets that were increasingly unbalanced, especially because of the rise in unemployment, put a heavy strain on company books. Social security contributions in France showed the greatest increase and appeared (given their base) to be the most burdensome. Thus, the increase in the share of employers' social security contributions in the value added between 1973 and 1980 was equivalent to nearly 75 percent of the rise in all the wage costs. On the other hand, the rise in financing charges, resulting from the companies' indebtedness, followed the same trend but remained limited in scope until the end of the 1970s. These interest fees were the most burdensome in Germany and Japan, which can be explained, in part, by the closer ties between banks and firms in these countries.

This decline in the share of profits was combined with a pronounced drop in the efficiency of capital related to both the lack of outlets and the low productivity gains (see chapter 6, p. 110). This resulted in a very marked drop in the profitability of capital that generally affected manufacturing much more seriously. Although a slight recovery got under way

Table 8.3

The Growth of Social Security Contributions and Finance Charges (1973-80)

Proportion of GNP (in %)	France	United States	Germany	Japan	United Kingdom	Italy
Firms' social security contributions						
1973	12.0	4.4	2.7	7.7	3.6	10.6
1980	15.7	5.1	4.2	8.8	5.1	11.2
Firm's interest charges						
1973	4.6	4.1	10.2	7.0	9.5[1]	3.5
1980	5.3	4.7	11.7	7.8	9.9[1]	6.1

Source: OECD, national accounts.
[1]With dividends.

from 1976 to 1979, this drop in profitability remained durable and was not followed by any real upturn (see Figure 6.4, p. 119). However, the recession that began in 1974 did not degenerate into a cumulative decline.

Absence of a Cumulative Decline

From 1976 on, most of the industrialized countries underwent a limited recovery owing to three groups of factors: the maintenance of the wage income through the protection of employment and the growth of the indirect wage (with certain exceptions); the spread of an overdraft economy on the national and especially the international level; and the effects of newly implemented budgetary policies, although these intervened in a more contradictory fashion.

Maintenance of Household Disposable Income

Although it was slower than during the 1960–73 period, the rise in real household incomes continued during the crisis and was more rapid than that of labor-market participation (Table 8.4). This phenomenon was very pronounced after the first oil crisis but considerably less so after the second.

Outside of the United States, several factors contributed to the increase in wage-earners' real income. These included first of all (except in the United States) maintenance of indexation mechanisms. Second, there was often the slowness of the adjustment in the numbers of personnel to the slowdown in growth, especially in Japan, Italy, the United Kingdom, and France. The Brechling equations remained stable (Boyer and Petit 1980),

Table 8.4

Evolution of Household Disposable Income (1973–1980)

	Real disposable income (annual rate of growth, in %)			Household disposable income/GDP (in %)	
	1973–75	1975–79	1979–81	1973	1980
United States	1.1	3.8	1.8	67.2	67.6
Germany	2.7	3.0	0.7	62.3	63.7
Japan	2.8	3.5	1.6[1]	67.1	71.7
France	3.9	3.3	1.3	72.3	73.8
United Kingdom	−1.0	3.2	1.2[1]	67.7	68.1

Source: OECD, national accounts.
[1] 1979–1980.

and labor productivity scarcely increased. In addition, the scope of social services was broadened, either automatically (via unemployment benefits) or relatively (via healthcare benefits). Finally, the rate of household savings also tended to decline from 1971 to 1979 (in the United States, Germany, and Japan, but not in France). Overall, excluding the case of the United States, where wage-earners' hourly gains dropped from 1975 to 1981 and the share of disposable household income in value added was stable, the crisis was cushioned by the fact that the majority of households (those that had jobs) were able to maintain their standard of living.

Growth of an Overdraft Economy

This factor continued to play a role—although less than is generally assumed—at least until 1979. The nonfinancial sector's balance-sheet structure (ratio of outstanding debts to total equity capital) deteriorated between 1970 and 1973 but then improved in the United States and Japan until 1979 (see Table 8.5). Debt phenomena were most pronounced on the international level. With the first oil crisis, the spread of international financing with the Eurocurrency market accelerated sharply. The emergence of significant surpluses in the OPEC countries, tied to the inadequate growth of their imports, implied a massive international financial intervention to avoid an adjustment in the form of a profound drop in production in the consumer countries. After 1974, the main industrialized countries succeeded, with varying speed, in reducing their foreign deficit, although this did not keep them from seeking international loans on the Eurodollar market to facilitate the financing of their balance of payments (the case of France's public enterprises was very significant). Several in-

Table 8.5

Balance Sheet Structure in the Nonfinancial Sector (outstanding debts/equity funds)

	1970	1973	1975	1979
United States	0.83	0.90	0.69	0.72
Germany	1.46	1.57	1.44	1.92[1]
Japan	—	6.36	6.54	5.32
France	1.91	2.27	2.59	2.43

Source: OECD, financial statistics.
[1]1978.

Table 8.6

Distribution of Manufactured Goods Exports from Industrialized Countries by Destination (in %)

	1973	1979
Industrialized countries	73.7	68.4
Oil-exporting developing countries	4.6	8.4
Other developing countries	14.1	15.7
Eastern bloc countries	4.4	5.0

Source: GATT.

dustrialized countries, the developing countries that were not oil producers, and the Eastern-bloc countries, because of a considerable trade deficit, were most likely to resort to international debt. These developments reflected a considerable change in the structure of worldwide demand. While trade among advanced capitalist countries constituted a growing share of exchanges of manufactured goods before 1973, the trend reversed itself between 1973 and 1979 (see Table 8.6): the developing countries and the Eastern bloc increased their share of purchases of manufactured goods coming from the advanced capitalist countries.

This increased external debt allowed a large number of countries to finance their imports of manufactured goods despite their oil deficit. The 1970s were marked by a kind of "Keynesianism on a planetary scale," which helped to maintain growth in the industrialized countries. But the growth of an international overdraft economy in which international loans became widespread as a means of financing chronic deficits and the expansion of trade reserves increased the dependency of international exchanges relative to the dollar and the American economy. Notwithstanding many vicissitudes, the dollar remained the hub of the international finance system. During the 1970s, the dollar notably played a growing role in international transactions, whether commercial or financial. While the circulation of dollars largely took place outside the United States, it nonetheless remained dependent on the American economy because of the way that international finance circuits were supplied in dollars. This overdraft economy and the dependence on the United States, as we shall see, were to have serious consequences.

The Ambiguous Role of Budgetary Policies

With the economic slowdown, public deficits automatically tended to grow, insofar as the increase in tax receipts and social security contributions was slowing down at the same time that the scope of expenditures was broadening. In 1975–76, these involuntary deficits were compounded by voluntary deficits when the oil surtax clearly appeared to be recessive. This was the case in France, more lastingly in Italy and Japan, and less clearly in Germany (see Table 8.7). Contradictory trends came into play with, in certain cases, the desire to reduce imbalances (France and the United States from 1977 on), even at the price of a sharp rise in tax and social security contributions, and in other cases, questions about the relevance of assuming the leadership role in world growth (Germany in 1979).

It should be stressed that a public deficit was much less disadvantageous in the 1970s. There was no cumulative debt process at work because of the level of real interest rates, which were negative and clearly lower than the rate of growth.

A whole group of factors thus came together in the course of the 1970s to permit a slower rhythm of growth to be maintained without setting off a cumulative decline along with a major financial crisis, as had been the case in the 1930s. These factors reflected the persistence of monopolistic regulation with the maintenance of a certain rise in real wages, the protection of employment, the growth of the indirect wage, and the pursuit of indebtedness. The existing institutional forms were maintained and, indeed, were even reinforced, whether this involved the supporting role of public finance or the nature of wage relations. While a certain resemblance in the evolution of the different countries could be seen in terms of real magnitudes, significant divergences emerged in the nominal magnitudes.

Sharp Disparities in Inflation

The growing dispersion of inflation rates within the industrialized countries was one of the main characteristics of the second half of the 1970s. This is a permanent feature of any period of floating exchange rates, and we have already observed it during the 1920s. Nonetheless, this development cannot be explained primarily by that of the exchange rates. The

Table 8.7

Evolution of Public Finances in the Leading Economies

A) Public spending in % of GDP

	1973	1974	1975	1976	1977	1978	1979	1980
France	35.8	36.9	40.6	41.0	41.2	42.0	42.3	43.2
Germany	38.2	41.0	44.6	43.9	44.0	44.1	43.9	44.3
United Kingdom	39.0	43.1	44.9	43.9	42.0	41.6	41.7	44.2
Italy	38.8	38.6	42.9	41.9	42.2	45.8	45.2	45.2
United States	30.2	31.7	34.1	33.2	32.3	32.0	31.8	33.8
Japan	21.9	24.0	26.8	27.3	28.6	30.2	31.3	32.9

Source: OECD.

B) Tax and Social Security contributions in % of GDP

	1973	1974	1975	1976	1977	1978	1979	1980
France	35.7	36.3	37.4	39.4	39.4	39.5	41.2	42.6
Germany	36.3	36.3	35.7	36.7	38.0	37.6	37.3	37.4
United Kingdom	31.9	35.4	36.1	35.7	35.5	34.0	34.0	35.8
Italy	26.3	28.3	29.0	30.3	30.9	31.3	30.1	31.7
United States	29.7	30.2	30.2	29.3	30.3	30.2	31.3	31.5
Japan	22.5	23.0	21.1	22.0	22.5	24.3	24.8	26.1

Source: OECD. Except for France; national accounts.

C) Public surplus or deficit in % of GDP

	1973	1974	1975	1976	1977	1978	1979	1980
France	1.2	0.6	−2.2	−0.7	−0.8	−1.7	−0.6	0.1
Germany	1.2	−1.4	−5.8	−3.6	−2.4	−2.7	−3.0	−3.4
United Kingdom	−3.5	−3.8	−4.9	−5.0	−3.4	−4.3	−3.3	−3.5
Italy	−8.5	−8.1	−11.7	−9.0	−8.0	−9.8	−9.5	−7.8
United States	1.0	0.5	−3.5	−1.5	−0.3	0.6	0.5	−1.2
Japan	0.7	0.4	−2.8	−2.9	−3.8	−5.9	−4.3	−4.2

Source: OECD.

different assessments of imported inflation show that in most cases this is much less important than indigenous inflation (OECD 1981). Leaving aside the small countries that are quite open to the outside, internal inflation is by far the most significant and generally the most stable element, and this is what we shall mainly be examining in this section. The divergence in the rates of exchange was often the sanction of the differing dynamics of incomes and prices. The evolution of the rates of exchange then intervened to amplify these trends, as was the case in Germany, where we can observe a virtuous circle of deutschmark reevaluation–disinflation, or in Italy and the United Kingdom, which, conversely, were marked by a spiral of depreciation–acceleration of inflation. We shall return to this issue at greater length below.

Inflation can be studied in the context of the analyses developed in chapter 6 to describe the acceleration of inflation at the end of the 1960s. The 1974–80 period seems to have been profoundly marked by the declining rate of profit, which, to varying degrees, affected all the leading economies. A comprehensive analysis would require integrating into a macroeconomic model the different forms of internal adjustment that allow the distribution of revenues to be described. In this study, we have limited ourselves to an informal approach focusing on the medium-term inflation differentials existing among the leading economies. It is possible to identify three main determinants reflecting the specific forms taken by monopolistic regulation during the 1970s in each country: the ways the nominal wage rate is fixed and the form of labor-force management, the medium-term slowdown in labor productivity, and the companies' markup behavior.

Sharp Contrasts in the Fixing of the Nominal Wage

Numerous econometric studies have explained the evolution of the nominal wage rate (Boyer and Mistral 1978; Artus 1983; Mazier, Dayon, and Galibert 1981), but no simple relation has been determined between a given degree of wage–price indexing and the more or less inflationary nature of an economy (Table 8.8)

Germany and the United States showed less indexing and, in the long run, brought their inflation under control. But England or Italy (with the exception of a cost-of-living adjustment that is indexed), with less indexing than France, underwent a sharp inflationary rise. Japan, with greater indexing, was to curb inflation after the first oil crisis. One explanation for these contrasting situations might be that intensive indexing can be helpful if it is rapid, in case of a reversal of inflationary expectations or forecasts of inflation. The institutional contexts deserve close examination because specific negotiating procedures are more decisive than the gen-

Table 8.8

Comparative Estimates of Wage–Price Elasticities

	France	United States	Japan	Germany	United Kingdom	Italy
P. Artus (1983) 1965–1980	0.96	0.87	1.32	0.72	0.57	
Ministry of Finance, Forecasting Department (1981), for 1962–1978	0.95	0.63	1.11[1]	1.04	0.94	0.72[2]
GRESP (1981) 1970–1979	1.0			0.7	0.9	0.6

[1]1967–1978   [2]1968–1978

Table 8.9

Real Wage and Inflation (annual rates of growth in %)

	France	United States(3)	Japan(4)	Germany	United Kingdom	Italy
Real hourly wage rate in manufacturing sector						
(1)	3.4	1.6	2.4	1.9	–3.1	4.2
(2)	3.8	0.6	1.9	2.3	1.4	3.9
Consumer price						
(1)	9.4	6.8	6.0	3.7	13.1	16.0
(2)	10.7	7.9	9.1	4.7	15.6	17.6

Source: OECD, national accounts.
(1) 1975–1979   (2) 1973–1980   (3) United States hourly gains   (4) Japan monthly gains

eral features of the system for managing nominal wages. In Germany, for example, indexing is prohibited by law. This is not the case in the United States, but wage agreements cover several years. In Japan, meanwhile, indexing procedures are not explicit, but the price elasticity of wages is greater than 1, which indicates the tenor of the implicit social compromise. Ultimately, the relationship between changes in real wages and inflation is far from uniform (Table 8.9).

On the other hand, a more significant contrast between the different economies emerges with regard to the sensitivity of the nominal wage rate to two major factors—the disequilibrium of the labor market and changes in labor productivity. In one group of countries (Germany, Japan, United States, Belgium, Netherlands), the "labor market" had to compensate—through reduced activity among women and foreigners in Germany, among young people and minorities in the United States, among employees of subcontracting firms in Japan. The dependency of the nominal wage on changes in labor productivity (which was slowing down) gradually became clear.

In a second group of countries (Italy, France, United Kingdom), continued strong wage pressure resisted any mobility weighing on wages, thus delaying adjustments in employment. In some cases, this situation favored a certain dualism. There was an increase in contingent work; the tertiary sector absorbed hidden unemployment, and production units were broken up (leading to the creation of the "second Italy"). In this second group, the nominal wage was more independent of the growing disequilibrium on the labor market and the changes in labor productivity. With the exception of Great Britain, where the real wage declined, developments temporarily maintained purchasing power but with a high level of inflation.

Uneven Inflationary Consequences of the Slowdown in Labor Productivity

The slowdown in the rise of labor productivity in the medium term exacerbated the tensions over income distribution. The social partners remained bound to procedures that had been established during the years of the greatest growth (when there was, as the French say, "food for thought" in the wage negotiations).

Thus, from 1973 to 1980, in most of the OECD countries, on the level of the economy as a whole, the nominal wage level was as rigid in periods of low productivity gains as when the value added showed high growth rates (Italy, Great Britain). The United States was able to achieve greater control of wage inflation in spite of stagnating productivity. Germany, Japan, and Austria, which had more stable productivity gains, also succeeded in controlling inflation. France occupied an intermediary position—sharp productivity gains in a few key sectors allowed increases in nominal wages, and these became contagious for employees in sectors where productivity showed lesser increases.

For manufacturing alone, Great Britain and Japan constitute two extremes: low productivity gains and high wages in the first case, stable productivity gains and controlled wages in the second. "Official" Italy, meanwhile, showed strong rigidities.

Defense of the Markup Rate and Inflation of Profit

The econometric analysis of the markup rate brings out certain contrasts within the leading economies (Artus 1983; Mazier, Dayon, Galibert 1981). Real markup rates declined sharply during the 1970s, but the desired markup rates, such as they can be determined, for example, by observing procedures for establishing production price scales, seem rigid and fairly insensitive to short-term developments in the United States, France, and Great Britain. In Germany, the decision to adopt a strategy of strong external competitiveness gave rise to a partial adjustment, and the same was true in Japan. These disparities among the leading economies affected the fixing of prices. With all other factors being equal, a greater rigidity of the markup rate led to sharper price increases. Conversely, the better control of inflation in Japan and Germany requires a new explanation.

These differences in profit inflation must be combined with differences in the processes of fixing wages and the slowdown in productivity that we have already described. They serve to explain contrasts in stagflation, which is the term applied to the unequal persistence of inflation in a context of slowed growth during the second half of the 1970s. Overall, it was in the countries where income distribution was best negotiated and where productivity gains were maintained at the same time that the firms abandoned their rigid markup behaviors that inflation was best controlled (Germany and Japan). Along with these internal determinants of inflation, the dynamic of the exchange rate amplified these tendencies.

Different Forms of Adaptation Through Exchange Rate and International Specialization

For the European economies in particular, growing internationalization and the accentuation of the horizontal nature of the international division of labor were reflected by greater openness to the outside in terms of both the penetration of the domestic market and the increased role of exports. For a given country, this growing openness would have all the more impact in reinforcing the weight of the external constraint if the country's specialization was of poor quality. The contrast between France and Germany is enlightening in this respect.

International capital movements and floating exchange rates amplified the impact of this constraint. Floating exchange rates had very destabilizing effects by increasing uncertainty and making any investment decision even more uncertain. But above all, they sharply increased pressures on the balance of payments through the short-term capital movements they engendered. If one country pursued a recovery policy by lowering its rate of interest and risking a deterioration of the foreign trade balance, the floating capital fled and caused a decline in the exchange rate. Even Germany, which was clearly competitive, underwent the experience in 1980. Conversely, if a government applied a heavily restrictive policy, even at the cost of threatening entire sectors of its industry, foreign capital flowed in, as was the case in Great Britain in 1980 (Baslé 1992). These mechanisms tended to bring the different countries in line with the one that had the most restrictive policy, and to limit general growth.

The rise in oil prices also led to significant foreign debts in many countries. Most of them sought to diminish these foreign imbalances by implementing programs to economize on energy, attempting to conquer new shares of the world market, and, especially in the least competitive countries, slowing growth, which in turn aggravated the world depression.

The reactions of the different industrialized countries in the face of this external constraint were of varying effectiveness, as witnessed by the contrasting changes in trade balances (Table 8.10). Multiple factors explain the varying nature of these changes, notably the quality of the specialization and redeployment strategies adopted, the exchange policy, the energy dependency, or the forms of macroeconomic regulation. Without underestimating the importance of the other factors, we shall limit ourselves to the first two.

Greater External Constraint for the Least Specialized Countries

Japan made the best use of its model of industrial and social organization to increase its shares of the world market through greater specialization within a protectionist context (CEPII 1983). Economies of scale linked to mass production were sought in electronics, automobile manufacture, machines, and the iron and steel industry, while many more traditional sectors remained protected structurally. Japan was thus able to achieve significant trade surpluses while reembarking on sustained growth.

The United States preserved major areas of competitiveness in high-tech industries, industrial equipment, and chemicals while maintaining its agricultural surpluses and engineering revenues. But the American positions declined, notably under pressure from Japan, in the automobile industry, mass-market electronics, and electrical equipment. Overall, American performances dwindled even if the position of the dollar, the size of the domestic market, and its relatively closed nature allowed the most drastic choices to be postponed.

The European economies, which were more open than those of Japan and the United States, assumed a position of relative weakness and fell increasingly behind in electronics. Even German industry did not entirely escape this phenomenon. It preserved major areas of competitiveness in chemicals, machines, automobile manufacture, and the iron and steel industry, which helped to bring its trade balance into equilibrium. But Germany lagged behind the Japanese thrust and maintained its positions without advancing (De Mautort 1981).

French industry, which was less specialized, found itself in a difficult position. The industrial trade deficit in relation to the OECD countries

Table 8.10

Trade Balance (average annual exports–imports of goods and services, in % of GDP) (1974–1980)

	France	United States	Japan	Germany	United Kingdom	Italy
1974–1975	−0.4	−0.5	−0.6	3.5	−3.3	−2.2
1976–1979	−0.1	−1.1	0.8	1.9	0.0	1.0
1980	−1.7	−1.0	−0.9	−0.4	2.5	−2.8

Source: OECD.

increased during the 1970s and was only compensated by surpluses with the developing countries and the Eastern bloc through the policy of major contracts. The strategy of industrial redeployment launched after 1974 did not bear fruit in terms of overall competitiveness. Heavy inter-mediate-goods industries were still aging. Consumer-goods industries were abandoned without being modernized. The rate of penetration of the domestic market rose, and specialization existed only on a limited level. France was a major exporter but also, and often for the same goods, a major importer, which led to great sensitivity to fluctuations in condi-tions of international competition. Industrial policy concerning engineer-ing and electronics was badly handled. Only a few sectors such as aeronautics, telecommunications, military hardware, or nuclear energy improved their situations, and this through significant public commis-sions. At that point, the French economy could not avoid a sharp external constraint, the impact of which was reinforced after 1978 by the strategy of the "strong franc."

Italy showed uneven foreign revenues, which reflected its profound economic and social dualism. The extremely unfavorable situation of heavy-industry sectors dominated by large groups contrasted with the good performances of smaller-scale firms in consumer goods, but also in engineering. Overall, through an original strategy of specialization that opted for complementarity rather than competition with Germany, Italy was in a position to improve its overall competitiveness.

The United Kingdom continued to pay the price of "stop and go" policies and underinvestment. Its traditional advantages in automobile manufacture, engineering, and the iron and steel industry were weak-ened. Fine chemicals showed greater resistance, and services became the area with the greatest surpluses. At the beginning of the 1980s, the United Kingdom gave the appearance of an independent economy owing to the North Sea oil deposits, with considerable service activities, a few very competitive multinational firms, and a sharp penetration of foreign, and notably American, capital.

Rates of Exchange and External Constraint

Exchange policy is not unrelated to the way production is organized. In the medium term, it has a considerable impact on specialization. Conversely, the quality of specialization affects the room for maneuver in the handling of exchange. Drawing on the problematic developed by Aglietta, Oudiz, and Orléan (1981), the analysis of exchange will be integrated into an overall framework taking into account not only price elasticities but also the dynamic of the industrial sector and changes in the distribution of wages and profits and investment. This approach shows that economies react quite differently to a fluctuation in exchange rates and that a given model cannot be applied universally. In the light of the experience of the major industrial countries during the 1970s, we shall examine in turn the conditions for a successful policy of reevaluation, the limits of a policy of overly sharp depreciation, and the advantages and risks of a policy of moderate depreciation.

Conditions for a Successful Policy of Reevaluation

The virtuous circle of the reevaluation of the German mark depended on three specific features (Figure 8.1). The first was the high quality of German specialization, which accounted for its position as price maker and a low price elasticity of exports. The second lay in the reduced sensitivity of industrial productivity gains to increases in production, according to the different tests of the Kaldor–Verdoorn ratio (Boyer and Petit 1981; Amable 1989). The third feature resulted from the moderation of domestic inflationary tensions as these have been analyzed above. In addition, the prices of services during the 1970s rose barely more quickly than industrial prices, owing, in part at least, to greater adjustments in service-sector employment than in other countries.

In this context, the reevaluation of the mark had relatively slight effects on import and export volumes, with the result that the increase in the terms of exchange led to an improvement in the balance of trade. The slowdown in growth remained moderate and practically without effect on labor productivity. The drop in import prices increased the brake on inflation. Because of its position as price maker, industry was able to avoid an overly large reduction of its markup rates. Furthermore, the limited rises in service-sector wages and prices also favored the profitability of capital.

Limits gradually became apparent, however. Germany's shares of the

Figure 8.1 **Exchange Rate and Price Competitiveness in Germany and Japan**

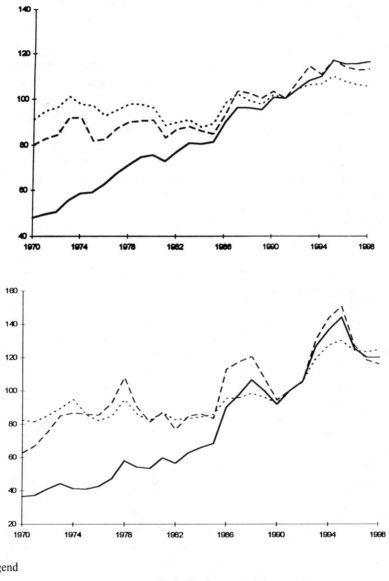

Legend

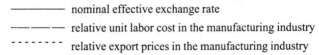 nominal effective exchange rate

relative unit labor cost in the manufacturing industry

relative export prices in the manufacturing industry

Source: OECD (1997).

world market declined considerably from 1974 to 1980 (see Table 8.11). Productivity gains were maintained by means of rationalization investments and downsizing, notably to the detriment of women and immigrant workers, and this trend reached its limits over time. The halt in growth led to a freezing of investment that, among other things, placed too much emphasis on rationalization and was not sufficiently oriented to new products and technologies. The microelectronics revolution was only belatedly recognized.

Japan offers an even more exemplary case of successful reevaluation. The reevaluation of the yen from 1971 to 1981, interrupted only during the two oil crises, led to a rise in unit wage costs in industry and consumer prices in international currency that were more rapid than those of Japan's partners. But this did not necessarily generate competitiveness in export prices. This lasting divergence between the two competitiveness indicators cannot be explained by a simple phenomenon of markup reduction. It goes back to the remarkable features of Japanese specialization and the heterogeneity of its industrial sector. The major export branches saw a much more rapid increase in productivity and a smaller increase in unit costs than the average for industry, which allowed price competitiveness to be preserved.

This specialization must be seen in the larger context of the Japanese economy's dual structure opposing the manufacturing and nonmanufacturing sectors. The latter functions as a kind of "shock absorber" that can make use of the surplus workforce or accept reduced profits or a decline in the purchasing power of non-wage-earners. This dualism explains the fact that the share of industrial profits rose in spite of the decline in relative industrial prices. Since the mid-1970s, Japan has opted for growth fed by the conquest of foreign market shares without opening its domestic market. Industrial specialization and dualism were the two factors that allowed Japan to implement this strategy and reevaluate the yen without compromising its price competitiveness until the mid-1980s.

In contrast to the previous two examples, reevaluation applied in a country with mediocre specialization runs the risk of deindustrialization. Belgium during the 1970s offers one striking example of this phenomenon, and the United Kingdom in 1979 constitutes another. The sharp real reevaluation of the pound between 1979 and 1981 struck British industry head on, leading to the collapse of entire activity sectors. As we shall see below, France's "strong franc" policy from 1978 on had something of the same effect, albeit more moderately.

The Limits of an Overly Sharp Devaluation Policy

The United Kingdom until 1978 and Italy until the mid-1980s pursued depreciation policies with uneven results (see Figure 8.2). English in-

Table 8.11

Market Shares by Value and Volume Relative to Total Exports of the Main OECD Countries (in %)

	1974	1975	1976	1977	1978	1979	1980	1981	1982
Value									
France	9.9	10.6	10.2	10.2	10.2	10.7	10.3	9.6	9.1
Germany	19.3	18.3	18.6	18.9	18.9	18.7	17.8	16.5	17.5
Italy	6.5	7.1	6.7	7.2	7.4	7.8	7.2	7.2	7.4
United Kingdom	8.4	8.9	8.5	9.2	9.6	9.9	10.7	9.7	9.6
United States	21.3	21.9	21.0	19.3	19.1	19.8	20.5	22.1	21.4
Japan	11.9	11.4	12.3	12.9	13.0	11.2	12.0	14.3	13.9
Volume (1)									
France	10.6	10.6	10.4	10.6	10.6	11.0	10.6	10.7	10.4
Germany	19.5	18.3	18.7	18.6	18.2	18.2	18.1	18.6	19.5
Italy	6.6	7.1	7.1	7.3	7.7	7.8	6.9	7.0	7.4
United Kingdom	8.7	8.9	8.7	8.9	8.8	8.6	8.5	7.9	8.1
United States	21.4	21.9	20.4	19.4	20.4	21.1	22.2	21.0	19.5
Japan	10.7	11.4	12.6	12.9	12.1	11.3	12.7	13.7	13.6

Source: Ministry of Finance, Forecasting Department.
(1) Based on 1975 exchange rates and prices.

dustry tended to use the depreciation to restore its export profits. Exports continued to show fairly slow growth. Combined with a reduction in real wages, the devaluation played its role of redistributing in favor of profits, but set off an inflationary spiral that accentuated already strong pressures domestically. In addition, the stagnation of domestic demand and the sluggishness of exports did not favor a lasting recovery of investment.

The depreciation of the lira was greater and longer lasting than that of the pound. The results in terms of foreign trade were more favorable than in the United Kingdom because of Italian industry's specialization in consumer goods with greater price elasticity. Italy was the European country in which manufactured goods exports by volume showed the greatest increase during the 1970s and where the rates of domestic-market penetration showed the smallest increase. The growth of profits in the export sector, the rise of industrial-goods prices on the domestic market, plus the recovery of productivity gains, contributed to reestablishing the share of profits in industry.

There was growing specialization in consumer goods and, upstream, in capital goods. These sectors were gradually modernized, with an improvement in product quality. The main disadvantage of this strategy was

Figure 8.2 **Exchange Rate and Price Competitiveness in the United Kingdom and Italy**

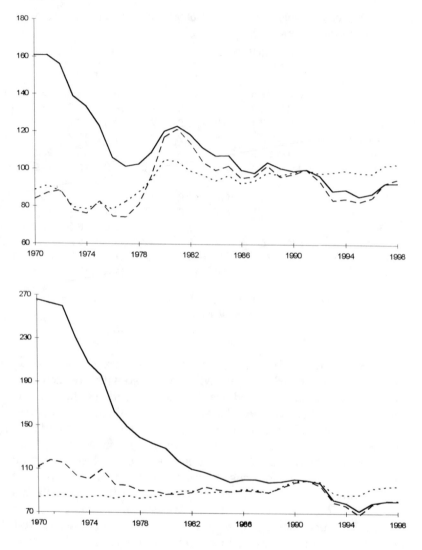

Legend

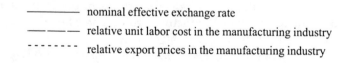

——————— nominal effective exchange rate

——— ——— relative unit labor cost in the manufacturing industry

- - - - - - - relative export prices in the manufacturing industry

Source: OECD (1997).

that it favored a depreciation–inflation spiral that reinforced already strong inflationary trends.

The United States constitutes a case apart because of its closed economy and the dollar's status as international currency that allows the monetary constraint to be avoided. The massive depreciation of the dollar between 1971 and 1974, which was continued on a more moderate basis until 1979, mainly confirmed the erosion of American positions during the 1960s (see Figure 8.3). In spite of their difficulty, international price comparisons suggest a transition from overevaluation to underevaluation as reflected by a marked drop in relative unit costs in industry (Mathis, Mazier, and Rivand-Danset 1988). In spite of the closed nature of the American economy, this ongoing depreciation of the dollar had significant structural effects. It permitted America's positions abroad to be stabilized without leading to a reestablishment of the balance of trade (Table 8.11). But above all, it allowed a resumption of industrial profits, which was the prerequisite for any recovery of investment in this sector. The United States was the only major industrial country where manufacturing investment showed a certain recovery between 1974 and 1980. But these developments were interrupted by the radical reversal of American monetary policy from 1979 on.

From a Policy of Moderate Depreciation to the
"Strong Franc" Policy: The French Case

France's de facto policy of moderate depreciation of the franc from 1969 to 1977 allowed it to maintain the real parity of the franc and export-price competitiveness at a relatively constant level (see Figure 8.4). This policy permitted a transfer toward the industrial sector, which was thus aided in its redeployment strategy. Export remained relatively healthy, but inflationary pressures were increased. Structurally, this policy led to reinforcing the specialization of French industry in relatively common goods. At the same time, the pursuit of major export contracts with developing countries permitted surpluses in industrial equipment that contrasted with its growing deficit in capital goods relative to the United States, Germany, and Japan. The issue here is not so much one of pursuing a prudent exchange rate strategy well adapted to production structures as it is the absence of a industrial policy to promote the private sector. Such a policy would have a better target public assistance to high-tech industries.

The arrival of a new government in 1977 marked a change in exchange policy that began gradually but became much more abrupt and subsequently emerged as a twenty-year choice in favor of a stronger currency that was rooted in a desire for stable parity with the

Figure 8.3 **Exchange Rate and Price Competitiveness in the United States**

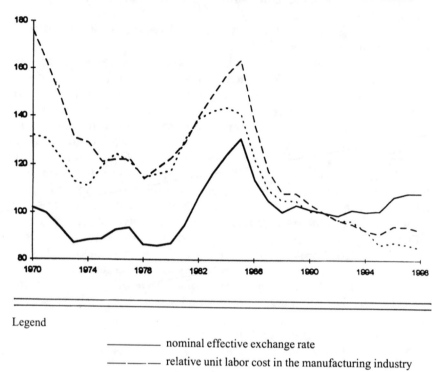

Legend

—————— nominal effective exchange rate

— — — — relative unit labor cost in the manufacturing industry

- - - - - - - relative export prices in the manufacturing industry

Source: OECD (1997).

mark. This new orientation was aimed at countering the perverse effects of monetary depreciation. But by subjecting French industry to a monetary constraint that it was basically unable to endure, this policy led to the disappearance of the weakest cogs in the industrial apparatus between 1978 and 1981, while businesses compensated for the reduction of their export markups with a sharp rise in domestic prices.

❖

Until 1979, the dynamics and policies of the industrial countries came under monopolistic regulation in a context of slower productivity gains and sharper conflicts over income distribution. The most significant differences among countries were mainly nominal—inflation rates diverged sharply in function of the forms of employment adjustment and fixing of income. In most countries, real wages continued to rise, albeit more

Figure 8.4 **Exchange Rate and Price Competitiveness in France**

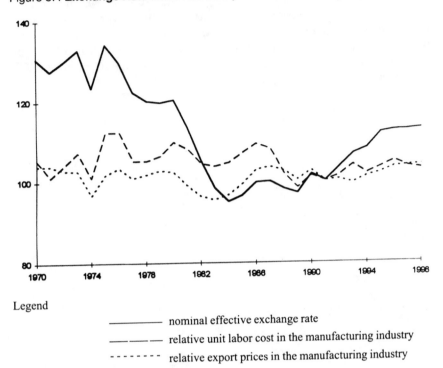

Legend

————————— nominal effective exchange rate

— — — — — relative unit labor cost in the manufacturing industry

- - - - - - - relative export prices in the manufacturing industry

Source: OECD (1997).

slowly; company profits were reduced, and the share of government spending in business increased considerably.

At the end of the 1970s, these developments were called into question. The most striking symbols of this were the elections of Ronald Reagan in the United States and Margaret Thatcher in the United Kingdom, on the basis of programs advocating a return to competitive regulation. This change had been anticipated by theoretical debates and spontaneous grass-roots movements alike. During the 1960s and 1970s, neoclassical theory had inspired new macroeconomic conceptions, such as monetarism and rational expectations, that led to conclusions diametrically opposed to those of Keynesianism. These theories spread the idea that the crisis resulted from failure to respect the laws of competition and from the excessive intervention of government and unions. At the same time, one sector of public opinion questioned the increase in compulsory payroll deductions and the growth of social assistance and public services.

During the 1970s, the idea that a transformation of the economies was necessary had not been absent, but it was limited to the restructuring or redeployment of industrial activities. After 1980, the very institutions of monopolistic regulation were called into question, including collective bargaining procedures, government intervention in economic life, or the validation of inflation by monetary policy. This change in economic policies marked a major turning point in the crisis.

CHAPTER NINE

From the 1970s to the 1980s: Contrasting Country Models

The 1970s were crisis years, but the basic forms of administered regulation were maintained. However, intensive accumulation was marking time, and international economic relations were profoundly disrupted. The initial response of the economies was more of a mechanical reaction than an adaptation to the new technological and organizational realities in the domestic and international arenas. However, when the slowdown in growth continued, when the first oil crisis was followed by a second, and when short-term domestic policies showed great difficulty in adapting to external constraints, public opinion and policy makers alike began to admit that "crises endure."

This situation was followed by a rash of theoretical and ideological debates between 1978 and 1983, with monetarism, supply-side economics, the idea of a global supply and a money supply that are rigid and vertical, and, more broadly, neoconservatism opposing Keynesian economics, the tenants of industrial policy and social democracy, and the supporters of greater supply-side flexibility in the context of more rigid prices. Thatcherism and Reaganism attracted a great deal of attention in particular because of their media tactics and the violence of certain institutional changes. But the differences among the various industrialized countries during this period of crisis were notable.

The United Kingdom in particular became a zone of confrontation with the unions and experimentation with attempts at new forms of wage flexibility and "exits from below" for the crisis. The United States also sought to change certain rules of the game. But British and American policies were often confused and contradictory, with, for example, an increase in credit, overheating of the economy, and disequilibrium of the foreign trade balance in the United Kingdom leading to the sharp recession of 1990-91, or, in the United States, the massive "twin deficits" of the domestic and foreign budgets.

In continental Europe, the accumulation of capital was slightly more sustained after the 1974-81 period. Germany and France continued to coordinate their efforts and adopted an exchange-rate system that was intended to impose stable parities along with monetary and budgetary discipline. Other countries tried to enter the system to gain credibility and become active partners in anti-inflationary policy. As a result, inflation subsided, putting an end to stagflation but not to the slowdown in growth. Germany was the only country to draw rapid but temporary benefits in terms of a decline in the real interest rates. France went against the tide in 1981-82 with an attempt at industrial policy and economic interventionism but limited its new ambitions from 1983 on for lack of long-term vision and under the triple constraint of the world recession, the concretization of the European Community, and the aggravation of its own public financing problems. The situation was somewhat improved in 1984-86, and the 1986-88 intermission, with the "cohabitation" of the Jacques Chirac government and Socialist president François Mitterrand, was to be above all a period of intense ideological confrontation. The most tangible reality, however, came from the fact that deadlines for the single European market were approaching, with hopes for a social surplus owing to forecasts of considerable economies of scale. But the macroeconomic shock stemming from the need to finance the German reunification with high interest rates led to a new slowdown on continental Europe after 1989. Aggravated by the Gulf War, this slowdown culminated in the acute European recession of 1993.

During this period, Sweden remained the example of an orderly Social-Democratic regulation that sought to arrive at new social compromises at home in order to play on a national strategy of export-led growth and replace the mainspring of domestic demand with foreign trade. The success was moderate but noteworthy until the late 1980s; afterward, increasing world competition became more aggressive for domestic norms and fixed wages, seemingly leaving Sweden's economic and social structure in need of in-depth adaptation.

In the Pacific, growth was lively, with the Japanese model vigorously imposing itself after 1979. Unlike the European scenario, capital accumulation resumed with considerable energy, and it led neither to inflation nor to foreign deficit because of strong labor-productivity gains (relative to those of other countries—an average of 3.2 percent for 1979-89, compared to 1.1 percent in the United States, 1.6 percent in Germany and the U.K., and 2 percent in France) and multifaceted protectionism maintained for the domestic market. Specialization was strengthened, and

Table 9.2

Production Growth and Labor Productivity Since 1960 in the United States
(annual average growth rate in %)

	1960–1968	1968–1973	1973–1979	1979–1986	1986–1995
GNP	4.5	3.2	2.4	2.4	1.6
Labor productivity	2.6	1.0	0.2	0.9	1.6
Capital per worker	2.4	2.5	1.3	1.9	
Real wage rate	2.3	2.1	0.5	0.7	0.4
Labor productivity					
In industry	3.2	3.5	0.9	3.3	
In services	2.3	0.6	0.0	0.4	

Source: OECD.

puter technology and the greater serviceability that goes along with it hinder standardization and time-saving. Proximity is sought after; competition is often strictly local; and in general, unlike sophisticated industrial plants, the facilities require little specialization (Petit 1988). Technical norms and monitoring are less developed in tertiary work, which leads to widely varying levels of productivity.

All of these general factors are particularly common in the United States. This is not a recent phenomenon; indeed, there has always been a visible contrast between the very large firms and the others. From the 1970s on, the rise of unemployment and inflation widened the gap in real wage levels between the two groups of this dualist economy. Employment equations suggest that this may have favored tertiary employment, especially since the gaps increased and the real cost of the least skilled labor force (e.g., household services often performed by women) even increased (Galibert and Le Dem 1986).

While considerable employment was generated during the expansion phases after 1982 (7 million jobs between 1982 and 1986) and after 1991, their nature and quality are open to discussion. According to the OECD, professionals, engineers, and managers accounted for nearly 50 percent of the jobs created between 1972 and 1982 (OECD 1986). During the 1980s, in absolute terms, businesses generated the most jobs, while in terms of the rates of growth, it was financial services and services to firms. What is most significant, however, is that the number of nonskilled jobs continued to increase in the United States while decreasing in Europe. One possible explanation is quite simple—the labor supply remains low-skilled when it comes from certain immigration flows or from failures and gaps in the education and vocational training systems.

The Paradoxes of American Industry

American industry underwent two surprising changes relative to the theory of industrial dynamics. First of all, in spite of the slowdown in profitability, the rate of capital accumulation increased after 1975, with the result that it was as high in the 1980s as it had been during the 1960s. Second, despite this accumulation that was comparatively stronger than in Europe, the United States continued to lose shares of the world market.

It may be recalled that the decline in profitability was due not to a rise in unit wage costs (real wages/labor productivity) but to a drop in the relative price of manufactured goods. These were not, as had previously been the case, determined by the strategies of the price-makers on the national market (see Table 9.3). Econometric analyses of the fixing of wages in the United States show that wage pressures were weak in the 1980s because of the decline of unions, the relocation of activities toward the South, and the spread of competitive ideologies. Even in companies where they remained influential, unions had to accept major concessions. However, econometrics does not indicate whether the slowdown in wage increases resulted from a temporary weakening of long-term trends or, on the contrary, a change in the parameters of wage elasticity to unemployment and prices (Kremp and Mistral 1988; Coe 1985). At the beginning of the 1970s, industrial value-added prices had declined relative to consumer prices because of the rise in imported basic goods. Between 1974 and 1980, the depreciation of the dollar attenuated the competition from imported goods, but this competition was to pick up in the 1980s, and relative industrial prices once again declined.

The recovery of the rate of investment in the manufacturing sector after 1975 paralleled sustained and/or renewed investment in research and development. The accelerator effect also played a part, insofar as after 1982 American industry benefited from macroeconomic conditions that were relatively more favorable than in continental Europe with more steady domestic demand. Industry enjoyed considerable government support through military purchases and research grants (Delmas and Roy 1988). And during the 1980s, accumulation remained steady because of increasing net capital entries through direct investments.

The loss of world market shares in this apparently favorable context can probably be explained by two groups of factors. First of all, as we have seen, growth was rather extensive. In more functional terms, company organization showed little solidarity, with low mobilization and high rotation of personnel. Low qualifications and wages offered few incentives. Pressure from stockholders doomed ambitious long-term planning programs for innovations and technological development. In certain cases, economies of scale for basic goods were neglected in order

Table 9.3

Investment and Profitability in Manufacturing Activities in the United States
(1968-1985)

	1968	1974	1979	1985
Wage rate/labor productivity	74	73	73	63
Value-added price index/consumer prices index	106	96	98	87
Gross profit/value added	31	25	25	27
Investment/value added	10	11	13	12

Source: OECD.

to concentrate on luxury products. Mass-consumption sectors were too quickly abandoned, given that their products still accounted for a significant share of international trade. The most skilled employees were channeled toward high technology and finance. In America's dual economy, control of the domestic market and economies of scale on mass-consumption goods could have permitted competitiveness abroad, but on the contrary, the trade deficit grew. Econometric studies of imports and exports bring out two causes for this deficit: the rise of the dollar in the 1980s and the positive growth differential relative to the rest of the world (OECD 1987-88; Marris 1985). The elasticity of imports relative to national income had been high since 1950, while the elasticity of exports relative to foreign income was not only low but lower than that of most other industrialized countries.

Geographical factors were also at work—the American deficit stemmed mainly from trade with the Pacific (Japan and the newly industrialized countries). These countries had made considerable efforts to develop their trade, and this was easier to achieve on the vast American market than in the national and linguistic mosaic of the different European markets. Mass consumer goods had been penetrated, but not exclusively (this is also true for electronics parts), which demonstrates Japan's aggressiveness and/or America's laxness during the 1980s.

Renewed Government Intervention and the
Plan for a New American Model

In the United States during the 1980s, the share of government expenditures continued to rise, and the federal budget deficit played a key role in the short and medium term in the revival of growth in 1982-83. Later on, the October 1987 crash was to lead to a reexamination of monetarist dogmatism (and the belief in governance by the money-supply aggregates M1, M2, or M3), which was replaced by a new pragmatism. This shift in the rates, and the intervention of the Federal Reserve Bank, are probably what avoided a greater financial crisis, while fiscal policy continued to be active, combining "fine tuning" and "policy mix" with gradualism and pragmatism.

This amounted to a turnaround. Indeed, early in Ronald Reagan's first term, supply-side economists had proposed tax cuts that were not supposed to lead to deficits (through automatic stabilizers, the induced recovery was to lead to new tax revenues). But the slowdown of inflation and growth sharply aggravated the loss of tax revenues while interest fees continued to accumulate because of the inertia of the rates. Between 1981 and 1985, the tax cuts increased the deficit while reducing levies on investments and the richest households. In terms of expenditures, welfare spending was whittled down through reduced access to healthcare benefits, unemployment compensation, food stamps, and housing assistance, but this decrease was insufficient to reduce the deficits (see Table 9.4).

The 1986 tax reform and subsequent decisions served to lower the marginal tax rates (those which are the most progressive) while eliminating many deductions. The rate for company profits was lowered from 46 to 34 percent while the taxable base was increased with the elimination or reduction of government aid for investment (thus weakening fiscal incentives for intensive accumulation).

Monetary policy, which was initially monetaristic, relied first of all on the monitoring of monetary aggregates. It then became more direct with the use of interest rates to halt growth and inflation while defending the dollar. At the outset, the rate differential with other countries was sufficiently high to lead to a real increase in the value of the dollar of some 35 percent between 1980 and 1984. The resulting drop in the prices of imported goods particularly weakened sectors producing consumer goods.

The 1986 oil counter-shock was fairly expansive until the recession of 1991, while monetary policy was one of accommodation, with a decrease in interest rates until 1987 that contrasted with the more restrictive choices made in Europe during the same period. The stock market crisis of October 1987 revealed the fragility of the financial system and by 1988 served to increase pressure on the reserves borrowed by the banks. As a result, the ratio of gross investment to the GNP reached a peak in 1988. The dollar's trade-weighted exchange-rate index decreased sharply between 1985 and 1988, which made labor in the manufacturing sector more competitive, thus compensating for the developments of the early 1980s.

By 1989-90, with the tightening of monetary policy and the cost of the Gulf War, the recession was under way, and by 1991 the unemployment rate had reached 7 percent. This recession was short-lived, however, and the recovery more gradual than usual. It was accompanied by low inter-

Table 9.4

Public Deficits in the United States (1960–1995)(% of GNP)

	1960	1970	1980	1990	1993	1995
Public deficit	0.7	−1.1	−1.4	−2.7	−3.6	−2.0
Net public debt	45.1	29.5	21.8	39.7	48.8	50.7
Public revenue	26.4	28.9	30.0	30.1	30.3	31.3
Total expenses	25.7	30.0	31.4	32.8	33.9	33.3

Source: OECD.

est rates until 1994, a dollar that was fairly stable between 1991 and 1995 in real exchange rates (apart from the effect of the Mexican exchange crisis), and a need for public financing going from 3 to 4 percent of the GDP.

The government sought to maintain its spending, but by redirecting it after 1989 toward public investments in capital that was physical (e.g., roads, water distribution) and human rather than, for example, military programs (defense activities lost 900,000 jobs between 1987 and 1992). Following a review and cost analysis of regulations, a first round of de-regulations took place in the 1980s, followed in 1992 by a moratorium on new regulations and an increase in cost-efficiency analyses and public-policy evaluations. Deregulation mainly affected tertiary activities (banking, transportation, telecommunications), with widely varying effects depending on the sector and an increase in competition that was often limited to the short term. Nonbanking financial intermediaries had proposed new products that could be countered by the banks. In the transportation industry, the modification of the rules of the game led to the creation and destruction of many companies. Budgetary policy was subsequently oriented toward the lowering of taxes rather than spending, which once again put pressure on federal funds with the deficit between 1990 and 1995, and the rise in interest rates in 1994 (which would soon slow down the recovery in Europe).

Overall, the United States maintained a coherent position, and this can be seen to have produced a new accumulation regime based more on product innovation and diversification than on standardization and economies of scale. Consumption was thus further stimulated by electronics goods and financial services. But the dualism was maintained or accentuated on the economic and social level. Wage regulation became more competitive while monetary regulation remained more administered and, at the same time, pragmatic. The foreign debt was considerable, but it was financed with national currency. In geopolitical terms, with the collapse of the Soviet Union, the United States became the only superpower capable of intervening anywhere in the world and remaining the bedrock of the world economic and financial system.

The United Kingdom: A Bifurcation Toward Deregulation and Continued Decline

Only the case of the United Kingdom appears to be close to that of the United States, and its success was limited. Between 1979 and 1990, the economy was guided by the Conservative Party government of Margaret Thatcher. The objective announced at the outset was to go against the tide in order to reestablish a competitive national supply. The means invoked or actually employed were the easing of restrictions on markets, the elimination of antitrust regulations, and the bringing into line, if not the backing down, of the trade unions. Ideology was used as a weapon against the status quo. It was necessary to change, or crush, mentalities and institutions in order to outdo what had been done before.

The results of these ten years are uneven and rather slim. Irregular short-term policies and structural reforms that were half carried out destabilized the United Kingdom and lowered its position among the world powers (in terms of per capita income, for example). The country lost market shares and had to leave the European monetary system after its very late entry. Certain appearances give the illusion that jobs were created. But English society became harsher, with greater inequality and less solidarity.

Privatization and Deregulation in Action

One element of the "new deal" were the privatizations. The most well known were those of British Telecom, Rolls-Royce, and British Airways, but the water, energy, and transportation sectors were all affected. The specific impact of these privatizations was not immediately apparent because they coincided with the upward phase of the cycle until 1988. The number of stockholders rose, and competition did not always increase because of the presence of numerous agents in a position to capture rents. The Monopolies and Mergers Commission carried out a major effort that showed itself to be increasingly complicated and yielded uneven results in terms of jurisprudence.

In dealing with wage issues and labor relations, the government's strategy was based on verbal and often frontal attacks on the unions (see the miners' strike of 1984-85). The reform of union laws was followed by a decline in the unions (12.2 million members in 1979, 8.7 million in 1988), the elimination of the closed shop, and the spread of the idea of "free, flexible areas" to attract direct investments by the multinationals. Flexibility largely depended on layoffs, the spread of part-time work, and more precarious employment after hiring, which are all factors that have not been favorable to productivity in the medium term. Inequalities in wages and/or among sectors and regions have increased. But paradoxically, in spite of these measures, unit wage costs compared to those of other countries of the European monetary system increased nearly 9 percent a year between 1988 and 1990, which explains why there was soon to be a necessary compensation through the devaluation of the pound.

Deindustrialization and Growing Dualisms

In terms of investment, it is probable, according to the OECD, that real capital stock stagnated during the 1980s with the recession of 1980-83, the pessimism, and the poor business climate. However, sharp contrasts were observed from 1979 to 1987 between, for example, energy and gas or banks and insurance companies and the more lifeless remainder of the economy. Manufacturing rose only 20 percent from 1979 to 1989, compared to 72 percent in the OECD member countries. Some industrial subsectors dominated by a few big foreign implantations (automobile manufacture, electronics, and office machines) nonetheless attained overall productivity gains that were above the average.

Deindustrialization took the form of major regional disequilibria leading to a division into "two nations." The north, which had been industrialized much earlier, fell victim to rapid restructuring, with a 30 percent drop in salaried employees between 1979 and 1988 (21 million fewer jobs). Even greater "records" were set in Scotland (–35 percent), the North, Northwest, and Yorkshire-Humberside, where a freeze on government aid and weak regional and local development policies increased the level of poverty still further. By contrast, the South profited from 1.16 million new jobs in private services to Europe, with the areas closest to the channel tunnel benefiting from the increased access to the continent.

Education remained backward. From 1979 to 1981, vocational training suffered heavy cuts (the budgets of the Manpower Services Commissions, the Industrial Training Boards, and the skills centers). Then, at the peak of the recession, new training programs were set up (the New Training Scheme) without compensating for inadequacies. The privatization of vocational training in the late-1990s made the Training and Enterprise Corails the local keystones of a belated overhaul.

An Open Economy in Industrial and Social Decline

The United Kingdom was probably one of the most open countries of the OECD in the 1980s. This situation weakened the autonomy of economic policies, and deindustrialization made the United Kingdom a "smaller country" that was not always competitive. Even in 1989, productivity gains, for example, left the overall U.K. economy below the standards of the major economies measured according to the 1986 purchasing-power parity. Deindustrialization accelerated after 1985 (20 percent less employment in manufacturing for 1985-95), while direct foreign investments tripled over the same period.

Increased openness led to a rising trade deficit in manufactured goods that was less and less compensated by massive petroleum extraction in 1983 and some food product surpluses. By 1986 the trade balance and the current balance had become continuously and sharply negative.

The search for an internal solution was difficult. On the other hand, direct investments or foreign portfolios and the incomes resulting from them increased until 1985, and this foreign income thus joined that accruing from North Sea oil. From 1985 on, loans abroad, from banks and residents, grew. By 1989, net foreign holdings in portfolios represented about 1,000 billion pounds, and this was still the case in 1992.

The intensive deregulation of the labor market was to make the United Kingdom a flexible country for employment conditions, working time, hiring, and firing. A quarter of the labor force was soon to work part time (45 percent for women). The increase in real wages was kept at a level below that of productivity during the 1982-89 period. Nonetheless, investment in the manufacturing sector, as a percentage of the GDP, showed a consistent decrease from 1985 to 1995; employment in the sector declined while total employment was not to regain the 1979 level until 1992.

At the beginning of the 1990s, English society was more advanced in its tertiarization than either France or Germany. Its investment rate was one of the lowest among the major countries. Its rank according to average standard of living (private consumption by inhabitant) declined; by 1993, the United Kingdom came after the United States, Switzerland, Belgium, Canada, France, Germany, Italy, and Spain.

The financial tradition remained a major feature with the Big Bang of the largest stock market in the European Community (40 percent of French stock transactions, for example, occur in London). The international role of the "City" made it imperative to maintain high interest rates. Ultimately this did not prevent the decline of the real exchange rate of the pound sterling in the 1980s or its devaluations (the real exchange rate went from the index of 109.5 in 1985 to 100 in 1992 to 88.9 in 1993).

The Case of the Social Market Economy and Social Democracy: An Orderly Regulation

West Germany: Slow Growth, Strong Mark, and Wage Compromises

Divergences between West Germany and the United States manifested themselves in the course of the 1970s. Over the next decade, the creation of jobs was greater in the United States, but industry, as well as foreign trade surpluses, were better maintained in Germany, despite the desire to keep the deutschmark strong and stable in contrast to the fluctuations of the dollar. Thus, the open model of the social market economy still provided a contrast with the model of the vast, closed country with its flamboyant competition. The German model was less directly opposed to the Japanese model, but Japan showed much more rapid growth (the most rapid among the OECD countries), and the introduction of new technologies and new forms of work organization was earlier in Japan (see below).

In general terms, the "Deutschland model" of the social market economy is a manifest version of Fordism with its combination of public spending of a social nature, wage negotiations with compromises, and a competitive spirit in the private sector open to the exterior and seeking cost competitiveness or competitiveness outside prices.

Germany's specificity had been reinforced during the 1970s. Price stability had become the primordial goal (with the historical fear of inflation dating from 1922-23, the Nazi period, and the Second World War). The Bundesbank stopped working toward the stability of the dollar in 1973; the sole exception to the policy that was to arise from this rule occurred during the 1979-81 period, at the time of the second oil crisis, when Germany had agreed to assume the leadership of national policies that were in principle coordinated. The choices of the 1980s did not make great waves before the new era that was to begin with the unification after 1989.

The Decline of Germany's Supply Conditions

The comparison with the averages of the OECD countries for this period permits us to bring out more capital-intensive growth with higher labor productivity gains (Table 9.5). There was a downward trend in capital productivity and a slowdown in labor productivity gains. The profitability of investments in the business sector declined at the beginning of the period (1979-82) and then slowly rose again (see Figure 6.4, chapter 6, p. 119). This led quite logically to a moderate rise in investments from 1983 to 1989.

The situation was less positive in manufacturing. The decline in profitability can be described by comparing the developments of total wage cost and labor productivity. Real wages followed labor productivity gains. On the other hand, the relative price of the value added (compared to the consumer price index) declined after 1981. After 1985, German industry benefited from more favorable circumstances—the American recovery, the drop in the short-term interest rate, wage moderation, the oil counter-shock, the rise of the dollar, and the decline of the real exchange rate for the mark all encouraged investment.

Table 9.5

West Germany's Growth Compared to That of the OEDC as a Whole (annual average growth rates, business sector, in %)

	1960-1973	1973-1979	1979-1986
West Germany			
Product	4.6	2.4	1.6
Capital stock	5.6	3.5	2.9
Capital by worker	5.9	4.5	3.3
Capital productivity	−1.0	−0.9	−1.3
Labor productivity	4.9	3.4	2.0
OECD			
Product	5.2	2.9	2.3
Capital stock	5.6	4.4	3.6
Capital by worker	4.5	3.1	2.5
Capital productivity	−0.4	−1.1	−1.3
Labor productivity	4.1	2.6	1.4

Source: OECD.

Contained Domestic Demand and Export-Led Growth

Wages and other income had showed considerable advances during the 1960s and 1970s. The increase slowed down in the early 1980s and did not resume until 1985, with the rise of monthly rates of contractual remuneration (from an index of 100 in 1985 to 118 in 1990). However, in 1990, the share of wages in current prices and percentage of GDP reached its lowest level since the 1960s (54.3 percent) (see Figure 6.3, chapter 6, p. 117).

The foreign trade balance had declined from 1974 to 1980, but at the time, there was talk of the virtuous circle of the strong mark—internal incentives for cost reduction, orientation to external performance exclusive of prices, foreign surplus, new rise in the value of the mark, domestic deflation. The reality was more complex, however. The decline in the German export-import ratio in value reached 17 percent between 1973 and 1980, and the export-import ratio in volume failed to compensate for the decline in terms of trade owing to the two oil shocks. This weakness in export volumes was related to the overvaluation of the mark. From 1980 to 1985, on the other hand, the export-import ratio in value rose 16 percent (but with a 3 percent drop in the terms of trade) at the time when the dollar began to pick up again and when the austerity of the German policy limited import expenditures (slow growth). Over the 1971-87 period as a whole, the 14 percent rise in the export-import ratio resulted above all from the decline in the share of German imports among OECD countries while the share of German exports in OECD exports in volume remained the same. Two contradictory factors were at play: the drop in price competitiveness on the one hand, offset on the other hand by a good international specialization in capital goods with low price elasticity of demand.

The other typical country pattern during this period was the geographical reorientation of trade among EFTA members toward the United States and the countries of the European monetary system. By contrast, German specialization by products continued and was even accentuated (Lafay and Herzog 1989). The current balance maintained its surplus until 1990. Trade surpluses allowed Germany to export capital, mainly in the form of short-term credits and initially to the United States, but also in the form of long-term credits and later direct investments.

The Persistence of Pragmatic Conservatism

Traumatized by its past, Germany consistently sought stability and openness to the outside during this period. At the outset, this stability was based on the rules of the game—regulations applied to the labor market, money markets, and financial markets alike.

Labor-force management was subject to strict legislation and largely depended on agreements signed with the unions. The law limited possibilities for firing and sharply restricted the flexibility of working hours. Wages were defined by collective agreements negotiated on the branch and regional levels with the federations of a single, powerful union organization. Unionization rates were high and differences between sectors minimal. A slow change began in 1985 with the spread of fixed-term contracts and very part-time work. Working time was negotiated, at 38.5 hours in 1985 and 37 hours in 1989, with the possibility of 35 hours proposed in 1995. Unemployment rose considerably after the German reunification, which had a high budgetary cost that the government did not seek to meet through the exchange rate or inflation. The adjustment was thus achieved through slow growth, lack of hiring, and stagnation of domestic purchasing power.

With regard to the financial sector, interest rates had indeed been deregulated since the 1960s, and there was freedom for capital movements. But the monetary market remained limited to banks, with few interventions by nonfinancial agents. Bank refinancing from the central bank mainly took place through limited rediscounting. The stock market was still marginal, and the number of firms quoted on the stock exchange reduced. On the level of corporate governance, the big companies often practiced self-monitoring, maintaining close links with the banks. The latter hardly developed their extra-banking activities and in particular limited their guarantees to short-term securities issued by the firms. The central and secondary banks remained very prudent.

More generally, deregulation proceeded very slowly during this period. Agriculture, iron and steel, energy, transportation, telecommunications, housing, and health services remained under government control. We can simply note the division of the Bundespost into three public enterprises specialized respectively in mail delivery, banking services, and telecommunications, and the opening up of the only new services (databases, Teletext) to competition.

The Reunification Shock

In 1990, Germany's territory and population increased by about 25 percent. The deutschemark was declared uniform. The impact of demand was brutal, with heavy labor-force migrations and unemployment tied to the restructuring liquidations, and privatizations. The demand for new productive capabilities, and urban and infrastructural needs, all implied massive budgetary accommodations, with an increased tax burden and the issuing of new public loans. But the ongoing commitment to a strong mark explained the desire to control monetary aggregates nonetheless, which was to be done only in 1993-95. The financial balance if the public sector in the broad sense was to go from a deficit of 2.6 percent of the GDP in 1990 to one of 5.4 percent in 1993 because of expenditures in solidarity with the Länder of the former East Germany. The total public-sector debt went from 48.7 percent of the GDP in 1990 to 59.5 percent in 1994, which was the limit of the criterion set by the Treaty of Maastricht.

The German model was thus inevitably confronted by a new slump in private investment in 1993-95, which can be related to the real interest rates that had long been elevated and a regular rise in the value of the mark in real terms. Total employment decreased in the west of Germany after 1991 while unemployment approached the fateful figure of 4 million. A dilemma was thus on the horizon: overly slow growth might be called into question, for lack of new flexibilities on the labor market, but the "German social pact" was also one of the keystones of low inflation.

Sweden, or Social Democracy Put to the Test

Germany is not the only example of Nordic capitalism that can be contrasted with market capitalism of the Anglo-Saxon variety. Sweden has been the classic example case of an internal accumulation of capital made possible by historic compromises between social classes, regulations, and social protection. The model was so strong that during the 1970s the per capita GDP was the highest in the world, with Sweden weathering the first oil crisis more easily than other countries. The percentage of business investments in the GDP increased until 1976, and the unemployment rate remained below 2 percent until 1979. On the other hand, by 1976-78, Sweden experienced rising supply costs: higher unit wage costs in the sheltered sector, domestic inflation with the slowdown in economic growth from 1979 to 1982. Stagflation was soon accompanied by budget deficits and repeated mini-crises in the balance of payments that were to lead to the 16 percent devaluation of 1982.

An Offensive Strategy from 1982 to 1986

The devaluation was accompanied by an export offensive and a domestic effort concentrated on household demand. What distinguished the 1980s was, until 1989, the minimal recourse to unemployment (less than 2.2 percent of the labor force) to reduce production costs. Employment in manufacturing remained at a high level (32.9 percent of total employment in 1989), with a slight decline over ten years (–1.5 points) and sectors such as wood, chemicals, and mechanical engineering still expanding. Sweden was thus a case apart. One part of its singularity lay in the way employment was organized: from 1980 to 1989, the manufacturing industries accepted a 10 percent drop in the number of hours worked, with a resulting average increase in hourly productivity gains of nearly 3 percent a year. Wage moderation was also introduced after the devaluation, and price freezes were instituted in the spring of 1984 to ease the acceptance of wage austerity. Occupational flexibility, on the other hand, was strong, with lifelong training to prepare employees for adaptations and vigorous measures to preserve the employability of the unemployed.

This offensive was complemented by an active budgetary policy. From 1980 to 1986, the cyclical budget deficit was accepted, while tax revenues swelled after the devaluation. Public employment continued to represent 40.7 percent of the total in 1987, with 8.7 percent in the public enterprises alone. Government aid to manufacturing remained high (3.1 percent of the GDP, compared to an average of 1.8 percent in the OECD countries), and additional aid was offered through public markets and the creation of special funds for industrial investment or reinvestment of profits with tax benefits.

A Little European Country with a Difference?

In the early 1980s, Sweden was a social-democratic country and also one of the rare net technology exporters in the OECD area. Its R&D spending accounted for 10 percent of the industrial value added (18 percent in electronics and 36 percent in the pharmaceutical industry). Many products had strong technological content, and exports of machines and non-electrical appliances, electronics, communications equipment, and industrial robots were thriving.

The acceleration of Sweden's opening to the world economy soon created tensions that, with the linking of the exchange rate to the European exchange mechanism, were no longer to be compensated by exchange. The free circulation of capital, the deregulation of the financial markets, and reduced aid to agriculture were also factors creating new challenges.

One of the problems of Swedish administered regulation arose from the trend toward cost inflation. Both relative wages (in national currency) and relative consumer prices (in national currency) rose more than 20 percent in relation to competitor countries during the 1980s, while by the end of the period, there was fear of a shortage of labor power.

The early 1990s thus opened the way to propositions for reform. Among them, a major tax reform in 1990-91 affected household and business incomes and the taxation of capital income; it attenuated the system's vertical redistribution and strengthened incentives for working and creating enterprises. Government was reformed through decentralization and rationalization in the public sector, and there were also reforms in social security. But the paths followed remain closer to the Nordic tradition than to rapacious hypercapitalism.

Social Liberalism à la Française

During the 1970s France had preserved the mixed-economy model. The two oil crises had practically been surmounted, and the economic problems seemed under control when the world recession took a turn for the worse in 1981-82. The Socialists' economic policy was caught off balance. The governments had to retreat and submit to external constraint. Unemployment rose between 1983 and 1985, while deflation set in because of a slowdown in growth and the de-indexation of wages to prices. The slow upturn in production investment became visible in 1984-85, beginning with manufacturing. But the imbalance in industrial trade also increased, hiding industrial weaknesses in certain fields (notably capital goods). Voluntarist industrial policy was soon replaced by withdrawal and an opening up to intra-European specialization that benefited Germany in several areas of industry. Tertiarization gained ground, in particular with financial deregulation and urbanization. France was characterized at once by the resistance of great national champions, the collapse of certain sectors, and the birth of companies with strong export performances. The social model moved toward a social free-market model with the opening up to the world economy. And the price to be paid was the pervasiveness and persistence of unemployment across all age groups, an unemployment that no policies and no measures have succeeded in checking. This has led in turn to the emergence of a two-tiered society.

The Abandoning of French-Style Planning
and the Decline of Colbertism

After its election in 1981, the Socialist government quickly undertook nationalizations of industry and banks. The expanded public sector accounted for 30 percent of manufacturing investment and 30 percent of total exports. Had this sector become manageable, it could have been the spearhead of a competitive industrial and financial supply.

International events and internal divisions were to abort this possibility. The Minister of Finance Jacques Delors incarnated the shift toward domestic austerity and the choice of European integration. Most of the major sectoral programs, such as the electronics or industrial automation plans, were thus abandoned or cut back. Industrial restructurings were initially positive within the expanded public sector but their negative impact began to be felt in coal mining, iron and steel, shipbuilding, and telephone equipment. An Industrial Modernization Fund created in 1983 had some success but suffered from lack of ambition.

The 1986-88 period of "cohabitation" between the Socialist president and the Conservative government reinforced and accentuated these choices of a shift toward less administered regulation and a capitalism that was more Anglo-Saxon than German. Industrial policy was watered down in favor of pragmatism and an orientation toward the improvement of the companies' economic environment alone through tax advantages for firms, public aid reoriented upstream (R&D), and new technologies. Planning Commission contracts between the State and the large public enterprises increasingly became simple exchanges of information, and the "priority programs" came up against refusals from the Budget Division of the Ministry of the Economy and Finance. Centralism (counterbalanced by the existence of 36,000 municipalities) was abandoned with, on the one hand, the decentralization law of 1982 that created regional collectivities invested with considerable authority and autonomy and, on the other, the deconcentration of the central government's administrative services.

The model was still social because the social security program remained intact, despite some financial difficulties. The improved economic situation between 1985 and 1989 allowed public finances to be balanced more easily. This equilibrium, however, suffered the consequences of rising unemployment on the net social transfers of social security contributions. Overall, the proportion of compulsory deductions in the GDP was reduced (43.8 percent in 1990 as compared to 44.6 percent in 1984), and the pressure toward an increase resulted more from the increase in local taxes (4.6 percent of the GDP in 1980, 6 percent in 1990) and social contributions (17.8 percent of the GDP in 1980 and 19.4 percent in 1990) than from the weight of the State per se (17.9 percent of the GDP in 1980 and 16.4 percent in 1990). In this sense, the Socialist governments, paradoxically as some would have it, played the card of decentralization and Europeanization rather than that of the Jacobin or Colbertist state.

The State's budgetary policy led to limiting the deficit (before interest on the public debt) to a maximum of 1.5 percent of the GDP in 1983. On the other hand, high interest rates and deflation led the governments into the trap of an increasingly heavy debt burden. The financial markets imposed a high price on governments that they did not initially consider credible, even though these governments ultimately liberalized the economy more than all their predecessors.

A More Inegalitarian Wage Relation Marked by the Search for External Flexibility

The redistributive measures taken in 1981 and those aimed at improving labor relations barely held up against the constraints of rigor. After 1983, the purchasing power of the wage rate stagnated, especially in net terms, because of successive increases in the rates of social security contributions. The de-indexation of wages and prices was invoked, often to an extreme because indexation continued to operate, but in another way. Indeed, new rules were tested according to two main principles:

- prior fixing of wage raises for the coming year in alignment with price objectives (rather than increases fixed earlier in function of observed price rises);
- adjustment at the end of the period in function of the results observed (on the national or company level), without any automatic aspect.

This procedure, associated with the price freeze implemented in 1982, played an important role in the 1982-84 deflation process, before imported disinflation amplified the movement in 1985. Company negotiation grew, but the weakness of the unions and the inertia of management did not allow the foundations of a real social compromise to be established.

It is more instructive to examine income distribution, because several indicators show that inequalities in income and wealth have increased since 1983. According to the CERC's 1989 report, income from property contributed most to the increase in real household income from 1982 to 1988, but the increase in the share of real estate in household wealth mainly profited the very rich. The range of wages opened up once again after 1984 with the spread of individualized forms of remuneration. The only factor of redistribution was the considerable improvement in the situation of the elderly between 1979 and 1984 and afterward. INSEE's 1991 study on household budgets shows that disparities also increased in terms of consumption. From 1979 to 1989, one-fourth of the most comfortable households were able to increase their spending by 20 percent in constant francs, while spending of the most modest households stagnated.

The labor market could not rely on either an internal flexibility (training-reconversion within the company, negotiated adaptation to new technologies) or an institutional flexibility based, as in Sweden, on a powerful public-sector employment program. Contrary to received wisdom, the French equivalent of such a program remained limited in scale by comparison with countries such as Sweden or even Germany. In 1988, for one person employed in a government job program, 93 people in France, 33 in Germany, and 8 in Sweden were unemployed (Brunhes 1989). If public spending for employment seemed relatively sustained in France, the proportion of "active measures" was small relative to "passive measures" designed to maintain income through unemployment compensation. At that point the employment service was not able to confront the extent of the imbalances existing on the labor market and provide services of the necessary sophistication and quality.

From 1986 on, emphasis was placed more explicitly on external flexibility, with the abolition of administrative authorization for dismissal and the easing of restrictions on fixed-term, part-time, and interim work contracts. These measures accelerated the growth of contingent, and it was only the resulting recovery and creation of jobs from 1987 on that permitted a decrease in unemployment, which stabilized around 2.5 million in 1988. Without questioning the basic trends, the new Socialist government introduced several measures after 1988 to diminish certain perverse effects and combat the most critical situations (notably the introduction of a minimum income for those not eligible for unemployment benefits). With the economic reversal that began in 1990, unemployment reached a new level.

Monetary Orthodoxy and Financial Deregulation

One of the characteristics of the Socialists' financial policy was the desire to win the confidence of international finance at all costs. At the time of its election in May 1981, the government chose not to devalue the franc, mainly to reassure its European partners while remaining within the European Monetary System. Devaluation was necessary, however, because of the deterioration of price competitiveness. Freeing itself from the EMS constraint, but not from Europe, would have allowed the government to maintain a policy of industrial restructuring under better conditions. The final choice was debatable and, indeed, it was sharply debated. From 1983 on, after three inadequate devaluations that were badly accepted, everything was done to defend the parity of the franc in spite of a decline in cost competitiveness and industrial trade. However, the parity of the franc did not come under attack. Foreign capital was attracted by the high levels of the real interest rates and reassured by the firmness of the official position. The economy and industry, in particular, were thus permanently sacrificed to currency.

Once this basic choice was made, the government could have taken measures to tone down certain perverse effects resulting from the defense of the franc, but this was not the case. At the beginning of the period, the short-term cost of money reached 16 percent, crushing businesses with financing charges because of their heavy indebtedness. Such rates largely contributed to reducing investment and induced companies to get out of debt, even if that meant reducing their production capacities. The State likewise incurred long-term debts at fixed rates of 16 percent while affirming its determination to fight inflation. The result was a rapid rise in finance charges that limited its margins for maneuvering, and it was only in 1984 that the State committed itself to more intelligent management of its debt.

Unlike the situation in other countries, the financial transformation in France was largely brought about by the public powers. It was partly desired and partly endured:

- partly desired because it facilitated nonmonetary financing of the budget deficit, because it helped Paris to become a financial center on the scale of continental Europe, and because it introduced greater competition into the overly protected banking sector;
- partly endured because the race for international savings forced the States to offer investments that suited investors of the 1980s, and because the growing opening up of the economy, notably in the context of Europe, necessitated a liberalization of the financial system.

This financial transformation was accompanied by profound changes in the behavior of the different actors. Businesses sought better financial returns. They tended to get out of debt, or at least to turn to bank credit, and to manage their liquid assets and debt better by making use of all the new financial products. They also had greater recourse to the market. Households, meanwhile, considerably modified the structure of their investments at the expense of nonremunerated deposits and savings invested in real estate and in favor of financial investments.

In the face of this upheaval, the banks reacted with a whole group of technological and financial innovations. They diversified their activities and developed new products. Various financial innovations sought to limit banking risks, the most significant of which was securitization, which meant transforming traditional loans into negotiable securities. The risks that had previously been assumed by the banks alone were thus redistributed throughout the financial community as a whole.

This securitization was probably excessive. In theory, more direct access to the capital market and the growth of competition should have reduced companies' finance charges. The existence of a unified market should have allowed savings to be directed toward the most high-performance companies. But this idyllic vision must be qualified in several respects. Only the major companies had access to the capital market, which accentuated inequalities among firms. The financial sphere underwent a kind of bloating, very visibly from 1982 to 1987 and again at the end of the 1980s.

This development had objective bases: the necessity for the Paris stock market to make up for lost time, the spectacular recovery of company profits, and a drop in the rates that pushed up bond prices. Nonetheless, the bloating of the financial sphere posed problems for several reasons. Financial markets tend to overreact to perturbations of the environment, and the prices of assets are by nature very volatile. One important consequence of the financial transformation concerned the handling of risks. In an overdraft economy, one function of the banks was to mutualize and take responsibility for risks. The elimination of financing intermediaries led to a demutualization and externalization of risks. Part of these risks were then assumed by the final securities holders, which, in the event of financial crisis, could make the system more fragile. In addition, the worst risks were concentrated on the banks, since the most solid clients turned to direct financing. And the different techniques for covering risks (forward or optional markets) were effective for microeconomic management but less so on the macroeconomic level.

The financial transformation altered the conditions of monetary regulation. Financial innovations and changes in behavior modified the traditional borders between currency and nonmonetary financial assets. The notion of money supply became ambiguous because of the greater interchangeability of assets. The increasingly indirect control of monetary emission through interest rates became more tricky. Instruments such as the control of exchanges or the supervision of credit, which had previously played a central role in case of monetary crisis, were eliminated. In many ways, the process of deregulating and financial liberalization of the French economy since the 1980s was overly rapid and probably excessive with regard to the risks it entailed.

Insufficient Industrial Competitiveness

The collapse of the trade balance in industrial goods from 1984 to 1990, followed by its recovery in the mid-1990s, reflects the fragility of France's industrial competitiveness (see Table 9.6). Traditional explanations permit only a partial description of this phenomenon. The sharp drop in price competitiveness from 1985 to 1987 brought about by the depreciation of the dollar and the swelling of export margins, despite strict control of wage costs, played a major role in the decline of export performances. Conversely, the effects of the competitive deflation strategy fully manifested themselves in terms of an upturn in cost competitiveness from the beginning of the 1990s, despite the devaluations carried out by some of France's European partners in 1992-93. The delayed recovery and the characteristics of domestic demand also played a role. A "healthy deficit" at the end of the 1980s that had been increased by exceptional capital equipment imports was followed by a readjustment spurred by the consequences of the German reunification and then an "unhealthy surplus" in the mid-1990s resulting from weak growth and stagnating investment.

In spite of the glowing results often cited, which were further improved by surpluses in agriculture and the service sector, French industry remained handicapped by weaknesses in nonprice competitiveness (Mathis, Mazier, and Rivaud-Danset 1988). France had neither poles of competitiveness like Germany or Japan nor a high degree of specialization in the form of "niches" with networks of successful SMEs. Outside of a few specific fields (luxury goods, food production, automobile manufacture), the most solid positions were tied to activities where there was considerable public intervention. Too often, French manufacturers have turned to the top of the line and ignored the middle. R&D efforts have favored state-of-the-art technology and have been inadequately funded by the firms themselves, partly because of the weight of military expenditures. As a result, R&D is badly articulated to the characteristics of specialization and does not adequately feed the whole of the industrial fabric (Amable and Mouhoud 1990). Nor have the modernization effort and the rise of automation been accompanied by a transformation in labor relations. The reorganization of work has not been pushed far enough in the direction of versatility and skilling of the labor force; rather, the search for external flexibility has been overly privileged.

Overall, France has not succeeded in defining an original model. Its initial advantages (a strong State structure, a large and efficient public sector, albeit one in need of restructuring, a tradition of planning that could allow the fragmentation of the social fabric to be avoided) were not put to use and were in fact viewed as limitations. Economic policy has

Table 9.6

Trade Balance in Manufactured Goods (billions of francs)

	1980	1984	1990	1995
Manufactured goods	19	98	−59	57
Intermediate goods	−10	8	−43	−16
Capital goods	10	68	5	60
Transportation				
equipment	28	33	25	26
Household goods	−5	−8	−14	−8
Consumer goods	−4	−3	−32	−5

Source: INSEE, national accounts.

been increasingly aligned to the norm imposed by France's foreign partners and the international markets. For lack of the advantages of German industry, the United Kingdom's financial power—and its oil—and Italy's flexible productive apparatus and social fabric, France has found itself increasingly constrained within Europe, while its traditional markets have been contracting. In social terms, growing inequalities and external flexibility have been the logical result. The improvement of the international economic situation in 1988-90 only allowed a temporary loosening of the stranglehold. Only the maintenance of a broad system of social security helped to diminish tensions.

Japan: Technological Revolution, Exports, and Foreign Investments

Japan was the only major industrialized country where manufacturing continued to increase its share of the GDP during the 1970s and 1980s. The country underwent a sharp slowdown in activity during the early 1970s, but it managed to stabilize the macroeconomic conditions of its growth after the first oil crisis and was little affected by the second. Its share of the world market began to increase once again through the compulsory modernization of its industry. With the exception of the financial domain, these successes were obtained without any in-depth questioning of the mode of regulation of previous years. But since the beginning of the 1990s, Japan has been affected by what increasingly seems to be a major crisis of change.

The Return to a Good Macroeconomic Configuration

At the beginning of the 1970s Japan was hard hit by a drop in growth and a sharp rise in inflation. The crisis was amplified by several specific factors: the shortage of land, which limited construction and increased nuisance problems, and the reevaluation of the yen when exports were largely concentrated in mass consumer goods.

The recovery came quickly, first of all through the control of inflation. Monetary policy, which was restrictive in 1974-75, was subsequently relaxed with a steady increase in currency and credit and negative real interest rates, while budget deficits were resolutely on the rise. What explains the moderate price rises is in fact the evolution of wages. In the context of central wage agreements and the lifelong employment system maintained by the major firms, wage increases have traditionally been dependent on short-term economic conditions. This situation can be explained by a certain degree of flexibility in some forms of remuneration such as annual bonuses, overtime not included in the monthly pay, or female work. The brief depreciation of the yen in 1978-79, and the appreciation of the dollar that followed, were also powerful stimulants for Japanese exports.

Growth remained intensive, unlike that of the United States, with a fairly steady rise in capital and an accelerated pace of substituting capital for labor. But the results varied greatly from one sector to another. In industry, the increase in labor productivity was maintained and capital productivity showed a recovery. In the services, by contrast, the efficiency of capital declined, and labor productivity gains were weak. The protected sectors served as a refuge for employment, which explains in part the continued low level of the unemployment rate (see Table 9.7).

But until 1985 at least, Japan avoided the logic of the prior mode of growth because foreign demand had become the most dynamic factor, while domestic demand had been the prime mover before the crisis. This extraverted dynamic was partially called into question after 1985 with the reevaluation of the yen.

The Successes of the Export Sector

Japan is familiar with large-scale industrial transformations in the context of public aid, and these comprise one of the forces behind the constant improvement of its international specialization. Heavy metallurgy, basic chemical products, shipbuilding, and textiles thus saw their capacities improve until the beginning of the 1970s. External pressure (energy costs, competition from the newly industrialized countries) necessitated planning for withdrawal. Thus, in 1977-78, laws provided for the creation of recession cartels that the Ministry of Foreign Trade and Technology (MITI) was to set up through negotiations with business on the one hand and the unions on the other. The cartels were organized by branch and company and supported by government aid. In 1983, a new law for im-

Table 9.7

Growth, Productivity, and Global Demand in Japan (1960–1986) (annual rate of growth in %)

	1960–1968	1968–1973	1973–1979	1979–1986
Product	11.1	10.3	3.6	4.5
Capital stock	10.8	13.1	6.8	7.5
Capital per worker	9.0	12.0	6.0	6.9
Labor productivity				
Industry	9.0	10.4	5.0	6.3
Services	7.5	4.4	2.2	1.3
Capital productivity	0.3	−2.8	−3.2	−3.0
Real wage	6.5	8.7	2.0	1.6
Private consumption	9.0	8.2	3.9	2.6
Exports	14.7	12.3	8.9	9.3
Imports	13.8	14.8	3.5	0.3

Source: OECD.

proving sectoral structures continued this policy of competitive restructuring, resulting in an adaptation to the reduced social cost. This also permitted incentives for the development of the electronics and automobile industries. The electronics industry's positions in mass-market goods (radios, TVs) had been reinforced since the 1950s through technological imitation and the protection of the domestic market (protective tariffs, quotas). In the 1970s diversification occurred upstream; this was made possible by a large R&D effort and direct or indirect public financing (procurement contracts). The coordination of research efforts was also rather specific to the Japanese economy.

The success of Japan's industry cannot be explained solely by this adaptability and industrial policy, however. Indeed, in the automobile industry, Japan had neither a natural advantage nor an enormous domestic market because of the relative lack of space. Companies nonetheless demonstrated unique organizational efficiency. A massive rationalization effect succeeded in integrating the impact of the electronics industry on facilities. Japanese automobile companies simultaneously instituted new forms of labor force mobilization and management on the basis of different principles from those underlying Taylorism. The experiment conducted by General Motors in the face of Japanese competition on the domestic American market is rather instructive about the productivity gap that resulted. The Japanese-style modernization of a California factory entrusted to Toyota yielded better performances than the parallel experiment in automation carried out in Michigan (Sautter 1987). The reasons for the difference were mainly better quality, better supplying, and low absenteeism.

The Taylorism still in effect in the automobile industry implied a fairly strict hierarchy and above all the total separation of conception and execution tasks. By contrast, Japanese organization—Toyotism—implied the recruitment of personnel with a high level of general training. This meant that jobs did not have to be defined as rigidly, personnel could change functions, and the circulation of technical and organizational information was facilitated accordingly. Production processes could be managed by a horizontal coordination procedure, with more rapid transmission of information and commands between shops (Aoki 1990; Coriat 1991). The zero supply system added to the intelligence of the whole and led to a sharp reduction in costs and a broad mobilization of personnel. The counterpart, however, was an immediate adaptation to the state of demand—daily or weekly working hours had to be modified in function of the company's needs. The internal flexibility seen in relations with subcontractors was thus very great. Lifetime employment, rather than constituting a factor of rigidity, constituted a means of integration that gave rise to confidence. It offered an incentive to make the maximum effort in terms of intensity, duration if necessary, and above all intelligence. Toyotism could thus beat Taylorism and Fordism once mass production was abandoned and the goal was one of satisfying a diversified, more unstable demand that is constantly renewed. Japan thus invented one of the most useful organizational models for adaptation in the 1990s.

By level, the productivity of Japan's industry caught up to that of the United States in the most modern branches. By rate of growth, the trend remains remarkable, generating a formidable challenge for industries in the rest of the world at the turn of the 1990s.

The Stability of Regulation Procedures and Financial Deregulation

The rapidity of technological and industrial transformations contrasts with the stability of institutions and modes of regulation. There has not been a real neoconservative revolution in Japan, or even a major debate on the organization of the economy. Japan's successes lie in part in the organization of cartels and the State's intervention in industrial choices.

On the labor market, regulation procedures were only slightly changed. The slowdown in wage increases fell within the traditional flexibility of remunerations, which is the pendant to job rigidity. The system of lifetime employment was not called into question. The decline of manufacturing's share in total employment slightly reduced its importance. But it remained one of the basic principles of the operation of major firms.

Questioning of the State's intervention also remained limited. While there were numerous regulations, the only profound modifications concerned the air-transport and telecommunications markets. Few public enterprises were privatized—Japan Air Lines; the telecommunications company, where the State retained a blocking minority interest; and the tobacco and salt company. MITI's strategic role in guiding industrial policy became less interventionist, but it remained essential.

The area that underwent the most structural adjustments was the financial sector. More than any concerted desire to accomplish a financial transformation, the changes resulted from shifts in the growth regime and Japan's new position in the world economy. Until the 1970s, the Japanese financial system was at once very compartmentalized and strongly regulated. Several financing circuits could be distinguished—the commercial banks, headed by the city banks, which were quite integrated into the big companies through the "main bank system"; establishments specialized in investment financing (trust banks and long-term credit banks); public and mutualist financial intermediaries that transformed the very abundant savings of households; and nonbanking institutions involved in consumer and real-estate credit and often dependent on the banks (*junsen* notably). This system was closely monitored by the central bank with the help of a credit-control system and a quantitative regulation of refinancing. It was reinforced by the control of exchange, which limited foreign investments in order to ensure domestic financing and discouraged the entry of capital in order to preserve the autonomy of the production system. The main objective of this system as a whole was to ensure low-cost priority funding for industry.

Since the 1970s, several convergent developments have led to deregulation. The drop in businesses' investment rate encouraged them to get out of debt, while the household savings rate remained steady. The banks were led to seek new outlets and succeeded in obtaining a relaxation of regulations allowing them to increase securities and international credit operations. The rapid growth of the public debt allowed the creation of a secondary market for bonds. The regulation on rates was relaxed, and the segmentation of financial activities diminished.

Japan's growing international power called into question the isolation of the financial system. During the first half of the 1980s, the control of exchanges was reduced and then eliminated, with the authorities abandoning an instrument that had systematically been used to influence the rate of the yen. Loans to nonresidents were authorized in 1986, as were exchange operations independent of foreign trade. This liberalization was carried out under pressure from the United States and in order to limit protectionist reactions from abroad, but also because it responded to the aspirations of Japanese operators who were increasingly oriented to the international arena.

The Major Crisis of the 1990s

Japan was the country that had managed to find the most effective responses to the crisis of the 1970s. Since 1990, however, it has been confronted by a profound recession that calls into question the very foundations of its growth regime and could be interpreted as a structural crisis.

The origin of this reversal lies in a financial crisis with fairly classic mechanisms (Geoffron and Rubinstein 1996). The speculative bubble that had developed on the financial and real-estate markets during the second half of the 1980s in the context of the deregulation and low interest rates burst in May 1989 following the central bank's raising of the rates. The financial crisis came in the context of a gradual slowdown in growth under the effect of overinvestments and the very sharp appreciation of the yen. The fragile financial situation of businesses, but also that of banks and financial institutions that had accumulated risky debts, notably in real estate, then became evident.

This financial crisis seems particularly difficult to overcome. In spite of a policy of very low interest rates, banks and nonbanking institutions are lastingly handicapped by the absorption of risky debts. Although the issue has given rise to debate, the difficulties encountered in auditing financial firms does not seem to have posed a major obstacle, in the form of credit rationing, to a lasting recovery from 1992-93 on. Rather, more structural factors have been at work, in terms of both financial relations and industrial competitiveness.

Japan is slowly learning the new financial rules that are profoundly different from the preceding ones. The "main bank system" and the privileged relations between bank and industry are on the decline as banks become more demanding and businesses seek other sources of financing. A new way of operating, less oriented toward long-term solidarities, is emerging within the financing system, thus making the financing of expenditures for innovation more difficult.

At the same time, a slow transformation of the elements of Japan's industrial competitiveness is under way. It is now more difficult for non-price competitiveness to compensate for the very high level of Japanese production costs. These have risen considerably with the reevaluation of the yen since the mid-1980s and the stagnation of labor productivity in industry—a reflection of the preservation of the lifetime employment system—since the beginning of the recession. But the very high costs of protected sectors within services and distribution, which traditionally served as a haven for employment, are also involved. Official reports emphasize the necessity of making successive adjustments that might have an impact on the unemployment rate (MITI 1996a and 1996b). Direct investments abroad also showed a sharp increase in the second half of the 1980s and have again been on the rise since 1993, notably toward the other Asian countries. This development is in sharp contrast with the stagnation of investment. In order to reestablish the basis of competitiveness, a new division of labor, based on international networks of production, is being set up and, for the first time in Japan, intrabranch exchanges are developing.

Overall, in a context of prolonged stagnation, the Japanese model has undergone profound upheavals, and its very identity has come into question in several areas. Institutional changes, structural transformations, and the setting up of new modes of regulation come together in the search for a new growth regime. These are all the characteristics of a major crisis, but in the past, Japan has demonstrated its ability to master such changes.

❖

The 1980s saw the crisis enter a second phase, marked by a deep recession from 1979 to 1982 that struck everywhere but in Japan, then by a recovery that grew after the oil countercrisis. However, the fragility of this recovery was illustrated by the extent of the new economic reversal after 1990, which was particularly serious in continental Europe and Japan. The industrialized countries, following very different national trajectories and with uneven results, attempted to reconstruct a consistent accumulation regime.

United States and Great Britain: Exploring a New Mode of Growth Through Renewed Competition

In the United States, the accumulation regime offered a marked extensive component, with low productivity gains and a downward shift of the demand structure from mass consumer goods toward more differentiated products (luxury goods, financial products, weapons). This regime was rather consistent with increased inequalities and the spread of jobs that were low-skill, not highly productive, and badly paid. But the United States also created skilled jobs in the high-tech and new service (finance, telecommunications) sectors. Although the labor market remained more competitive than elsewhere, deregulation actually penetrated only a limited number of activities. Government intervention remained a strong element of the American accumulation regime, which was, however, faced with a double contradiction: on the one hand, the excessive indebtedness of the actors (State, households, and numerous businesses) constituted a limit to growth, but on the other hand, the decline of industrial competitiveness posed the problem of U.S. integration into the world economy despite the fact that on the geopolitical level it remained the only dominant economy.

In spite of certain common features, the path followed by the United Kingdom was rather different. The return to more competitive regulation was noteworthy in terms of the labor market, with the spread of precarious work and recourse to defensive flexibility. The apparently rosy results in terms of reduced unemployment in the mid-1980s and again in the mid-1990s can be explained in this context and owe more to phenomena of discouragement and exits from the labor market than to real creation of jobs. The labor force, moreover, was more difficult to mobilize, which limited productivity gains. The inadequate training level of the labor force contributed to the same effect and generated tensions around certain qualifications. There were considerable inequalities among regions or incomes. Overall, with the exception of a few sectors, the introduction of an active policy of competition and privatization had only a rather limited impact. De-industrialization and internationalization were more accentuated than in the United States. The decline of industrial competitiveness was made up for by service incomes, the financial activities of the "City," and, temporarily at least, oil. The British economy, which had become more cyclical, was far from having defined a healthy growth regime.

Germany and Sweden: Social-Democratic Management of the Supply Crisis

By relying on a powerful unionism and the codetermination system within the companies, social compromises were reached in order to reorganize production methods and exploit all the possibilities of the new technologies while seeking a certain wage moderation. Germany thus recovered its competitiveness in the 1980s by strengthening its specialization in capital goods, but it met with relative failure in the information technologies. In spite of the spread of precarious forms of work, there was no neoconservative revolution. Financial deregulation was more limited and more prudent than elsewhere. By contrast, budgetary and monetary rigor was the rule during the 1980s, with the choice of slow growth and the acceptance of rather widespread unemployment that could only be reduced gradually. The shock of reunification called this strategy into question by creating a significant budget hike and opening the way to more extensive accumulation.

The Swedish methods were more diverse. The preservation of full employment remained a central objective until the end of the 1980s. An active employment policy was set up and competitive devaluations carried out. This strategy reached its limits with a level of compulsory payroll deductions that was held to be excessive. Since the beginning of the 1990s, the Swedish model has undergone significant modifications, notably with the (temporary?) acceptance of higher unemployment.

France: The Unsuccessful Search for a New Model

France's economic policy gradually approached a norm inspired by both German orthodoxy and Anglo-Saxon "liberalism," in the sense of a neoconservative, free-market approach to economic policy—halting of structural policies, freeing of prices, financial deregulation, recourse to defensive flexibility in wage relations. The strategy of competitive disinflation was successful but quite costly in terms of unemployment. Handicapped by the failure to modernize its productive apparatus sufficiently, the political desire to link the franc to the mark, and the lack of advantages enjoyed by its European partners, France found itself increasingly constrained within the Community. Only the preservation of a broad social security system permitted the alleviation of tensions created by the rise of mass unemployment and growing inequalities.

Japan: New Challenges Following an Early End to the Crisis of the 1970s

By relying on its distinctive social relations, Japan created new forms of work organization based on automation and "just-in-time" production combined with a strong mobilization of employees. This model became a worldwide reference. Japanese industry, structured around large groups and operating with a network of subcontractors, also managed to redeploy itself toward products most responsive to world demand. The performances of the Japanese model have little to do with neoconservative logic, although dualism is a major element in Japanese society. Government intervention remained considerable in the areas of industry and research, while liberalization was most pronounced in the financial sector, under the effect of both internal pressures and Japan's new position in the international arena.

Since the early 1990s Japan has been faced by a major crisis that was set off by classic factors in financial terms but that affects many fundamentals of the Japanese model—learning the new financial rules, accelerating relocation in response to declining industrial competitiveness, and questioning excessive costs in the protected sector.

CHAPTER TEN

The Accumulation Regime of the 2000s, An Open Choice

The preceding chapter brought out the contrasting experiences of different countries and the scope of the changes incurred since the beginning of the world crisis. A more horizontal analysis is needed to identify the issues of the 2000s by exploring what the characteristic institutional forms of a new accumulation regime might be: wage relation, nature of the State, monetary constraint, and forms of articulation with the international regime. Particular attention will be paid to the prospects for European economic and monetary integration and the changes in Eastern Europe. In each case, it will be seen that the choices are more open than is often admitted.

Transformation of the Wage Relation and Technological Changes

In a context of slowed growth, intense restructurings, and increased international competition, the wage relation had undergone profound changes since the 1970s. The constraints of competitiveness and the need to restore and then maintain the profitability of capital led firms to seek greater labor flexibility. At the same time, the need to surmount the crisis of Taylorism and Fordism led to significant organizational innovations based on early experiments with the reorganization of tasks. As firm strategy evolved, greater emphasis was placed on product quality and product differentiation. The development of the new electronics and computer technologies also contributed to profound changes in production methods.

The Search for Greater Labor Flexibility

Most elements of the wage relation (adjustment of employment, fixing of wages, social protection) were affected by this search for greater flexibility, but the differences from one country to another were considerable (Boyer 1986b).

Adjustment of Employment to Cyclical Fluctuations in Economic Activity

West Germany had a number of forms of adjustment at its disposal. These included the speed of employment adjustment, greater sensitivity of the labor-market participation rate, greater reductions in female employment and recourse to immigrant workers, or the rapid expansion of part-time work. Labor relations based on a timeworn system of negotiations with strong unions allowed the adjustments to function more smoothly. The 1980s, and especially after the conflict of 1984, were more dominated by the demand for a reduction of work time, but in exchange for shorter hours the unions had to accept a greater flexibility of work schedules (variable hours, work time calculated on an annual basis). Within this framework, negotiations tended to be more decentralized on the company level.

In Italy, the high elasticity of the length of the workweek in response to fluctuations in activity was initially the favored means of adjustment. It allowed for compensations in the sluggishness of employment and the strict control of temporary work in the large plants that had, in part, been engendered by the introduction of worker legislation in 1970. Subsequently, the legal system itself was to be circumvented with the rapid rise of employment in small and medium-size enterprises and greater recourse to undeclared labor and homework, which permitted the growth of a significant underground economy. By guaranteeing incomes and formally maintaining the relation between the employee and the firm, the Cassa Integrazione facilitated downsizing.

France occupied an intermediate position, whether in terms of the speed of employment adjustment, the elasticity of work time, or the recourse to part-time work. Since the end of the 1970s, the government did its best to introduce a certain degree of flexibility into the legal system through a vast range of measures undertaken within the framework of employment policy (management of early retirement, solidarity contracts, in-company internships for young people). Beginning in the mid-1980s, greater emphasis was placed on the search for external flexibility.

In the United Kingdom, the early period was marked by fairly great rigidity concerning employment (closed shop, strong union positions), but this was offset by increased recourse to part-time work and the flexibility of labor-force participation rates. From 1979 on, a systematic policy was implemented, including the reduction of union powers, diminished authority for the wage councils, relaxing of laws on hiring and firing, and fewer obstacles to professional and geographical mobility.

The United States is often cited as a model of flexibility. In fact, the two-tiered nature of American society has been reinforced since the 1970s by playing on differences in labor law from one state to another and differences in status among social groups (young people, women, racial and ethnic minorities). There was a trend toward relocation from the traditional industrial centers in the Northeast to Southern states where the workforce is less skilled and less unionized, but also to the Pacific Northwest, a privileged area for the development of new technologies. The seniority system, which limited management's freedom, notably in conversion industries, was gradually called into question.

In Japan, the singular functioning of the labor market favored an over-all adjustment of the economy after the first oil shock. The guarantee of lifetime employment within the large firms carried with it significant internal mobility, even geographically, and vocational training at the employer's expense. However, the proportion of these guaranteed jobs within total employment diminished. The cost of the adjustments was largely passed on to the employees of SMEs, workers with precarious employment status, and women. The adaptation of overtime was an additional factor of adjustment.

Less Rigid Wages

West Germany profited from the greater sensitivity of the direct wage to the disequilibria of the labor market and changes in productivity. A "wage pause" was nonetheless imposed by the employers' organizations and the government at the beginning of the 1980s. The individualization of wages spread in conjunction with the flexibility of working hours despite the distrust of the unions (remuneration based on output, bonuses, constraints of difficult working conditions). The German compromise was characterized by a delicate balance between concessions and guarantees with a constant, negotiated, and sometimes conflictual effort to adapt.

In Italy, employers sought to call into question the principle of the mobile scale that had been one of the main union objectives during the 1970s by limiting it to a fraction of the wage and excluding the price of imported primary goods from the basic price index. Italy's parallel economy, moreover, constituted a significant factor of flexibility on the wage level.

In France, the growth of the real wage rate was more steady until the beginning of the 1980s, especially in brute terms because of the increase in payroll deductions. From 1983 on, the disindexation of wages to prices became an important issue, and new rules for programming raises were tested, with some success. Different elements of employment policy contributed to locking young people into jobs with low wages. A similar phenomenon may be observed in the United Kingdom on a much greater scale. There, however, the systematic policy of fighting against "rigidities in wages" and the union power imposed since 1979 seem to have had only a moderate effect on the growth of the real wage rate.

In the United States, employers' organizations obtained the suspension of the old formula for wage negotiations, which were held responsible for the inflationary trend of the 1970s, in 1982–83. The union organizations, when they were present, had to concede significant wage cuts in hopes of limiting the number of layoffs. But no new formula was really elaborated, despite the need for a certain codification of wage negotiations. In the deregulated sectors, two-tiered wage formulas were tried out in order to arrive at greater reductions of wage costs. More generally, the two-tiered nature of the American labor market became more pronounced.

In Japan, the role of seniority in wage increases within the large firms was never called into question but was more than offset by other factors (moderation of raises during spring offensives, reduction of bonuses). Constraints were reinforced in the least favored sectors of the Japanese economy.

Given the gap that had been increasing since the 1970s between the net wage received by employees and the total cost borne by the firms, social security systems were at the core of debates on flexibility. Efforts at rationalization led to a reduction of social coverage in all countries, including France and Germany (limiting of certain services, less favorable indexing of retirement benefits). Alternatives were explored, including local solidarity networks and the privatization of certain risks. But on the whole, the cleavage between social security systems, which were more extensive in Europe than in the United States and Japan, was not called into question.

From this rapid survey, the search for greater flexibility of labor and greater labor-market segmentation emerge as general trends since the 1970s. These take specific forms depending on the nature of social relations, production structures, and international integration of the countries concerned. Following the schema of Boyer (1986), we can contrast offensive and defensive flexibility. Thus, in West Germany and Japan, flexibility could be termed offensive, or positive. In West Germany, the practice of negotiations with the union partners (including those on the decentralized level), the vocational training system, and the emphasis placed on the qualification of the labor force created a favorable context for adjustments in spite of the tensions that emerged at the beginning of the 1980s. Similarly, in Japan, positive elements included internal flexibility and employees' ability to adapt within the large firms, as well as the originality of the subcontracting system, although these should not make us overlook the bipolar nature of Japanese society.

By contrast, British flexibility seems to have been more defensive, or regressive. Indeed, it was characterized by a return to mechanisms that were more competitive in terms of employment and wages, without any search for new forms of social compromises or intervention. France, meanwhile, occupied an intermediate position. In many respects, external flexibility was privileged, as demonstrated, for example, by the development of particular forms of employment. But at the same time, numerous solidarity measures were undertaken during the 1980s, and the need to promote a more active employment and training policy gradually made itself felt, although its implementation came up against the constraints of short-term management.

Beyond this initial characterization of flexibility-related phenomena, it is now necessary to consider the changes that occurred in firm strategies.

The Search for a New Organization and Changing Firm Strategy

On the firm level, the crisis years were indeed marked by a double interrogation. On the one hand, the need to go beyond Taylorist principles of work organization led firms to explore new forms of organization (Coriat 1990). On the other hand, forms of competition were considerably transformed with the increased role of product quality and product differentiation.

The Emergence of New Forms of the Organization of Work

The problem of going beyond Taylorism and Fordism was raised at the end of the 1960s with the rise of the unskilled workers' struggles against the fragmentation of tasks as well as with growing absenteeism and waste in production, which seriously harmed labor productivity. An initial group of responses involved attempts to enrich tasks and humanize work. These were followed by more ambitious experiments in the reconstitution of tasks, the introduction of breaks, and variable rhythms on the assembly lines. If dehumanized, fragmented, and repetitive work did not disappear, these experiments nonetheless contributed to forging new principles in the organization of work.

Work was no longer individualized and fragmented, but better distributed among small units of workers who were responsible for transforming a given product and managing a homogeneous group of tasks. Continuous assembly lines were replaced by a system of networks of small-scale feeder lines able to supply different areas simultaneously. Rhythms were no longer rigid, but became flexible in function of needs. These new organizational principles allowed a potential increase in the flexibility of the productive apparatus, and in this context, automation was able to achieve its full development.

The Search for Product Quality and Product Differentiation

On a totally different level, the forms of competition were profoundly modified during the 1970s and the 1980s. In a difficult economic situation, with markets that were unstable and undergoing slow growth, companies had to follow fluctuations in demand as closely as possible and adapt to increasingly specific, segmented markets. Mass production with goods that were undifferentiated and slow to change appeared as an increasingly inappropriate response. Thus, product differentiation and quality became essential elements of competition, which required greater flexibility in production. Starting from the same basic organization, plants had to be able to adapt, without major transformations and within fairly short time periods, in order to fabricate products from the same family but with specific features. Here, too, automation and the possibility of programming were to prove particularly useful.

The Emergence of a New Technical System

The 1970s saw the gradual affirmation of a new technical system centered on the information technologies and their applications in the area of capital goods. A whole group of new production tools involving electronics emerged (robots, programmable automatons, numerical controls, flexible shops, handling management), and changes in this area are far from over.

These technological innovations, which were only able to be fully developed because they were linked to organizational innovations, had a double consequence. On the one hand, they led to a more intensive integration of production sequences allowing the reduction of slack time, whether in the case of active work, storage of finished or nonfinished goods, or the utilization of the machines. On the other hand, they permitted greater flexibility of production, which made it possible to fabricate differentiated product lines because of the automatic and programmed adaptation capacities of the new facilities. Considerable productivity gains were thus able to be obtained.

This technological transformation could not have been conceived, however, without the definition of a new model of work relations. The work required was indeed more indirect, oriented toward management and supply tasks and the optimization of maintenance and machine utilization time. It required greater versatility and cooperation on the part of employees. In contrast to the old functional division within the company, new relations had to be established between the different departments, notably between sales and production to minimize stocks and between engineering and fabrication to improve quality. Productivity became much more social and dependent on relations forged not only within the company but also with clients, suppliers, and subcontractors.

This process of change was thus extremely coherent. Organizational innovations were based on technological innovations and new generations of production tools. They responded to needs for greater product differentiation and quality in order to keep up with more segmented and fluctuating markets. But obviously, this transformation did not lead to a single "model."

On the contrary, quite different solutions were adopted depending on the nature of each social formation. The reorganization of work, the forms of appropriating new techniques and mobilizing employees, and the recourse to defensive or offensive flexibility all constituted elements of differentiation within the new wage relation that was being created.

Two Diametrically Opposed Scenarios

To be sure, various combinations can be imagined. By simplifying the typology proposed by Coriat (1990), two main scenarios can be identified—one neoconservative and bipolar, the other cooperative. Obviously these are only stylized forms, and they are, in addition, rather marked by the industrial dimension.

The Neoconservative Bipolar Scenario

In this scenario, automation is carried out without any profound transformation of the organization of work. The most skilled tasks are entrusted to a few high-level operator technicians or subcontracted to maintenance companies. A large part of the staff remains in fairly general, repetitive functions (surveillance, supplies). The company focuses on the most strategic activities and makes broad use of subcontracting.

In the area of labor relations, forms of defensive flexibility predominate, with a return to more competitive practices. Wage formation accords a greater place to bonuses tied to individual or company performance. Company agreements replace collective bargaining and branch agreements. There are growing differences between the status of employees in large and small firms. The society's two-tiered nature is accentuated by the trend toward deregulation spurred by the government, notably in the area of employment and wages.

The Cooperative Scenario

This scenario would seem to synthesize all the positive trends at work in the transformation of the wage relation, firm strategies, and technological changes. Automation is accompanied by a thorough reorganization of work, with an effort to promote a more skilled, versatile workforce. Negotiation, a greater training effort, and the pursuit of contractual agreements are privileged, leading to the negotiated involvement of employees. Subcontracting is stabilized and contractualized in order to arrive at forms of partnership and alliances permitting the reconciliation of flexibility and quality for externalized activities and modernization and growth for the subcontracting firms.

In the area of labor relations, new wage agreements are negotiated to guarantee both stable income (notably in function of anticipated inflation and productivity gains) and a certain ability to adapt to diverse situations (in function of the branches, the companies, or the economic situation). Employee mobility is encouraged by an active, decentralized training policy and reconversion in close collaboration with the companies. Such a scenario implies the definition of a social compromise according to modalities that may vary from one country to another.

Weakening or Restructuration of Public Interventions

The 1980s, and especially the beginning of the decade, were marked by the rise of a strong antigovernment ideology. The role of the public sector was often called into question, with any number of tax reforms, and the frequent cancellation of public aid measures deemed anticompetition. Expanded markets were invoked as a universal remedy for problems of efficiency and even justice. The grave imbalances on the labor market, inequalities in lifestyles, and the rise of violence were considered as passing difficulties related to phases of structural adjustment.

By the beginning of the 1990s, however, the relevance of this ideology came to be qualified, and the demand for government intervention was often quite strong in the areas of industrial reconversions, unemployment, or maintenance of social order. The idea of a genuine complementarity between private and public sectors gained adherents, with each sector obviously required to accept adaptations. Administered regulation was thus able to make a comeback with a new face, at least in the leading economies that were not the Great Powers (i.e., outside the case of the United States, which probably remained in a very asymmetrical situation relative to the rest of the world because of the continued role of the dollar and its probable undervaluation during this period).

The Yield and Legitimacy of the Tax Systems
Partly Called into Question

As we know, the role of taxes in the economy has never increased linearly over the long term. Periods of war or crisis have been more propitious to the birth of new taxes and public debt. The crisis of the 1970–82 period with its rebound in 1989–93 was no exception to the rule, even if its tax-crisis profile is uncommon. Taxes initially increased, followed by attempts at stabilization that were often accompanied by the rise of public debts, which, in some cases, wound up being problematic for growth as long as inflation remained low. The new dilemma for regulation as a whole thus became tax consolidation versus reduction of public spending.

Increasing Taxes Until 1983–1985

Before 1983–85, and in spite of the repeated crises in demand and the length of the overall crisis in question (1970–83), tax revenues continued to flow in easily in the leading economies, owing partly to inflation and partly to routine. Between 1970 and 1984, the share of taxes in the GDP thus rose 2 points in the United States, 10 points in Japan, 7 points in Germany, 9 points in France, 2 points in the United Kingdom, 7 points in Italy, and more than 12 points in Sweden (for an average of 5 points in the OECD countries). But with the help of inflation and ideology, the United States and the United Kingdom were the first to seek a halt to this increase by turning to the logic of "supply-side economics." Subsequently, in Germany, Belgium, Austria, the Netherlands, Denmark, Greece, and France, the high points were reached in the 1983–87 period, and this was followed by a leveling off, or even a regression of the share of taxes (United Kingdom, Greece, Netherlands). Where the regression was obtained without increased public debt, there was a relative impoverishment of government administrations (because of the differential evolution of productivity in the tertiary sector) and/or a trend toward the reduction of the share of government investment (as was the case in the EEC after 1984–87). This might be counterproductive for the private sector in the medium or long term insofar as public infrastructures probably play a role that is complementary to that of business activity. Everything here depends on the more or less positive content of public spending and the effective use made of public resources (absence of waste, absence of overlap between levels of government administration, productivity gains, computerization, modernization).

Partially Voluntary Drying Up of Tax Resources After 1985

Between 1985 and 1990, the share of current public revenues generally leveled off. This was particularly clear in the EEC countries (43.5 percent of the GDP, including 29.4 points for 1990 tax revenues). (See Table 10.1.) Between 1984 and 1990, the average structural deficits of the GDP decreased by 1.4 percent in the OECD zone. The economic situation was thus better, mainly because of the oil counter-crisis. But this anti-State

Table 10.1

Total Tax Revenues Excluding Social Security in Leading OECD Countries (in % of GDP)

	1985	1990	1993
European Union	28.0	28.4	29.0
France	25.2	24.4	24.3
Germany	24.2	22.9	23.9
United Kingdom	31.2	20.2	27.6
OECD	27.9	28.7	28.5

Source: OECD (1995).

determination was to continue at the beginning of the new crisis of 1989–91, especially in Germany, the United States, and the United Kingdom. In the U.K., for example, the official goal was to balance the real budget of the public sector over the medium term by reducing public expenditures and interest on the debt. The British government also undertook privatizations and a recentralization of public expenditures (a phenomenon that was often underestimated abroad).

This anti-State determination was illustrated by various actions, notably fiscal reforms. Often inspired by the Laffer Curve, these reforms proposed lower rates of taxation (for income taxes or the VAT), but also—in order to provide incentives for the most wealthy—reductions in the progressiveness of tax rates for higher incomes. These reforms did indeed seek to reduce the complexity of the tax systems, but the results in this respect were uneven, and what decreased most clearly was the taxation of large private incomes, incomes from capital, and savings (Baslé 1990). Thus the reforms contributed partly to the drying up of a tax resource with the recession of 1990–93 and partly to a restructuring of taxes imposed. This was especially true in the United Kingdom, where the gross sum of personal income tax and that of taxes on incomes and profits declined between 1990 and 1993 with a rise in general and value-added taxes. In France, revenues from value-added taxes stagnated with the recession of 1990–93. In Germany, by contrast, following the reunification in 1991, income taxes and household social security contributions were increased voluntarily until 1992–93.

The ideological debate during this period remains all the more unclear in view of the fact that the aggregates used to speak of the share of the State and taxes are probably not the most relevant. The share of current public receipts excludes indebtedness, while that of compulsory deductions includes social security contributions, which have as their primary objective insurance and social redistribution of wealth. The one indicator that might be useful is not employed—the rate of tax deduction net of those receipts that are used to finance social transfers and public services aimed at individuals (such as education or health). For example, this indicator of the net real weight, strictly speaking, of the public administrations (financing the "general expenses" of the society) was only 13.1 percent in France in 1985 and 12.5 percent in 1990, which means that over thirty points of the GDP passed only temporarily through the public financing circuits.

The Rise in Public Debt Charges and the Fear of So-Called "Financial Crowding Out"

At the end of the 1970s, real long-term interest rates were negative, which meant that debt could thus be a source of wealth. This trend was reversed from 1978–79 on, whether through the introduction of very restrictive monetary policies under the label of monetarist policy and the belief in the efficiency of a quantitative control of the money supply, through the defense of overly high exchange rates, or through the recession itself, which weakened inflationary pressures. Certain critics blamed the drop in public savings (which, in the CEE countries, Japan, and the United States, represented 5 percent of the GDP in 1970 and –1.5 percent between 1981 and 1984), arguing that the excess demand for public credit was the main threat to interest rates. This explanation, however, is far from being complete and econometrically verified.

It is true that the gross public debt increased between 1979 and 1987, especially in the CEE countries, and in certain cases, because of the fear of a tax revolt that led to avoiding increased taxes. But in 1990, the situation was far from homogeneous. Net public debt in Japan was only 10.9 percent of the GDP; that of Germany and France was below 25 percent; and that of the United Kingdom and the United States, 28.9 and 32.6 percent, respectively. On the other hand, the cases of Italy (98.2 percent), Ireland (116.9 percent), or Belgium (120.6 percent) constituted excessive debt, although the ratio of debt stock to GDP flow is hardly relevant (Baslé 1990). In the latter cases, the new budget deficits and the rise in real interest rates created cumulative effects. Within a poor economic climate, there was an increasing gap between the rate of real economic growth and the real interest rate, which led to automatically growing deductions aimed at financing the public debt. The smaller, open countries were thus prisoners of a situation where they could not use multipliers for a national recovery and where decision makers seeking private investments would have difficulty obtaining loans, thus raising the possibility of a crowding-out effect. The situation was not the same everywhere, however. The continental CEE countries paid interest charges that went from

2.8 percent of the GDP in 1983 to 4.9 percent in 1991. France and Germany, however, found buyers for their public debts without unduly increasing the differentials in their rates, and, in addition, the high rates attracted foreign capital that maintained the high rates of exchange relative to the dollar. The crowding-out effect has not been proven in France, where the self-financing of the large companies (the case of the SMEs was different) was nearly total in the early 1990s and where the public sector's need to borrow was easily offset (Deniau, Fiori, and Mathis 1989).

The situation in the United States was more ambiguous. The country is large but only slightly open. Its private domestic savings are limited, and the lack of public savings has an impact on the rates. This may explain the pursuit of budgetary economies in a situation where new taxes are impossible.

Restructuring of Public Expenditures and Privatizations: Changing Frontiers Between Private and Public?

Between 1979 and 1989, public consumption and public investment were reduced in Japan, the United Kingdom, Germany, and Sweden. On the other hand, social transfers rose slightly almost everywhere (2.3 points of the GDP in Japan, 3 points in France, 3.8 points in Italy, 2 points in Sweden), and with the rise in interest payment on the debt, this marked a very sharp restructuring of public charges (social spending and finance income, with their opposing effects in terms of social justice). The stated goal was to "widen the scope of the market and improve its operation," but with slight growth or recession and the persistence of unemployment and problems of inequality, the Welfare State still served as a safety net.

The most extreme case of announced "marketization" was the United Kingdom, where privatization was especially pronounced because of the belief in a causal relation between public ownership of stocks, low productivity, and its effects on the decline of the English economy. The reality of the action and its effects was more complex than anticipated. The sale of stocks at prices that were attractive for savers certainly allowed the situation of current public accounts to be improved. But the technical difficulties of implementing real competition in the privatized sectors were considerable (notably the revival of oligopoly and the considerable requirements imposed by the regulatory authorities). The heavy costs of transition (corruption, wages of new administrators) were often absorbed to the detriment of the quality of the services provided in, for example, water, electricity, or rail transport. The medium-term results, which cannot yet be assessed, may be even worse (low investment in the long term) unless a financial recentralization is envisioned.

In France during the 1986–88 period of "cohabitation" between Socialists and Conservatives, the expression of "industrial policy" was banished, public aid to industry pruned, and privatization extended to the industrial (Dassault) and financial (Paribas) sectors. After his reelection in 1988, President Mitterrand adopted a doctrine of "neither–nor" ("neither nationalization nor privatization"). The equity capital of public enterprises was strengthened and internal restructurings undertaken. Partial privatizations soon followed. But the strength and modernity of the public sector—Electricité de France, Gaz de France, high-speed trains, France-Télécoms—remained obvious, and France's transportation infrastructures were the envy of Europe. It was only with the single market of 1993 and the deregulations and open markets anticipated in the Treaty of Maastricht that the organization of the branches on the European scale was called into question.

The most tangible change in public interventions has undoubtedly been the pronounced effort in the social domain. In many countries, countercyclical social spending has limited the effects of unemployment, but this spending is sometimes difficult to finance. Thus, Germany faces three major challenges: the growing proportion of both young and old people in the population, the unemployment and reemployment of people from the former *Lander* of East Germany, and the determination of a level of social protection extended to all Germans and capable of being financed. In France, there is recurring debate over the deficits of the social security system. Until 1990, demographic factors had little impact—the working-age population had increased by 5 percent during the 1980s, and demographic effects remained indirect, in terms of education costs and unemployment benefits. On the other hand, the health system has continued to follow an autonomous trajectory; with no limits to the quantitative prescription of treatment, it calls for a structural reform. As for retirement benefits, an increase of 5 percent in old-age contributions would seem necessary in order to meet the requirements of the 2005 deadline. The collective system of intergenerational distribution might well be affected if measures are not taken. Some would envision the possibility of introducing formulas for individual capitalization of retirement points (closer to private insurance than national solidarity), but the transition between the two systems can only be anticipated over a very long period.

In the United States, at the heart of the 1989–91 recession, domestic policy came into the spotlight, and there was talk of a New Deal for the 1990s with the Clinton presidency. A shift of public opinion in favor of certain government interventions (education, environment, etc.) was manifest, and this offset certain past weaknesses. Between 1979 and 1990, for example, public investment had represented only 1.7 percent of the GDP, and public services such as education, health, and housing had considerably deteriorated, while public employment had been cut back. New limits seemed attainable in terms of the control of energy and the reduction of pollution and urban congestion.

As in the case of Japan, where public investment had represented 5 percent of the GDP between 1987 and 1990 (and with the exception of the United Kingdom), the idea of a consolidation of the basic role of public spending in infrastructures, the reduction of externalities, and social justice thus gradually reappeared during the 1990s. In other respects, however, this period gave the impression of a chaotic globalization, with the weakening of nation-states and the protections they provide. In fact, spending has been restructured, just as a restructuring of authority can be observed in many countries—in America as well as Europe—according to the level of public intervention, from local to national or federal.

Thus, the choices among various modes of regulation simply do not include the possibility of eliminating collective public action. Depending on the outcome of conflicts between interest groups, administered regulation will persist, but with different forms, with different levels of incentives for accumulation, and probably with greater social injustice and social violence.

Financial Changes and Transformations in Economic Cycles

The financial sector of the industrialized countries underwent major changes during the 1980s, along with significant transformations in short-term dynamics. These developments suggest that the metamorphosis of the financial institutions considerably modified the regulation procedures that were characteristic of Fordism.

Changes in the Financial Systems During the 1980s

These transformations, which were initiated in the 1970s and thoroughly developed in the 1980s, can be divided into three main categories. The first concerns the rise in real interest rates. As Blanchard and Summers (1986) indicate, the causes of this phenomenon remain quite controversial, and several of the explanations initially proposed have been refuted by subsequent developments. The chronological origin of the rise in short-term rates can be pinpointed to the 1979–82 period, with the change in American monetary policy. It follows that one of its causes lies in the decision of American authorities to make the fight against inflation a priority, in contrast to the permissive policy they had adopted during the 1970s. Between 1980 and 1982, massive entries of capital into the United States had forced other central banks to raise their interest rates. But subsequently, with the strengthening of the European Monetary System, the European rates, which were less dependent on the American rates, nonetheless remained high. During the recession of the early 1990s, the central banks of the United States and Japan opted for a sharp decrease in their short-term rates while European rates were still quite high. This divergence, as we shall see later on, is easily explained by different choices in monetary policy. It thus seems clear that the level of short-term rates largely depends on the choices of the central banks, which have, overall, accorded increasing weight to the objective of price stability since the beginning of the 1980s.

Among the explanations that have not withstood the test of time, two must at least be cited in passing. The first maintains that the agents badly anticipated the disinflation of the first half of the 1980s and thus continued to demand high premiums, but that when the low level of inflation was subsequently confirmed, the real rates remained high. The second thesis targets budgetary deficits, but in fact those of all the OECD countries went from a level equal to 4.5 percent of the GDP in 1985 to 1.2 percent in 1989 without any significant decrease observed in the real rates. It is plausible that part of the rise in long-term rates can be explained by that of the short-term rates. For one thing, the rise in the former began at the same time as that of the latter, between 1979 and 1982. For another, the most commonly accepted theories of the investment yield curve according to term are based on the idea of possible substitutions between short-term investment and loan operations carried over from year to year, forward operations on short-term securities, and operations on long-term securities, the conclusion generally being that the long rate is equal to the average of the short rates anticipated for the future periods plus a risk premium. It is likely that since the early 1980s agents have anticipated restrictive monetary policies and high short-term rates, which helps to explain the high level of the long-term rates. It is not certain, however, that this is the only factor at work. It is possible that the decline in the rate of household savings in the developed countries, the increase in economic and financial ups and downs, or greater demands of profitability also played a role.

The second major transformation involved the growing role of the financial markets, as manifested by the appearance of new products. These have been the focus of numerous studies, notably those of De Boissieu (1987) and Aglietta (1987). Financial innovation in the strict sense of the term was reflected by the appearance of instruments intended to cover the risks inherent in investments. Until the end of the 1960s, the security of assets was basically the responsibility of the public authorities, who limited inflation and guaranteed the stability of interest and exchange rates. With the spread of the crisis and growing international mobility of capital, national regulation procedures lost their effectiveness. The agents thus sought to cover themselves on the futures and options markets.

But these new tools had the effect of transferring the risks to the other agents, since covering operations imply speculative operations as a counterpart. The overall risk, resulting mainly from the mimetic behaviors generated during panics, was not reduced. Another aspect of the financial innovations was the appearance of new securities that broadened the traditional range of Treasury bills, bonds, and classic stocks. These were intended to enlarge the possibilities open to capital bearers and borrowers and constituted a weapon for financial institutions facing increasingly sharp competition in the context of globalization.

The growing power of the financial markets was accompanied by the "securitization" of financial operations. In most countries, the proportion of financing in the form of securities rose considerably to the detriment of credits. Households and small companies could not finance themselves by issuing securities, however, and they remained dependent on bank credits. Among the causes that favored this expansion of security transactions, those most often cited are the changing behaviors of capital bearers and borrowers. Households considerably reduced their housing acquisitions, which favored financial savings; the rise in investments in the form of securities rather than monetary or quasi-monetary deposits can be explained mainly by the significant increase in the difference between the returns on these two forms of investment. In the course of the crisis, the financing needs of OECD member countries rose quickly, and these were met by the issuing of securities. In 1970–73, the public administrations most often had balanced budgets or showed a slight surplus, but deficits accumulated until around 1980–81 and remained high during the first half of the 1980s. The rise in financing costs also encouraged large companies to turn to the financial markets in order to avoid intermediation costs.

The decompartmentalization and deregulation of financial activities constituted the third major transformation, and one where the will of the public powers played an important role. Deregulation diminished or eliminated the specializations imposed on financial intermediaries, which placed them in competition with one another. The forms of privileged financing accorded to certain sectors had been largely suppressed and the control of exchanges abandoned, with the result that capital circulated freely between sectors and countries. These open-market policies had several motivations. The growth of the international capital market allowed large banks and companies to get around the regulations, which thus lost their effectiveness. In the intensive accumulation regime, with its well-known sectoral dynamic, government interventions ensured a certain selectivity of credit to encourage the development of growth sectors or favor the modernization of traditional ones. During the crisis, some of these interventions came at an inopportune moment and, notably in Europe, may have contributed to freezing productive structures. These failures helped to reinforce the idea that the State should not intervene in processes of allocating capital. Competition among financial markets encouraged each government to deregulate in order to favor innovations and preserve or improve the share of markets located on its territory in the international financial flows. The priority accorded to the fight against inflation also led governments to favor financing through the issuing of securities over monetary financing.

The 1990–1993 Recessions: New Features

Overview

This recession offered new features relative to those that preceded it. The first was the low intensity of the American recession. For at least a century, the United States had been considered more cyclical than the European countries, but its last recession was clearly less violent than that of the Europeans. The same observation may be made for France and Sweden: before 1990, the economic situations of the two countries were viewed as stable; Sweden had not undergone a recession during the two oil shocks, and in France, the drop in activity was limited. By contrast, the 1992–93 recession was, in both countries, the most violent in forty years. In Sweden, the unemployment rate went from 1.5 percent in 1989 to 8.2 percent in 1993, which amounted to a veritable collapse. As of 1992, Japan underwent four years of stagnation, whereas its previous growth performances had been far superior to those of the other industrialized countries.

In the Fordist accumulation regime, recessions sanctioned overheating, in other words, an excess of overall demand, which translated into an acceleration of inflation or an increase in foreign deficits. In 1988 and 1989, inflationary pressures remained very limited, except in Germany, where the overheating can be explained by the exceptional event of reunification. At the end of the 1980s, prices of goods and services increased only very moderately while the prices of assets, and notably real-estate assets, underwent a massive rise.

This particular situation helps to explain why professional forecasters were unable to predict the scope of the 1990–93 recession, for there was no habitual overheating–recession schema. It was thus necessary to find new explanations for the length and intensity of the recession. For most specialists, these were to be sought in the area of balance-sheet readjustments and asset prices, as can be seen from the semi-annual reports of the OECD and the annual reports of the BIS. These analyses propose the following scenario: during the 1980s, the deregulation of the financial systems increased competition among financial intermediaries and pushed them to a massive increase in credit supply. Financial innovations gave the nonbanking sector new opportunities for loans and investments, which led to a speculative boom between 1985 and 1990. During this time, households and businesses greatly increased their loans, which they used to speculate on assets such as securities and real estate. During this process, the banks accumulated risky debts, and the nonbanking sector, assets that were artificially inflated in value. A slight rise in the interest rates at the end of the 1980s was enough to burst the speculative bubble and force financial agents to clean up their balance sheets by reducing expenditures, which caused the price of assets to plummet. We shall thus take a closer look at this thesis of the debt–deflation process as it applies to the 1990–93 recession.

Indebtedness and Depression

In order to identify the causes of the depression, it is necessary first of all to examine the role of the different components of demand with the help of an accounting calculation (see Table 10.2). In the five countries analyzed, investment played a more important role than consumption in the recession. This is perfectly normal—the sluggishness of consumption as opposed to the instability of investment is commonplace in macroeconomics. A comparison with the recessions of 1974–75 and 1980–82 provides additional details. In the United States, it is usual for consumption to decline during a recession because of the purchase of consumer durables; thus, 1991 is hardly exceptional. In Japan and Germany, similar brakes on consumption were observed during the preceding recessions. By contrast, in France and especially in Sweden, the slowdown or decline in consumption was greater in 1993–93 than before. These indications may be complemented by data on indebtedness and the rate of household savings (see Table 10.3). For our purposes, the important element is the share of interest payments in disposable household income as an indicator of the share of the debt. In fact, national accounts mainly record flows, so that interest payments are more apparent than outstanding debts. Since debt generally accumulates during a boom and interest rates rise at the end of expansion, interest payments often reach a maximum at the beginning of a recession. This is why Table 10.3 compares the share of interest payments in household income in 1974, 1980, 1990, and 1992. In the long term, this ratio remained fairly stable in the United States and Germany while rising moderately in France and sharply in Japan and Sweden. It is in these last two countries above all that we can speak of excessive debt. In a period of recession, the savings rate usually declines, thus playing a countercyclical role. This was the case in Germany and to a lesser extent in Japan, but it

Table 10.2

Contribution of Domestic Demand Components to Growth

	1989	1990	1991	1992	1993
United States					
Household consumption	1.4	1.0	−0.25	1.9	2.2
Changes in inventories	0.5	−0.3	−0.2	0.1	0.2
Investment	0.3	−0.1	−1.0	0.8	1.7
Japan					
Household consumption	2.5	2.3	1.3	0.9	0.6
Changes in inventories	0.2	−0.3	0.3	−0.5	−0.1
Investment	0.9	0.8	0.6	0.6	0.1
Germany					
Household consumption	1.6	2.9	3.1	1.2	0.1
Changes in inventories	0.2	−0.1	0.2	−0.8	−0.2
Investment	1.3	1.7	1.2	0.1	−1.7
France					
Household consumption	1.7	1.5	0.8	0.8	0.3
Changes in inventories	0.0	0.2	−0.8	−0.6	−1.4
Investment	4.7	2.1	−0.4	−1.8	−3.0
Sweden					
Household consumption	0.7	−0.1	0.6	−0.7	−1.9
Changes in inventories	0.2	0.2	−1.6	1.1	−0.3
Investment	3.4	2.4	−1.7	−4.0	−5.4

Source: OECD national accounts.

The contribution of an expenditure C to the fluctuation of the GDP growth variation Y is equal to: $100\,(C_t - C_{t-1})/Y_{t-1}$

rose moderately in France and the United States and quite sharply in Sweden. This allows us to conclude that the excessive debt of households and the readjustment of their balance sheets played an important role, especially in the Swedish recession. By contrast, Germany shows neither an excess of indebtedness nor a rise in the savings rate during the recession, and in the United States, Japan, and France, the readjustment of household balance sheets probably played only a modest role.

As we have seen above, in strictly accounting terms, capital formation (investments and stock fluctuations) played a major role in the recession. We shall thus turn to the situation and behavior of businesses during this period (see Table 10.4). During the recessions of 1974–75 and 1980–82, the proportion of company profits in the value added declined. This phenomenon of reduced profit had resulted from the sluggishness of employment and the indexing of wages to prices, so that the decline in terms of exchange linked to the oil shocks, along with the slowdown in productivity gains, was above all reflected in a deduction from company incomes.

Table 10.3

Household Indicators of Indebtedness and Rate of Saving

	1974	1980	1990	1992
Interest payments/income (in %)				
United States	2.3	2.4	2.7	2.4
Japan	3.7	4.5	6.1	5.8
Germany	1.1	1.4	1.3	1.5
France	3.0	4.0	5.9	5.6
Sweden	6.1	10.5	15.6	12.8
	1990	**1991**	**1992**	**1993**
Rate of saving (in %)				
United States	4.3	5.1	5.2	4.6
Japan	14.1	15.1	15.0	14.7
Germany	13.8	12.7	12.9	12.3
France	12.5	13.2	13.7	13.8
Sweden	−0.6	3.1	7.7	7.9

Source: OECD.

In 1990–93, profit margins showed a slight decline in the United States and Japan, but they improved in France and Sweden. As a result, at the time when production was decreasing, the real wage bill was sharply reduced, contrary to what had occurred in the earlier recessions. In macroeconomic terms, the labor market became more flexible, especially in France and Sweden, where the share of profits increased during the 1990–93 recession. In the short term, the flexibility of the wage bill includes the risk of an intensifying of the recession because it can lead to a drop in consumption; a first buffer was the possibility of a drop in the savings rate, but as we have seen, it hardly played a role. A second buffer was the Welfare State, which slowed the drop in household revenues by increasing its services, and the recession increased budget deficits in all five countries, notably in France, where it went from 1.6 percent of the GDP in 1990 to 6 percent in 1993. In Sweden, the fluctuation was even more severe: in 1990, there was a surplus representing 4.2 percent of the GDP, and in 1993, a deficit totaling 13.4 percent of the GDP, which reflects both the gravity of the recession and the importance of automatic functions linked to the Welfare State.

The hypothesis of excessive debt among companies in the 1980s is not generally confirmed by the data of Table 10.4: in Germany, Japan, and France, the ratio of interest payments to the gross operating surplus was lower in 1990 than at the beginning of previous recessions. Given the fact that the level of real interest rates was much higher in 1990 than during

Table 10.4

Companies' Profitability and Interest Fees

	1990	1991	1992	1993
Share of profits in company value added (in %)				
United States	33.5	33.1	33.1	33.1
Japan	32.0	31.8	31.2	30.6
Germany	37.1	37.7	37.5	37.5
France	37.6	37.9	38.3	38.3
Sweden	27.4	28.7	31.0	33.7
	1974	**1980**	**1990**	**1992**
Share of interest payments in gross operating surpluses (in %)				
United States	29.8	38.3	38.8	32.7
Japan	48.3	45.0	38.0	37.0
Germany	27.6	25.3	19.4	25.5
France	33.5	35.9	29.8	34.7
Sweden	30.6	35.1	49.1	46.9

Source: OECD.

the earlier recessions, this shows that in these three countries, companies got out of debt during the 1980s, which can be related to the reconstitution of profits. Only in Sweden can a sharp rise in company indebtedness be observed.

The sharp drop in capital formation in Germany and France thus cannot be explained by either a decline in profitability or an excess of company debt. Rather, it is necessary to invoke the decline in demand or the high level of interest rates. To reach a clear conclusion, it would be necessary to have full adjustments of the investment functions. The equations tested on previous decades mostly show that company investment was above all influenced by demand or profits and that the influence of the interest rate was minor or nonexistent. It is possible, however, that the financial transformations of the 1980s increased the role of the interest rate. For one thing, they equaled or surpassed the rates of growth, whereas they had previously been much lower than them, and the risks of insolvency linked to debt accumulation thus increased. For another thing, securitization increased the possibilities of a trade-off between physical capital and financial investments, and this may have led companies to make their choices in function of not only the profitability of physical capital but also the gap between the interest rate and profitability.

One particular feature of the French economic situation that has been little studied is the massive role played in 1992–93 by destocking, which was much greater than in the past in France and in the recent situation of the other countries. In the very short term, destocking can be a channel for transmitting the recession between sectors—businesses and industries downstream interrupt their orders to sectors upstream and simply satisfy their demand with existing stocks. The data from the quarterly accounts show that this phenomenon took on an exceptional dimension in France between summer 1992 and spring 1993. It coincided with a sharp drop in investment and a fundamental change in the capital account of the companies, which had always needed financing but since 1992 had shown a capacity for financing in spite of the recession. This new situation visibly resulted from voluntary decisions—the cutback in employment in order to lower the wage bill, the decline in investment, the reduction of supplies. This abrupt change can be related to the considerable gap between high rates of interest and a low or negative growth since 1990, which encouraged agents to interrupt their recourse to borrowing by reducing their costs and capital formation.

The Role of Monetary Variables

The interest and exchange rates can be influenced but not totally controlled by monetary authorities. On the monetary markets, the central banks have the means to provide considerable quantities of liquid assets, but their efforts may be countered by international capital movements, especially under a regime of fixed exchange or managed float. The authorities can also influence exchange rates, but only indirectly, because capital exchanges represent much greater sums than hard-currency reserves.

As we have already seen, the interest rate clearly affects domestic spending. Between 1990 and 1993, they followed opposing trajectories: the United States and Japan lowered the rates in order to fight against the recession, while in Europe they remained high. On the one hand, the Bundesbank implemented a restrictive policy to counter the recession. France and Sweden, already undergoing recession and on the verge of deflation, maintained high rates in order to protect the parity of their currency relative to the mark, which accentuated the recession. Thus, France and Sweden practiced countercyclical monetary policies.

Exchange rates are likely to affect export-market shares on the condition that their fluctuations are too great to be offset by inflation differentials. Three countries have experienced considerable fluctuations in their exchange rates, beginning with the yen, which underwent a sharp increase in value from 1986 on, thus reducing price competitiveness in Japan. Between 1974 and 1986, Japanese growth, which remained vigorous, basically relied on the rise in exports and increased market shares, but this thrust disappeared by the end of the 1980s. Germany has also suffered losses in market shares since 1990; these were initially related to the demand crisis resulting from reunification, which reduced the exportable surplus in 1990 and 1991. Subsequently, Germany continued to lose market shares despite the return to calm in 1992–93, but the increased value of the mark and the rise in wages sharply decreased competitiveness through industrial costs. Following the EMS crisis, Sweden underwent a sharp depreciation of its currency in 1993, which permitted an increase in its market share, but these gains did not compensate for the depression of domestic demand related to excessive debt and the rise in interest rates.

The Lessons of Change

The 1990–93 recession shows that monopolistic regulation procedures were partly maintained and partly transformed. In the United States and Germany, short-term dynamics remained similar to those of the past. In the United States, a slight rise in inflation was followed by monetary restrictions, then by a moderate recession because of expansive policies; the economic situation was controlled by the authorities' countercyclical measures, which succeeded in smoothing over the fluctuations. West Germany was subject to a violent shock from exogenous demand, which required a response in the form of very restrictive policies.

In France, Sweden, and Japan, on the other hand, the recession offered atypical features relative to the past. In France, these stemmed above all from the change in the objective of macroeconomic policies, which were no longer aimed chiefly at stabilizing economic activity but at maintaining parity relative to the mark. In Japan and Sweden, the deregulation of the financial systems increased the instability of the economic situation and weakened the effectiveness of macroeconomic policies. It favored the development of a speculative bubble, excessive debt, and the accumulation of risky debts, while the opening of international capital movements made it more difficult to control exchange rates. This situation is particularly clear in the case of Japan, which had previous modulated the regulation of capital entries and exits in order to make the exchange rate fluctuate in the direction sought by the authorities.

The Evolution of International Regulation

The Impossibility of Fixed Exchanges and the Drawbacks of Floating

The evolution of the exchange rates since the 1970s shows that it is nearly impossible to maintain a fixed exchange regime. At least these are the lessons that can be drawn from the collapse of the Bretton Woods system in

1973 and the breakup of the European Monetary System (EMS) in 1992–93. But experience also shows that fluctuation is not very satisfying.

The collapse of the monetary system established in 1944 has been the subject of many analyses, and these have yielded several widely accepted conclusions on several points. The abandoning of gold as international currency in 1971 resulted from the fact that there was no reason for the world money supply in gold, which depended on world gold production, to correspond to the needs of the central banks' reserves at a given price level. It follows that instruments of liquidity such as the currencies of the major countries or monetary units created by international agreement can be added to gold and reduce its role in international liquid assets. The demonetarization of gold does not imply the floating of currencies because these can theoretically be stabilized relative to a key hard currency or a basket of currencies.

The abandoning of the fixed-exchange regime in 1973 is an illustration of Mundell's Triangle, according to which it is impossible to reconcile the three principles of fixed exchanges, strong international mobility of capital, and autonomy of monetary policies, even if it is necessary to find a compromise among them. In the Bretton Woods system, none of these principles was completely applied. Exchanges were fixed, but adjustable; after the war, exchange markets were gradually reestablished, but many countries monitored short-term capital movements. Fordism implied active policies for stabilizing the domestic economic situation, but countries with persistent foreign deficits were forced to adopt restrictive policies in order to reconstitute their exchange reserves because capital movements were limited. This compromise was called into question by both the increase in international capital mobility and the fact that the major powers had adopted different policies during the first phase of the crisis. The rapid expansion of trade in goods and, more important, the growing internationalization of businesses and banks greatly contributed to the massive increase in capital exchanges. The erosion of Fordism was reflected first of all in an acceleration of inflation, which West Germany vigorously countered with positive real interest rates and the increased value of the mark, while the United States and several European countries accepted negative real interest rates and the depreciation of their currency (see Table 10.5 and Figures 8.1–8.4, pages 159, 162, 164). In addition, the asymmetries of the Bretton Woods system were less and less accepted. On the one hand, this system allowed the United States to finance foreign deficits by the creation of international liquid assets that other central banks were forced to absorb when they intervened to stabilize their currencies in relation to the dollar; this situation was less and less accepted by the central bank of Germany, which feared the inflationary effect of an increase in its hard-currency reserves. On the other hand,

Table 10.5

Growth and Monetary Variables (1973-1993)

	1973-1979	1979-1983	1983-1989	1989-1993
GNP (annual rate of growth)				
OECD	2.3	1.4	3.6	1.7
United States	2.5	1.0	3.9	1.7
Germany	2.4	0.5	2.6	2.9
France	2.8	1.5	2.8	0.8
Real interest rate (annual averages)				
United States	−0.2	3.8	4.4	2.0
Germany	0.9	4.8	3.0	4.8
France	−1.3	2.4	4.3	6.8
Effective exchange rate (annual average rate of growth)				
United States	−1.0	4.5	−5.2	0.5
Germany	4.8	2.2	2.5	3.6
France	−1.4	−4.7	0.3	3.2

Source: OECD.

since the different countries fixed the parity of their currencies in dollars, the United States could not, within the Bretton Woods system, make its exchange rates vary. Before 1971–73, the dollar was clearly overvalued, with the result that the United States' share of the market declined. After the collapse of the Bretton Woods system, the dollar depreciated in the long term, and the United States' market share practically ceased to decline.

The experience of floating currencies from 1973 on led to many disappointments. Partisans of flexible exchanges had argued that floating ensured the equilibrium of the balances of payments and the autonomy of monetary policies. In the long term, to be sure, fluctuations in the exchange rate had the effects on trade flows that had been announced by the theory. In the short term, however, exchange rates depend above all on capital movements set off by the operators' expectations; since these are self-realizing, there is no reason for the exchange markets to stabilize themselves, and great fluctuations in the exchange rates have been observed, far in excess of the "fundamentals." It is impossible for the central banks to determine their economic policy solely in function of domestic objectives, without taking parity into account. They must intervene frequently on the exchange markets in order to even out the rates.

In addition, if the exchange rate is affected by persistent movements that distance it from the value corresponding to the fundamentals, the authorities are forced to apply monetary and even budgetary policy to the stabilization of the exchange rate. Floating entails the risk of continued depreciation over the long term when wages are totally indexed to prices (see chapter 4). On the other hand, if wages do not follow prices, and if monetary policy is not too expansive, the inflationary effects of deflation remain limited, and it is possible that the depreciation of the exchange rate may be followed by a recovery. Nonetheless, in a floating regime, given the abundance of capital movements and the volatility of expectations, it is very difficult to bring the exchange rate to an adequate level and stabilize it, especially since floating does not eliminate the constraints that weigh on economic policies.

At the end of the 1970s, when the disadvantages of flexible exchanges had become apparent, the European countries set up the European Money System. This was designed to eliminate the effects of asymmetry, since official parities were to be determined in an accounting unit created for that purpose, the ECU. In addition, it was anticipated that when a bilateral exchange rate attained the limits of the margins of fluctuation, the central banks of the two currencies, strong and weak, would intervene. It turned out, however, that an asymmetry persisted in favor of the mark. Periods of heavy uncertainties, which were frequent during the crises, led operators to fix themselves on refuge currencies, including the mark. In the case of such behaviors, the mark rose in relation to other European currencies, and Germany's partners were forced to intervene on the exchange markets and borrow hard currencies.

The EMS grew stronger during the 1980s; parity readjustments were less and less frequent, and an increasing number of currencies participated. But this apparent success was called into question during the 1990s. On the one hand, following the crisis of autumn 1990, the range of fluctuations was expanded to such an extent that it was no longer possible to characterize the EMS as a fixed exchange system. On the other hand, it became clear that for Germany's partners, the EMS had a deflationary bias.

Several causes can be cited for the European monetary crisis of 1992. The first stems from the asymmetry of the EMS, which means that the interest rate of the European countries depends on Germany's monetary policy because the mark is the key currency of the system. The shock of unification prompted the Bundesbank to raise its rate sharply, which led the other European countries to apply restrictive monetary policies at a time when a slowdown in the economic situation was already under way. Germany's partners reacted differently. In the United Kingdom, the liberalization of the financial systems had led to massive indebtedness among economic agents and the accumulation of risky debts. The bursting of the speculative bubble had led to a violent recession in 1991–92; it became essential to lower the interest rate rapidly in order to help the agents put their balance sheets back in order and, as a result, permit the pound to be depreciated. In Italy and Spain, less advanced countries that were in the process of catching up, the "Balassa effect"—which implies that such countries should have an above-average rate of inflation—came into play, and the deterioration of price competitiveness could only be offset by a depreciation of the exchange rate.

France had a low inflation rate and, for the first time, foreign trade surpluses, while its unemployment rate was higher than the OECD average. These conditions called for implementing restrictive monetary policies and letting the mark–franc parity increase, but these measures were not applied, and France underwent the most serious recession of the postwar period. The 1992–93 choices continued the economic policy options adopted in 1982–83, thus marking a break in the evolution of the French economy. Between 1945 and 1983, France maintained accommodating monetary policies and experienced rates of inflation and growth that were higher than those of the OECD average. Since 1983, it has maintained very restrictive monetary policies (see Table 10.5) and has one of the lowest inflation rates in the world, lower growth than that of the OECD, and particularly high unemployment rates. During 1983 and 1986, the EMS served as an anchor for restrictive policies that allowed the rate of profit and the rate of accumulation to be raised, but during the 1990s, such a policy was no longer justified because of the high level of profitability. In France, the fixed mark–franc parity has been a major factor in the continuation of the crisis.

The fact that neither fixed nor floating exchanges are truly satisfactory solutions offers a powerful argument in favor of measures aimed at reducing the international mobility of capital. Proposals for taxing capital movements have been made, but such a solution is only viable if all countries adopt it, and this, for the moment, is a utopian goal. The European countries have chosen to set up a single European currency, which would eliminate the problem of exchange rates. However, this currency must not lead to the same deflationary bias as the EMS. Unfortunately, as we shall see in the following section of this chapter, the Treaty of Maastricht does not provide such a guarantee.

International Regulation Through Debt

When the most developed countries undergo a phase of slump or stagnation, it is logical that their capital is invested in regions that are less developed but which have potential for rapid growth; this process encourages development and helps to stabilize the world economic situation. This kind of international regulation has certain weaknesses, however, as shown by the crisis of the developing countries that erupted in 1982.

During the 1970s, the surpluses of the OPEC countries and the expansive monetary policy of the United States sharply increased the total of liquid

Table 10.6

Debt/Exports Ratios in Value (%)

	1972	1974	1977	1978	1980
All developing countries	100	69	92	104	89
Main borrowers	133	89	117	129	102
Latin America	98	75	117	135	104

Source: World Bank, debt tables.

assets in dollars. These were recycled by certain Eurobanks, which granted considerable credits to developing countries that seemed to have good prospects for growth. The Eurocredits constituted an innovation in financing, for the developing countries had previously been financed by public credits at low rates; as a result, the consequences of the Eurocredits were little known, and their spread resulted in a major financial crisis.

The causes of this crisis have been the subject of much debate, but as Krueger (1987) indicates and the World Bank data demonstrates, it seems that until 1978 the borrower countries were not excessively indebted (see Table 10.6).

Indeed, the debt–exports ratio did not really deteriorate between 1972 and 1980, even for the largest debtors. The main reason for this is that during the 1970s, raw materials prices rose very sharply, with the result that exports in value showed a dramatic increase; the American real interest rate, which was crucial for the Eurocredits, was far lower than that of inflation on the basic goods markets. In addition, the investment rates of the developing countries rose in the 1970s, which dispels the idea that the loans were systematically wasted. In reality, the financial crisis of the developing countries was the result of the change in monetary regime around 1980—the nominal interest rates rose sharply, and the rise in raw materials prices was followed by a drop.

This analysis might suggest that the financial crisis of the developing countries was no more than an accident related to transitory factors such as the adjustment to deflation on the part of banks and debtor countries. Unfortunately, Mexico underwent a new financial crisis in 1994–95, which cast doubt on the stability of the emerging markets. After the difficulties caused by the spread of banking Eurocredits during the 1980s, the developing countries had managed to improve their financial situation, at a cost of drastic austerity plans and liberalization measures. By the end of the 1980s, these policies allowed them to amass funds by issuing securities. But this kind of loan is even more unstable than bank credits because the funds that are loaned can be quickly withdrawn. The

present state of monetary regulations increases this instability. The floating of most currencies encourages speculative investments, and in addition, the interest rates of the leading powers are quite variable following
the liberalization policies that succeeded in making monetary policy
practically the exclusive tool for adjusting the economic situation. Thus,
on the world level, there are no stable financing procedures with the
exception of direct international investments.

European Integration and the New Accumulation Regime

To conclude this examination of the transformations that have affected
the industrialized countries since the 1970s, two major changes must be
taken into account on the specifically European level. First of all, a new
logic in the building of the European Community was adopted with the
signing of the Single Act in 1986 and the prospects of Monetary Union.
Second, the acceleration of changes in the countries of the East as of late
1989 introduced a major break; this will be examined separately because
of its importance.

Until the mid-1970s, the European Community had been set up
through a process of harmonization and structuring of the European
zone through common policies. But as of this period, and notwithstanding certain advances, European integration seemed to be blocked. The
signing of the Single Act in 1986 thus opened a new perspective. The
recourse to the market, conceived as a "European-style supply-side policy," seemed to be a magic solution for surmounting obstacles to European integration. But the complete liberalization of capital movements,
which was one of its components, called into question the EMS and imposed a change in monetary regimes. The choice of the single currency
adopted in Maastricht in 1991 raised formidable problems, and the unre-
alistic nature of its underlying scenario became clear with the monetary
crises of 1992 and 1993.

These changes on the Community level mark the beginning of a mode
of regulation that is partly supranational, and they are leading to a profound transformation of the institutional forms and national modes of
regulation. After the shift from the flexible EMS to the rigid EMS, three
stages may be distinguished.

Single Market: The Perverse Effects of Increased Competititon

The abolition of nontariff barriers, the broadening of the markets, the
exploitation of economies of scale, and the reinforcement of competition
were, theoretically, supposed to encourage a drop in costs and prices as
well as an increase in the competitiveness of the European economies.

The liberalization of capital movements was supposed to improve the means of financing and allow a decrease in interest rates. In the medium term, increased growth and marked creation of jobs were expected. But these mechanisms have hardly had such a pronounced impact, and many perverse effects have emerged.

A certain number of factors have limited the play of competition and returns to scale. The simple abolition of nontariff barriers does not suffice to create a single market. National markets continue to be marked by sharp particularities that structure private behaviors, whether in terms of industrial relations, the funding of social security, the organization of the education and training system, or the nature of relations between banks and businesses. In a certain way, the real barriers continue to exist. The search for optimal scale and the pressure of competition lead to concentration trends that may, in the long run, bring back monopoly rents and halt the dynamic of innovation.

All the expected advantages stem from cost reductions and restructuring spurred by the play of the market. The principle of "mutual recognition," based not on the harmonization of national regulations but on their confrontation and competition, allows certain obstacles to be overcome but runs the risk of favoring the least constraining regulations. In the case of the flexibility of labor, a regressive logic has been privileged in terms of the reduction of personnel and pressure on wages in function of the constraints exercised by international competition and the opportunities for relocation offered by the Single Market. The improvement of labor-force training and the search for greater versatility and negotiated involvement of employees, which are characteristic of an offensive kind of labor flexibility, are preoccupations reflected in official discourse, including those of the conservative governments and the White Paper on Europe. In practice, however, they are hardly being implemented with the exception of Germany.

Government interventions, which are closely monitored by the European Commission, are considered factors that can distort competition. Only certain public aid is authorized—support for R&D or regional development and, more generally, policies aimed at improving the business environment. Such a position ignores the particular institutional features that determine the role of the State and the forms of public intervention in each country. France does not enjoy the quality of bank–business relations that permit successful industrial restructuring in Germany. Nor can it rely on the flexibility and dynamism of SME networks as in Northern Italy. On the other hand, France's State apparatus and mixed-economy tradition constitute advantages that should be accepted without seeking to cast all the European countries in the same institutional mold.

The restrictions on national government interventions have not been adequately compensated for by an expansion of Community interventions. The technological programs have not received new impetus and remain very limited financially. Outside of a few categories where a single operator has been set up (aeronautics, space), the Community's shortcomings are particularly flagrant in the high-tech sectors. The reform of the structural funds intended for less developed regions allowed these to be doubled in real terms between 1987 and 1993, but they still represent only 0.3 percent of the GDP and suffer from a multiplicity of participants and a lack of coordination that compromises their effectiveness.

The absence of a Community trade policy is one of the most pressing problems. The Community has at its disposal a certain number of tools (antidumping and antisubsidy procedures, among others) that are used rarely or with extreme slowness. The opening of public markets and the liberalization of services are carried out unilaterally, without a counterpart among the non-European partners. In sectors where there were import quotas on the national level, the definition of a policy on the European scale proves to be difficult, as seen in the case of the automobile. In the GATT negotiations, the EEC appeared in a position of weakness and allowed itself to be cornered in the handling of its bilateral relations with the United States.

The liberalization of capital movements seems to be a decision with heavy consequences. The instability of the financial sphere has increased; in the face of risks of capital flight, taxation on savings income has been lowered, which has reduced budgetary resources and accentuated the inegalitarian nature of the growth pattern. The financial markets have become the main, if not the only, reference for judging the validity of economic policy, yet their vision of the economic and social reality is only partial, subject to change, and often erroneous. The result is a strengthening of the orthodox wing of economic policy.

The Prospects for Monetary Union and Its Contradictions

By depriving monetary authorities of all possibility of modifying inter-European parities and by setting up a European central bank, the shift to a single currency changes the nature of the monetary constraint and modifies the growth pattern more profoundly than the creation of the Single Market.

The choice of a European central bank that is independent of the political power and has price stability as its primary goal has significant implications. The underlying idea that monetary policy is the best means of controlling inflation has not really been demonstrated to be correct. The separation of monetary policy from other aspects of economic policy and, in particular, national budgetary policies will accentuate problems of coordination and may lead to a lack of coherence. The choices that have been made are also disturbing in terms of democratic principles insofar as supranational authority has no clearly established legitimacy in Europe.

The advantages of the single currency cannot be ignored. The disappearance of the premium for exchange risks will permit a lowering of interest rates, and the variability of exchange rates between European currencies will be eliminated. Likewise, transaction costs resulting from the use of different hard currencies will disappear. Like any system of fixed exchanges, the Monetary Union will enjoy greater macroeconomic stability in case of shocks. And external financing will be facilitated, at least with respect to its intra-Community component. The external constraint will thus be reduced in the short term, although problems of solvency and dependence will remain in the medium term.

The abandoning of any modification of exchange between European currencies will, however, constitute a major problem for carrying out the real adjustments that will be confronting European countries. One kind of adjustment will stem from increased economic integration. In the countries of the periphery, which are less advanced and which specialize in mass-market goods, high rates of investment and productivity gains that are differentiated by sector will favor continued inflationary pressures that will lead to an increase in real exchange rates. In the countries of the center, where competition is more dependent on product differentiation, the improvement of nonprice competitiveness will permit greater room for maneuvering. A second kind of real adjustment will be related to the existence of specific shocks that will continue because of the survival of strong national characteristics and the accentuation of the process of sectoral specialization.

In the face of these adjustments, modifications of real parities can only occur through flexibility of relative prices, wages, and employment. Such a development is disturbing insofar as it will imply a modification of the wage relation in the direction of a regressive flexibility of work that will accentuate the trends already under way with the Single Market. There are also perverse effects stemming from the competitive deflation strategy, which operates very slowly, is very costly in terms of the rise in unemployment, and runs out once the rate of inflation has reached a certain threshold. The strengthening of competitiveness by product quality and diversity will allow these constraints to be diminished, but only in the countries of the center and in the medium/long term.

The recourse to the flexibility of relative prices will not be adequate for the real adjustments that the European countries will have to face. Institutional changes will only manifest themselves gradually in the dynamic of wages and employment. The American case shows that the growth of employment is always more rapid in certain states than others. Flexibility of employment and wages does not allow states affected by negative shocks to reestablish competitiveness and maintain employment. Two mechanisms for reestablishing equilibrium, present in the American case but not in the European one, intervene: the geographical mobility of the labor force, which limits imbalances in local unemployment rates, and federal budgetary transfers (Eichengreen 1990; Blanchard and Katz 1992).

Sharp disequilibria will thus emerge among European regions, either in the form of trade deficits, which will eventually pose problems of solvency and dependency, or in the form of stagnant growth, rising un-employment, and increased income disparities among regions. Interregional labor-force mobility will only be able to attenuate these imbalances to a limited extent because of persistently strong linguistic, cultural, and social barriers.

In principle, budgetary policies would seem to offer certain possibilities for restoring equilibrium. In a regime of fixed exchanges and capital mobility, national budgetary policies will enjoy greater effectiveness. The constraints weighing on budgetary policies will also be attenuated within the framework of the Monetary Union, notably because of the lessening of the external constraint in intra-Community trade. Conversely, several factors will limit the room for maneuvering in terms of budgetary policies—the increasing openness of national markets will diminish their effectiveness; and downward competition will affect European tax systems, as has already been the case since the late 1980s. Even more serious, is the fact that the generalized fear concerning excessive levels of public debt will now have a concrete focus on keeping budget deficits within very tight limits set by the Stability Pact of 1997. Overall, the national budgetary policies will not be able to respond to regional imbalances in the face of shocks and structural adjustments.

Because of its extremely limited size relative to national budgets and the GDP, the Community budget will also have a very limited impact. Community interventions will play only a reduced role of redistribution between regions, unlike the federal systems where the normal interchange between public revenues and expenditures serves to restore equilibrium. The degree of redistribution among the regions of federal states, calculated in relation to primary revenues, may be estimated around 30 percent.

In sum, the profound transformations that will mark the creation of the Monetary Union will hardly permit the establishment of a sufficiently stable growth pattern in Europe. The components of national regulations (ways of fixing wages, forms of social protection, etc.) will remain quite heterogeneous. National economic policies will be subject to constraints, and regional imbalances will increase. The wage regime will be one of the main factors of adjustment in the direction of regressive labor flexibility, and the economic context will hardly be favorable to growth.

At the beginning of the transition, however, these prospects were affected by two sets of factors:

- the shock of German reunification and the severity of the 1991–93 recession, which made the criteria of the Treaty of Maastricht particularly constraining;
- the fall of the Berlin Wall and the transition of the Eastern-bloc countries to the market economy, which poses the problem of the enlargement of the European Union in radically new terms.

The transition period 1992–98 toward a single currency proved especially costly in terms of slow growth and mounting unemployment in a majority of European countries. Yet a large number of countries managed in the end to defy initial predictions and comply with the convergence criteria of Maastricht. That success was not least due to the Southern European countries using these constraints to attack the corporatist and archaic structures of their economies which had handicapped them for so long. A large monetary union, comprising Italy, Spain, and Portugal, thus became possible. With this decision, made in early May 1998, several scenarios can be envisaged for the near future.

Scenarios for European Integration

Federal Utopia

In spite of its utopian nature, the federal scenario deserves to be examined because it corresponds in a certain way to the realization of the Single Currency. As a permanent regime, the creation of a federal budget would indeed allow the effects of asymmetrical shocks and regional imbalances generated by heightened competition within a unified monetary space to be countered. In the short term, it would facilitate the implementation of a program for European recovery. Wages and employment would not be the only variables of adjustment, and the recourse to regressive labor flexibility would no longer be the rule. The heterogeneity of wage relations would slowly be reduced. The existence of increased budgetary means on the federal level might make it easier to strengthen structural policies in the areas of research, industry, and major infrastructures. The gradual affirmation of a European identity would also help to define a more offensive trade policy.

This scenario has a certain coherence, but it remains very unlikely in the present context. For lack of a sufficiently strong feeling of involvement, the richest European countries are not ready to assume the considerable transfers that would be involved. Certain member states, such as the United Kingdom and the Scandinavian countries, are extremely hostile to a federal vision. Without going this far, many other countries are guarded about setting up supranational political bodies that would infringe considerably on national prerogatives. And the creation of such a European bloc would hardly permit the establishment of balanced ties with the countries of Eastern Europe hoping to join the European Union. Their integration within a federal framework would clearly be untenable, even ten years from now, and their resulting feeling of exclusion could produce very destabilizing effects.

A Powerless Europe

In contrast to the first scenario, there exist also strong tendencies which, if allowed to prevail, may render Europe powerless. Important institutional reforms have yet to be realized, in particular those that would allow a better balanced functioning of Monetary Union, as well as those that would provide more favorable conditions for the integration of Central European countries with whom negotiations concerning their eventual inclusion in the European Union have already started (i.e., Hungary, Poland, Czech Republic, Estonia, and Slovenia.) Neither of these reforms seems imminent in the current political climate. The Euro Council put in place in 1997 only has an "informal" advisory function, not enough to give democratic legitimacy to monetary policy that will remain under sole control of the technocrats at the European Central Bank. No effective coordination will thus be possible between national budgetary policies and the supranational monetary policy. Those factors slowing growth and exacerbating inequalities will continue to make their weight felt in the Euro zone. They may even be make worse by an excessively restrictive monetary policy, one solely oriented toward the fight against inflation, and an overvalued Euro. Only a few initiatives on the European level will be taken to enhance the reequilibrating role of structural policies (research policy, technological cooperation, regional policy). Under those conditions, underlying tensions may accumulate to such a point that certain observers are today tempted to predict the failure of the Euro project.

The entry of the Central European countries into the Union will in such a context only serve to intensify the problems. The political paralysis on the European level is likely to become even more pronounced. The still existing community-wide policies, such as the common agricultural policy and the structural funds, face long-term decline. Europe will then simply revert to becoming a free-trade area that is submerged into an even larger North Atlantic Free Trade Area without preserving any autonomous space. We can imagine under these circumstances a sort of

Anglo-Saxon Europe, or even more likely an Anglo-German Europe. The latter idea corresponds after all to the ancient preferences of the United Kingdom, as well as the interests of Germany, which will have a vast zone of influence in Eastern and Central Europe.

A Europe of Recovery

We can also easily imagine a rosier scenario. The practices of the Euro Council could manage to evolve over time into a kind of supranational economic government endowed with greater power. Limited forms of budgetary federalism are progressively introduced, be it in the guise of a fiscal insurance system (meaning an automatic stabilization mechanism in favor of countries affected by negative shocks) or certain taxes particularly well suited for collection on the Europe-wide level, such as those on income from savings or effluent taxes concerning CO_2 emissions. The acceptance of a small deficit for the community budget (around 1 percent of the GDP) and its financing through issue of Euro–denominated bonds would be a first step in this direction. The social dimension of the European Union, moving beyond general declarations on employment, could gain greater weight on the basis of common standards for minimum wages and income–maintenance allowances. Parallel to that, European–wide collective bargaining may be given gradually more impetus. Renewing a tradition dating to the first steps in the postwar construction of a united Europe, structural policies could be relaunched. A more pragmatic vision with regard to competition policy would be adopted to give more space for national specificities.

Such proposals have a certain level of support in France, but are much less widespread in other European countries, which remain strongly attached to a more conservative free-market tradition. Under these circumstances it is hard to see how a scenario such as the one described here could be realized, except perhaps in response to a salutary shock that may come about with the next business cycle downturn or with a convergence of social movements on the European level.

The Impact of Changes in the Countries of Eastern Europe

At the same time that the pace of European economic and monetary integration was changing, a new situation emerged with the acceleration of transformations in the Eastern countries at the end of 1989. German reunification and the transition of the countries of Eastern Europe and the former USSR toward market-economy systems profoundly modified the European dynamic and the very logic of Community integration.

The evolution of these countries, and especially those of the ex–Soviet

Union, is one of the major unknowns for the coming years. Structural reforms and the transition to a market economy have been accompanied by disruption and drops in production. It is only in the medium term that an upturn in productivity, the development of private activities, and the contribution of capital from the West should allow a resumption of growth. The mechanisms of such a recovery remain uncertain, however, and a clear distinction should be made among several cases: East Germany involved in a process of unification with West Germany; the Visegrad countries (Hungary, Poland, ex-Czechoslovakia), where the recovery is under way; the Balkan countries, which are much less advanced; and the countries of the ex-Soviet Union, where the uncertainties and problems to be resolved are the greatest.

The New Integration of the Eastern Countries into the World Economy

With their gradual integration into the world economy, the countries of Eastern Europe have completely redefined the organization of their commercial exchanges as well as the specialization of their productive system. From 1988 to 1992, exports toward the OECD increased an average of 15 percent a year, while imports from the OECD increased 23 percent per year. This commercial redeployment was particularly significant in relation to the European Community, which absorbed more than half the exports from the Eastern European countries in 1984. Rather logically, these exports have mainly increased in sectors where the Eastern countries had developed comparative advantages during the 1970s and 1980s—basic manufactured goods (iron and steel industry, building materials, glass) and industries relying on low-skilled labor (clothing manufacture and leather goods). As a result, such exports remain situated in sensitive sectors where access to the Community market is controlled, despite the elimination of a large number of restrictions since 1990. In a small number of sectors (textiles and leather goods), they also compete with the countries of North Africa (Lemoine 1995).

In spite of major inertia, the evolution of industrial exports increasingly tends to differentiate the countries of Central Europe from those of the Balkans. The first group is beginning to develop specializations in new sectors (mechanical engineering and electrical industries, transport materials) in conjunction with European firms' relocation operations and inflows of direct investments. The reduction of their cost advantages relative to the countries of the second group is pushing them to promote better-quality goods and develop intra-industrial exchanges in the context of integration into multinational networks.

Prospects of membership in the European Union would encourage such developments, but apart from questions of an institutional or legal nature, this membership presents two major problems: the costs of expanding the common agricultural policy and the costs of access to the structural aid funds for less developed regions. The membership process will be lengthy, and transitions suited to the variety of situations must be found.

Inflows of private capital have turned out to be modest and particularly hesitant. Fears that the Eastern countries would take the place of developing countries in terms of capital transfers or that interest rates would rise because of an excessive drain on savings have hardly been founded. From 1990 to 1994, the Eastern European countries received some 13 billion dollars in direct foreign investments, which amounts to an annual flow of about 2 percent of the direct investments of the OECD countries and about 10 percent of the total net direct investments received by all the developing countries. These flows were concentrated in two countries—Hungary and, to a lesser extent, the Czech Republic where, relative to the number of inhabitants, they represented considerable contributions (between $199 and $150 per inhabitant, sums that are comparable to Portugal).

The countries of the former Soviet Union constitute a very different case. For many of the republics, foreign trade represented over 50 percent of the national income. The breakdown of these very close trade relations led to a decline in intra-CIS (Community of Independent States) trade of nearly 50 percent in 1991–92 and contributed to the drop in production in the whole of the CIS (Gros 1993). Exports outside the zone remain largely dominated by raw materials and energy and constituted the only dynamic demand factor between 1993 and 1995. Redeployment toward the European countries has been more limited than for the East European countries. In terms of capital flows, the basic component of external financing has remained in arrears on the principal and finance charges on the debt ($45 billion in combined flows between 1992 and 1994 for the Federation of Russia). Because of the major uncertainties that persist, direct foreign investments amounted to less than $4 billion during the same period.

The Impact of German Reunification

Economic and monetary unification with West Germany offered East Germany a shock therapy. Initially, the direct effects of reunification resembled a Keynesian recovery. The additional demand coming from the East German market was due to the reevaluation of wages and social services and massive transfers to local communities (100 billion marks in 1990 and an average of 5 percent of the GDP from 1991 to 1994).

But the initial desire to finance unification through borrowing caused a sharp rise in the interest rates, especially since the Bundesbank used this weapon to limit inflationary pressures. The very high level of the interest rate slowed growth and led to a revaluation of the mark and currencies belonging to the EMS. Rising taxes and the reduction of certain spending as of 1991 increased the downward trend and plunged West Germany into a severe recession in 1992, from which it only emerged in 1994, mainly because of renewed exports. In a context of considerable concessions on the part of German wage-earners, the easing up of inflation allowed a slow, prudent reduction of short-term interest rates, which were brought down to 4.5 percent in 1995.

Other equally fundamental choices were also called into question. The initial decision to exchange the Eastern mark with a Western mark and the complete and immediate opening of the East German market to goods from the West led to the collapse of the East German economy. In one year, industrial production plunged 50 percent, and by early 1991, unemployment hit 800,000 people, plus over 2 million people who were partially unemployed. Privatization by the Treuhandanstadt had excessively favored the most immediately profitable units to the detriment of a prior stabilization of the largest number of companies. Modernization of infrastructures was not sufficiently recognized as a priority. In 1991, there was a shift toward greater pragmatism and greater decentralization of the Treuhandanstadt's activity.

In terms of the whole of reunified Germany, a drastic reduction in spending and a rise in compulsory payroll deductions allowed the budget deficit to be brought down to 2.5 percent of the GDP in 1994. In the medium term, public spending will remain limited because transfers to the Eastern *Länder* will remain substantial (some 3 percent of the GDP around the year 2000) and the assuming of the debts of the former West Germany and the Treuhandanstadt in 1994–95 increased the federal debt by nearly 10 percent of the GDP.

The Impact of Changes in the Other East European Countries

There is greater uncertainty concerning the other countries of the East and especially the former Soviet Union. Similarly inspired reforms have been instituted at very different paces depending on the country (liberalization of prices, banking reform with the breakup of the former central bank, monetary reform to make currency convertible, privatizations, tax reform). In the short term, production dropped, and the rapid rise of private activities, most often in services, compensated only very partially for the collapse of industrial production. An inflationary process that in some cases amounted to hyperinflation got under way and was controlled with varying degrees of rapidity through reductions in real wages sometimes exceeding 30 percent. There was a considerable effort to redeploy foreign trade, while contrasting choices prevailed in the management of the foreign debt. Poland has thus enjoyed significant debt reductions since 1990, which has considerably lessened the constraints weighing on its public finances and the current balance and helped it to resume healthy growth. Hungary, by contrast, refused such concessions in order to preserve its financial credibility and has since been struggling under the weight of a double deficit in current payments and public finances (Sgard 1995a).

Beyond such developments, the capacity of these countries to resume sustained growth depends on their ability to carry out a complex package of reforms. The role of privatizations in the restructuring process is a crucial issue that raises the question of the control exercised over the management of the large companies by the new stockholders (investment funds or employee stockholders) (Nuti 1995). Similarly, the slowness of the restructuring of the banking systems, which are neither very solvent nor very competent, may well block the recovery with a risk of evicting companies that can no longer finance their expansion with their own resources or, conversely, with an accumulation of debts favoring an inflationary crisis (Sgard 1995b). An excess of Anglo-Saxon "liberalism" may lead to ignoring the positive role that the State might play in at least three areas: the rehabilitation of infrastructures and the renovation of the public services, the carrying out of industrial restructuring through privatizations and the channeling of foreign investments, and the definition of a new wage relation. The importance of this last point has not been sufficiently stressed. The old social compromise based on near-guaranteed employment, social services provided by the companies, and low prices relative to consumption has come to a sudden end. A whole complex of new institutions and finance mechanisms must be set up.

The issues are more complicated in the former USSR, which is faced with both the institution of radical reforms and a problem of redefining new relations among the republics and states born from the breakup of the Soviet Union. The Russian transition has followed particular kinds of logic relative to the other experiences. Production has dropped sharply without an increase in unemployment; the freeing of prices has led to only a partial correction of relative prices, and inflation has exploded since 1992, but without having an autonomous monetary origin (Sapir 1993; Aglietta and Moutot 1993). The persistence of scarcities, the existence of significant price differentials between regions, the continuation of bilateral bargaining relations between firms, and the strong rise in inter-company credit have kept the monetary constraint from operating globally. In addition, companies have preferred to sacrifice their profitability and increase their losses rather than lay off their employees. The contagiousness of bankruptcy risks and the fragility of the financial system, which is undercapitalized and underregulated, have also prevented the central bank from applying a harsh monetary constraint. From 1993 to 1995, nearly 120,000 companies were privatized, but half of their capital belongs to their employees, which hardly helps to modify their form of management. The reintroduction of State authority, the creation of a social protection system, and the consolidation of the financial apparatus seem to be prerequisites for the reestablishment of a coherent economic system.

The ex-USSR formed a very economically integrated entity with a strong dependence on Russia. This heavy complementarity could not be preserved to the extent that the relatively little developed regions had fewer incentives to trade with each other and new axes emerged with neighboring countries, notably Iran and Turkey, which attracted the Asian republics. But the most significant gains are to be expected through growing trade with the European Union. These brief indications stress all the uncertainties of the transition in the East.

CONCLUSION

This book analyzed the different growth patterns and accumulation processes in the world's leading industrial nations over the last century. A great variety of trajectories have been identified on the basis of some "stylized" facts. Yet, beyond the diversity, many similar trends are visible that point to a co-evolutionary pattern in the long-term growth dynamic of advanced capitalist nations. In this context we have applied the major hypotheses of the so-called "French School of Regulation," a heterodox approach to economic theory that emphasizes the succession or confrontation of different accumulation regimes and modes of regulation as the principal form of economic evolution.

Our "regulationist" approach rests on three key arguments. First of all, long-run conditions for the accumulation of capital are characterized by a succession of stable growth patterns and recurrent crises. Technological change, besides being a vector of innovation and differentiation, is also a means for sustained growth that can postpone the return to a Schumpeterian phase of stationary state. But continuous investment in new capital goods incorporating such technological change may well encourage excess capacity, thus eventually creating conditions of increased risk at the national level and intensifying competition in international trade. Such overinvestment is produced in decentralized fashion and requires some form of readjustment, especially when effective institutional control mechanisms are lacking.

Second, any accumulation regime has a dual dimension. The distribution of income between wages, profit, interest, and taxes is a source of considerable conflict among the different income groups. Growth in capitalist economies is characterized by rather unequal distribution of payments and incentives, prompting attempts by diverse classes and the political authorities to rearrange the benefits of growth. The instruments of such redistribution are laws and regulations, taxes and income transfers, as well as defining the "rules of the game" in terms of commercial and contract laws, consensual notions of solidarity, and the production of public goods and services. The other, more hidden side of any accumulation regime concerns the evolution of the mode of regulation at different levels.

Finally, regulation—in the sense used in our theoretical approach—deals with procedures of conciliation between different categories of agents. We can observe in this context a divergence of interests, a diversity of strategic games, and a variety of temporal and technical trajectories as empirical facts. Economists tend to postulate the existence of some mechanisms of coordination among different agents. Usually they emphasize prices as the most important mechanism. But because of imperfect competition and recurrent periods of persistent disequilibria in different markets, price regulation cannot be the only coordinating mechanism. Coordination on the basis of well-established rules, common knowledge, a consensus with regard to the implementation of contract laws, and a variety of elements that we Regulationists characterize as "institutional forms" (e.g., forms of money, forms of competition, type of wage contracts, public policy) all contribute at least for a while to a stable accumulation regime. The failure of the correct mechanisms sets the stage for a new crisis at the national level that can have some serious consequences for the rest of the world.

Theoretically, a crisis, whether at the national level or the international level, is the inevitable consequence of eroding institutional forms and mounting imbalances which destabilize an economy's growth pattern. Yet at the same time we can also look at such a crisis as a mode of regulation that comes to the fore when other modes have failed. As such it can be an opportunity for good or bad change. For over a century, culminating in the Great Depression of the 1930s, crises appeared generally as deadly events causing heavy social burdens for poor people, excessively high unemployment, wars, and movements toward authoritarian forms of governance (e.g., fascism). Under these conditions it was imperative to develop new modes of social and international regulation whenever economic crisis endured. After the World War II the leading economies seemed to have found new ways for accelerated capital accumulation, regular growth, and liberalization of external trade.

But this success of the postwar period, giving us the longest boom in capitalism's history, did not last. Rapid growth in the 1950s and 1960s gave way to a new form of crisis, namely stagflation, in the early 1970s. We have argued in this book that the downturns since then were not just short-term recessions in the normal course of the business cycle. Instead we looked at them as manifestations of a long-term process of transformation toward a new technological and institutional age, as necessary stages in the direction of a new accumulation regime.

The United States has explored a new growth pattern by relying once again more heavily on the mechanisms of competition, with relatively weak productivity gains and an aggravation of inequalities as consequences, while managing to preserve its advances in high-tech sectors. The principal weakness here remains America's mode of insertion on an international level. The United States remains on the global level the only superpower, and has constructed a new style of governance toward the rest of the world. But this position does not correspond to the real economic weight of the United States. The size of U.S. trade deficits and external debt will eventually come to pose problems that will not be without consequence for the status of the U.S. dollar and the organization of the international monetary system.

Elsewhere the crisis resumed during the early 1990s. The excessive degree of financial liberalization weighed heavily in that resumption of crisis, above all in Japan and more recently in the rest of East Asia. Other emerging market countries seem vulnerable as well. The growing complexity of international finance and its increasingly determinant economic impact require new forms of regulation at the international level.

Japan, which managed to get out of the crisis of the 1970s quite early, now has to confront new challenges. The foundations of its growth model will have to be redefined not only to overcome the crisis of its banking system and to construct new financial regulations, but also to provide appropriate answers to the erosion of its industrial competitiveness and to reduce the excessively high costs of its protected sector.

The European countries have by and large been stuck in a slow growth pattern since the 1980s. Ill-conceived economic policies are, in our opinion, more responsible for this stagnation than the often-cited wage rigidities. The introduction of new forms of labor-market flexibility, whether regressive as in the United Kingdom or offensive and cooperative as in Germany, constitute an important development. The introduction of the "Single Market," followed by the introduction of a single currency, marks the beginning of a new mode of regulation, in part supranational and thus in theory better adapted to the strong degree of interdependence existing among European economies. But, in the absence of a federalist perspective, the project of Economic and Monetary Union has had to go through important contradictions that are related to the inadequacy of rebalancing mechanisms as well as to the difficulties associated with the coordination of economic policies. The challenge of bringing the emerging-market nations of Central and Eastern Europe into the European Union exacerbates the uncertainties regarding the future functioning of the union.

REFERENCES

Aglietta, Michel (1976). "Monnaie et inflation: quelques leçons de l'expérience américaine des dix dernières années," *Economie et Statistique,* no. 77, INSEE, Paris, pp. 49–72.
——— (1979). *A Theory of Capitalism Regulation: The U.S. Experience* (London: New Left Books).
——— (1982). *Regulation and Crisis of Capitalism* (New York: Monthly Review Press).
——— (1986). *La fin des devises-clés* (Paris: La Découverte).
———(1987). "Structures économiques et innovations financières," *Revue d'Economie Financière* Paris, pp. 43–58.
Aglietta, Michel, and Moutot, Philippe (1993). "Redéployer les réformes: comment adapter la stratégie de transition?" *Economie Internationale,* no. 54, 2ème trimestre, pp. 67–103.
Aglietta, Michel, and Orléan, André (1982). *La violence de la monnaie* (Paris: Presses Universitaires de France).
Aglietta, Michel; Oudiz, Gilles; and Orléan, André (1981). "Des adaptations différenciées aux contraintes internationales," *Revue Economique,* no. 4, juillet, pp. 660–712.
Amable, Bruno (1989)."Economies d'échelle dynamiques, effets d'apprentissage et progrés technique endogène: une comparaison internationale," *Revue de l'IRES,* automne, Paris, pp. 31–54.
Amable, Bruno, and Mouhoud, el Mouhoub (1990). "Changement technique et compétitivité internationale: une comparaison des six grands pays industrialisés," *Revue d'Economie Industrielle,* no. 54, pp. 22–43.
Aoki, Masakiko (1990). "Towards an Economic Model of the Japanese Firm," *Journal of Economic Literature,* March, no. 1, pp. 1–27.
Artus, Patrick (1983). "Formation des prix et des salaires dans cinq grands pays industriels," *Annales de l'INSEE,* pp. 5–52.
Artus, Patrick, and Debonneuil, Michèle (1979). "Les conséquences d'un pétrole plus cher," *Economie et Statistique,* no. 115, octobre, pp. 21–26.
Artus, Patrick, and Muet, Pierre-Alain (1980). "Une étude de l'influence de la demande, des coûts des facteurs et des contraintes financières sur l'investisse-ment," *CEPREMAP,* no. 8015.
Asselain, Jean-Charles (1984). *Histoire économique de la France, de 1919 à la fin des années 1970* (Paris: Le Seuil).
——— (1995). *Histoire économique du 20ème siècle: la montée de l'Etat, 1914–1939* (Paris: Dalloz).
Balderston, T. (1983). "The Beginning of the Depression in Germany 1927–1930: Investment and the Capital Market," *The Economic History Review,* pp. 395–415.
Balke, Nathan S., and Gordon, Robert J. (1986). "Historical data" in R.J. Gordon, *The American Business Cycle, NBER* (Chicago: University of Chicago Press).

Barou, Yves (1978). "L'économie britannique: difficultés et renouveau," *Notes et études documentaires* (La documentation française).

——— (1979). "La croissance japonaise," *Statistiques et Études Financières, Série Orange*, no. 39, Paris, pp. 1–40.

Barou, Yves; Dollé, Michel; Gabet, Christian; and Wartenberg, Erwin (1979). "Les performances comparées de l'économie en France, en RFA et au Royaume-Uni," *Les Collections de l'INSEE, série E*, no. 69, Paris, pp. 3–273.

Baslé, Maurice (1990a). "L'analyse financière de l'endettement public: essai d'appréciation des méthodes courantes," *Revue d'Economie Politique*, mars-avril, pp. 283–296.

——— (1990b). *Systèmes fiscaux* (Paris: Dalloz).

——— (1992). "Britain: Financial Sophistication and Industrial Wastelands," in Maclean, Mairi, and Howorth, Jolian, *Europeans on Europe, Transnational Visions of a New Continent* (London: Macmillan), pp. 57–73.

Baslé, Maurice; Mazier, Jacques; and Vidal, Jean-François (1979). "Croissance sectorielle et accumulation en longue période," GRESP, *Statistiques et Etudes Financières, Série Orange*, no. 40, pp. 3–51.

Bathia, R. (1961). "Unemployment and the Rate of Change of Money Earnings in the United States," *Economica*, pp. 286–396.

Bernanke, Ben (1983). "Non-Monetary Effects of the Financial Crisis in the Propagation of the Great Depression," *American Economic Review*, pp. 257–276.

Bernis, Gérard de (1977). *Relations économiques internationales* (Paris: Dalloz).

Bertrand, Hugues (1978). "La croissance française analysée en sections productives," *Statistiques et Études Financières, Ministère de l'Economie et des Finances*, no. 35, pp. 3–36.

Bettelheim, Charles (1945). *L'économie allemande sous le nazisme* (Paris: Marc Rivière).

——— (1947). *Bilan de l'économie française: 1919–1946* (Paris: Presses Universitaires de France).

Blanchard, Olivier J., and Summers, Lawrence (1986). "Pourquoi les taux d'intérêt sont-ils aussi élevés?" *Annales D'Économie et Statistique*, pp. 53–100.

Blanchard, Olivier J., and Katz, Laurent (1992). "Regional Evolutions," Brookings Papers on Economic Activity, no. 1, Washington, pp. 1–75.

Boeda, Michel (1975). "L'adaptation de l'économie au choc pétrolier: quatre scénarios," *Economie et Statistique*, no. 71, INSEE, Paris, pp. 49–56.

Boissieu, Christian de (1987). "Mutations financières," *Revue Française d'Economie*, pp. 74–109.

Bolch, Ben; Fels, Rendings; and MacMahon, Marshall (1971)."Housing Surplus in the 1920s," *Explorations in Economic History*, pp. 259–283.

Borchardt, Knut (1982)."Waschtum, krisen, handlunggsspierlräume der wirtschaftspolitik" (Göttingen: Vandenhoeck and Ruprecht).

Bouvier, Jean; Furet, François; and Gillet, Michel (1965). *Le mouvement du profit en France au 19ème siècle* (Paris: Mouton).

Boyer, Robert (1977). *Approches de l'inflation: l'exemple français*, tome 3 (Paris: CEPREMAP).

——— (1979a). "La crise actuelle: une mise en perspective historique," *Critique de l'économie politique*, avril-septembre, pp. 5–113.

——— (1979b). "Wage Formation in Historical Perspective: The French Experience," *Cambridge Journal of Economics*, 3 (3), pp. 98–118.

———, ed. (1986a). *Capitalismes fin de siécle* (Paris: Presses Universitaires de France).

——— (1986b). *La flexibilité du travail en Europe* (Paris: La Découverte).

——— (1986c). *La théorie de la régulation: une analyse critique* (Paris: La Découverte).

Boyer, Robert, and Mistral, Jacques (1983). *Accumulation, Inflation, Crises,* 2nd edition (Paris: Presses Universitaires de France).

Boyer, Robert, and Petit, Pascal (1980). "Emploi et productivité dans la CEE," *Economie et Statistique,* no. 121, avril–mai, pp. 35–59.

——— (1981). "Progrès technique, croissance et emploi," *Revue Economique,* no. 6, novembre, pp. 1113–1153.

Boyer, Robert, and Saillard, Yves (1995). *Théorie de la régulation: l'état des savoirs* (Paris: La Découverte).

Brunhes, Bernard (1989). "Un Service Public de l'Emploi pour les années 1990," Rapport pour le Commissaire au Plan, mars.

Calomiris, Charles W. (1993)."Financial Factors in the Great Depression," *Journal of Economic Perspectives,* spring, pp. 61–85.

CEPII (1983). *L'économie mondiale 1970–1990: la montée des tensions* (Paris: Economica).

CEPII-OFCE (1995). Équipe MIMOSA, "Quand les marchés triomphent: une projection de l'économie mondiale à horizon de 2002," no. 55, pp. 95–150.

CERC (1989). "Les Français et leurs revenus" (La documentation française).

Coe, David (1985). "Salaires nominaux, taux de chômage non inflationniste et flexibilité des salaires," *Revue Economique de l'OCDE,* automne, pp. 97–141.

Coriat, Benjamin (1979). *L'atelier et le chronométre* (Paris: Christian Bourgois).

——— (1990). *L'atelier et le robot* (Paris: Christian Bourgois).

——— (1991). *Penser à l'envers* (Paris: Christian Borgois).

Delmas, Philippe, and Roy, Geneviève (1988). "Dix ans d'une politique d'aide à l'industrie sans précédent," *Economie Prospective Internationale,* no. 36, 4ème trimestre, pp. 33–60.

Delorme, Robert, and André, Christine (1983). *L'Etat et l'économie* (Paris: Seuil).

Deniau, Claire; Fiori, George; and Mathis, Alexandre (1989). "Impact de la dette publique sur quelques variables macroéconomiques françaises," *Economie et Prévision,* no. 90, pp. 87–96.

Divisia, François, Dupin, Claude, and Roy, René (1956). *A la recherche du franc perdu* (Paris: Hommes et monde).

Dollé, Michel (1979). "Les branches industrielles avant et aorès 1974," *Economie et Statistique,* no. 108, INSEE, Paris, pp. 3–20.

Dumenil, Gérard, and Lévy, Dominique (1993). *The Economics of the Profit Rate: Competition, Crises and Historical Tendencies in Capitalism* (Aldershot: Edward Elgar).

Eckstein, Otto, and Girola, James A. (1978) "Long Term Properties of the Price–Wage Mechanism in the United States: 1891 to 1977," *Review of Economics and Statistics,* pp. 323–333.

Eichengreen, Barry (1990). "One Money for Europe? Lesson from the U.S. Currency Union," *Economic Policy,* no. 10, pp. 117–187.

——— (1992). "The Origins and Nature of the Great Slump Revisited," *Economic History Review,* May, pp. 213–236.

Eichengreen, Barry; Tobin, James; and Wyplosz, Charles (1995). "Two Cases for Sand in the Wheels of International Finance," *Economic Journal,* January, pp. 162–172.

Encaoua, David, and Franck, Bernard (1980). "Performances sectorielles et groupes de sociétés," *Revue Economique,* mai, pp. 397–429.

Etudes de politique industrielle (1976). "La division internationale du travail" (La documentation française).

Fayolle, Jacky (1981). "Capital et capacités de production dans l'industrie," *Economie et Statistique,* no. 136, INSEE, Paris, pp. 3–16.

Feinstein, Charles H. (1976). *Statistical Tables of National Income, Expenditures and Output of the U.K. 1855–1965* (Cambridge: Cambridge University Press).

Friedman, Milton, and Schwartz, Anna (1963). "A Monetary History of the United States" (Princeton, NJ: Princeton University Press).

Gabet, Christian; Honoré, Geneviève; and Houssin, François (1974). "Les répercussions mécaniques de hausses de prix énergétiques," *Economie et Staistique*, no. 56, INSEE, Paris, pp. 45–50.

Galibert, Alain, and Le Dem, Jean (1986). "Les services au secours de l'emploi? Une analyse comparée des évolutions en France, en Allemagne, aux Etats-Unis et au Japon," *Economie Prospective Internationale*, no. 28, pp. 5–35.

Gardes, François (1983). "L'évolution de la consommation marchande en Europe et aux Etats-Unis depuis 1960," *Consommation* no. 2, pp. 3–32.

GATT (1966). "Le commerce mondial en 1965," Genève.

GATT (1979). "Le commerce international en 1977–1978," Genève.

Geoffron, Patrice, and Rubinstein, Marianne (1996). *La crise financière du modèle japonais* (Paris: Economica).

Girardin, Eric (1986). "Estimation en longue période d'une fonction d'investissement pour le Royaume-Uni: 1881–1979," *Economie Appliquée*, no. 2, pp. 297–336.

Goldet, Hélène; Nicolas, François; and Séruzier, Michel (1975). "L'endettement des entreprises et des ménages de 1954 à 1974," *Economie et Statistique*, no. 73, décembre, INSEE, Paris, pp. 21–38.

Goldstein, Morris, and Kahn, Moshin S. (1985). "Income and Prices: Effects on Foreign Trade," pp. 1040–1105, in Jones, Ronald W., and Kenen, Peter. B., *Handbook of International Economics* (Amsterdam: Elsevier, North Holland).

Gordon, Robert (1975). "Wages, Prices and Unemployment 1900–1970," *Industrial Relations*, pp. 273–301.

——— (1980). "A Consistent Characterization of a Near Century of Price Behavior" *American Economic Review*, May, pp. 243–249.

Gros, Daniel (1993). "Mettre un terme à la désintégration monétaire dans la CEI: une banque inter-Etats pour le financement des échanges," *Economie Internationale*, no. 54, 2ème trimestre, pp. 121–135.

Grubb, David; Jackman, Robert; and Layard, Robert (1983). "Wage Rigidity and Unemployment in OCDE countries," *European Economic Review*, pp. 11–39.

Grubel, Herbert G., and Lloyd, P.J. (1975). *Intra-industry Trade: The Theory and Measurement of International Trade in Differentiated Products* (London: Macmillan).

Guibert, Bernard (1975). "La mutation industrielle de la France," INSEE Collections E31–32.

Haberger, Arnold C. (1957). "Some Evidence on International Price Mechanism," *Journal of Political Economy*, pp. 506–521.

Hamilton, James D. (1992). "Was the Deflation During the Great Depression Anticipated? Evidence from the Commodity Futures Market," *American Economic Review*, pp. 157–178.

Hau, Michel (1994). *Histoire économique de l'Allemagne, 19ème et 20ème siècles* (Paris: Economica).

Hickman, Bert G. (1961). *Growth and Stability of the Post War Economy* (Washington, DC: Brookings Institution).

Hill, T.P. (1979). "Bénéfices et taux de rendement," OECD.

Homer, Sidney (1968). *A History of Interest Rates* (New Brunswick, NJ: Rutgers University Press).

Hoffmann, Walther G. (1965). *Das Wachstum der deutschen Wirtschaft seit der Mitte des 19. Jahrhunderts* (Berlin: Springer Verlag).

INSEE (1975). "La fresque historique du système productif," Collections de l'INSEE, série E, no. 27, Paris.

INSEE (1981). "La crise du système productif," Paris.

INSEE (1991). "Le bilan social," Paris.

Jacquemin, Alexis (1979). *Economie industrielle européenne* (Montrouge: Dunod).

Joshua, Isaac (1994). "La grande crise et le rêve américain," *Economie et Sociétés*, no. 3, Paris, pp. 167–203.

Kalecki, Michael (1954). *Theory of Economic Dynamics: An Essay on Cyclical and Long Run Changes in Capitalist Economy* (London: Allen and Unwin).

Keese, Dietmar (1966). "Die Volkswirtshaftlichen gesamtgrössen für das deutsche Reich in den Jahren 1925–1936," in *Die Staats und Wirtschatskrise des deutchen Reiches* (Stuttgart: Ernst Klette Verlag).

Keiser, Bernard (1979) "Le modèle économique allemand: mythes et réalités," Notes et études documentaires (La documentation française).

Kendrick, John W. (1961). *Productivity Trends in the United States, NBER* (Princeton: Princeton University Press).

Kenwood, A.G., and Lougheed, A.L. (1971). *The Growth of International Economy 1820–1960* (London: Allen and Unwin).

Kindleberger, Charles P. (1986). "Histoire financiére del Europe occidentale," (Paris: Economica).

———— (1988). *La grande crise mondiale 1929–1945* (Paris: Economica).

Kravis, Irving; Heston, Alan W.; and Summers, Robert (1978). *International Comparisons of Real Product and Purchasing Power* (Baltimore: John Hopkins University Press).

Kremp, Elisabeth, and Mistral, Jacques (1988). "Flexibilité des salaires: l'impact des années Reagan," *Economie Prospective Internationale*, no. 36, 4ème trimestre, pp. 87–113.

Krueger, Ann O. (1987). "Origins of the Developing Countries' Debt Crisis: 1970 to 1982," *Journal of Development Economics*, pp. 165–187.

Kuznets, Simon (1967). "Quantitative Aspects of the Economic Growth of Nations, Levels and Structure of Foreign Trade: Long Term Trade," *Economic Development and Cultural Change*, pp. 1–140.

Lafay, Gérard (1979). *Dynamique de la spécialisation internationale* (Paris: Economica).

Lafay, Gérard, and Herzog, Colette (1989). *Commerce international: la fin des avantages acquis* (Paris: Economica).

Laubier, Dominique de, and Richemond, Alain (1981). "Interpénétration des capitaux et concurrence industrielle mondiale," *Economie Appliquée*, tome 34, Paris, pp. 469–515.

Lemoine, Françoise (1995). "La dynamique des exportations des PECO vers l'Union Européenne," *Economie Internationale*, no. 62, 2ème trimestre, pp. 145–172.

Le Pors, Anicet (1976). "Les transferts Etat–Industrie en France," Notes et études documentaires (La documentation française).

Lewis, W. Arthur (1952). "World Production, Prices and Trade 1870–1960," *Manchester School of Economics and Social Studies*.

Linder, Burenstam S. (1961). "An Essay on Trade and Transformation,"(New York: John Wiley and Sons).

Lipsey, Richard (1960). "The Relation Between Unemployment and the Rate of Change of Money Wage Rates in the United Kingdom 1862–1957: A Further Analysis," *Economica*, vol. 27, February, pp. 1–31.

Lorenzi, Jean-Hervé; Pastré, Olivier; and Toledano Joelle (1980). *La grande crise du 20 ème siècle* (Paris: Economica).

Lucas, Robert (1988). "On the Mechanics of Economic Development," *Journal of Monetary Economics,* no. 22, pp. 3–42.

Maddison, Angus (1982). *Phases of Capitalist Development* (Oxford: Oxford University Press).

—— (1985). "Deux crises: l'Amérique Latine et l'Asie: 1929–1938 et 1973–1983," (OECD).

Mairesse, Jacques, and Delestrè, Henri (1978). "La rentabilité des sociétés privées en France 1956–1975" (INSEE).

Maizels, Alfred (1971). *Industrial Growth and World Trade* (Cambridge: Cambridge University Press).

Mandel, Ernest (1978). *La crise 1974–1978* (Paris: Flammarion).

Marris, Stephan (1985). "Deficits and the Dollar: The World Economy at Risk" (Washington, DC: Institute for International Economics).

Marseille, Jacques (1980). "Les origines inopportunes de la crise de 1929 en France," *Revue d'Economie Politique,* juillet, Paris, pp. 648–684.

Mathis, Jean; Mazier, Jacques; and Rivaud-Danset, Dorothée (1988). *La compétitivité industrielle* (Montrouge: Dunod).

Mautort, Laurent de (1981). "La désindustrialisation au coeur du modèle allemand," *Economie Prospective Internationale,* no. 8, octobre, pp. 2–96.

Mazier, Jacques; Dayon, Anne-Françoise; and Galibert, Alain (1981). "Les ajustements internes et externes des économies européennes face à la crise 1970–1979," GRESP, Université de Rennes.

Mercer, Lloyd J., and Morgan, W. Douglas (1972). "The American Automobile Industry: Investment Demand, Capacity and Capacity Utilization 1921–1940," *Journal of Political Economy,* pp. 269–290.

Miége, Jean-Louis (1977). *Expansion européenne et colonisation de 1870 à nos jours* (Paris: Presses Universitaires de France).

Milleron, Jean-Claude, and Younes, Yves (1980). "Productivité du travail et substitution entre les facteurs: points de repères," *Economie et Statistique,* novembre, pp. 55–62.

Mishkin, Frederic S. (1978). "The Household Balance Sheet and the Great Depression," *Journal of Economic History,* pp. 918–937.

Mistral, Jacques (1978). "Compétitivité et formation du capital en longue période," *Economie et Statistique,* février, INSEE, Paris, pp. 3–23.

—— (1986). "Régime international et trajectoires nationales," pp. 167–201, in Boyer, Robert, ed., *Capitalisme fin de siècle* (Paris: Presses Universitaires de France).

MITI (1996a). Small business in Japan.

MITI (1996b). White paper on international trade.

Muet, Pierre-Alain (1979). "Modélles econométriques de l'investissement: une étude comparative sur données annuelles," *Annales de l'INSEE,* no. 35.

Neisser, Henry, and Modigliani, Franco (1953). "National Income and International Trade: A Quantitative Analysis" (Urbana: University of Illinois Press.

Nelson, Daniel B. (1991). "Was the Deflation of 1929–1930 Anticipated?" *Research in Economic History,* pp. 1–65.

Nuti, Mario (1995). "Corporate governance et actionnariat des salariés," *Economie Internationale,* no. 62, 2ème trimestre, pp. 13–34.

OECD (1981). "L'inflation," Etudes Spéciales.

OECD (1986). "Etudes par pays, Etats-Unis," Paris.

OECD (1987–88). "Etudes par pays, Etats-Unis," Paris.

Olney, Martha L. (1989). "Consumer Durables in the Interwar Years: New Estimates, New Patterns," *Research in Economic History*, pp. 119–150.

Petit, Pascal (1988). *La croissance tertaire* (Paris: Economica).

Phillips, Andrew (1958). "The Relation Between Unemployment and the Rate of Change of Money Wage Rates in the United Kingdom 1862–1957: A Further Analysis," *Economica*, vol. 25, November, pp. 283–99.

Polak, Jacques J. (1954). *An International System* (London: Allen and Unwin).

Robinson, Joan (1962). *Essays in the Theory of Economic Growth* (London: Macmillan).

Romer, Christina D. (1993). "The Nation in Depression," *Journal of Economic Perspectives*, spring, pp. 19–39.

Romer, Paul (1986). "Increasing Returns and Long Run Growth" *Journal of Political Economy*, no. 5, October, pp. 1002–1037.

Rybczynski, T.M. (1978). "Structural Change in the World Economy," *The Three Bank Review*, no. 4.

Sachs, Jeffrey (1980). "The Changing Cyclical Behavior of Wages and Prices: 1870–1976," *American Economic Review*, pp. 78–90.

Sapir, Jacques (1993). "Forme et nature de l'inflation, pourquoi les thérapies de choc sont vouées à l'échec?" *Economie Internationale*, no. 54, 2ème trimestre, pp. 25–65.

Sautter, Christian (1973). *Le prix de la puissance* (Paris: Seuil).

——— (1987). *Les dents du géant: le Japon à la conquête du monde* (Paris: Odile Orban).

Sgard, Jérëme (1995a). "Faut-il payer ses detes? Hongrie et Pologne, cinq ans après," *Lettre du CEPII*, no. 138, septembre, Paris, pp. 1–4.

——— (1995b). "Le financement de la transition en Europe centrale et balkanique," *Economie Internationale*, no. 62, 2ème trimestre, pp. 61–102.

Shapiro, Edward (1976). "Cyclical Fluctuations in Prices and Output in the United Kingdom," *Economic Journal*, December, pp. 746–758.

Singer-Kerel, Jeanne (1961). *Le coû de la vie à Paris de 1840 à 1954* (Paris: Armand Colin).

Temin, Peter (1971). "The Beginning of the Depression in Germany," *The Economic History Review*, pp. 240–248.

——— (1976). *Did Monetary Forces Cause the Great Depression?* (New York: Norton).

——— (1993). "Transmission of the Great Depression," *Journal of Economic Perspectives*, pp. 87–102.

Thorning, Margo (1975). "Cyclical Fluctuations in Prices and Output in the United States," *Economic Journal*, March, pp. 95–100.

Tyszynski, H. (1951). "World Trade in Manufactured Commodities 1899–1950," *Manchester School of Economic and Social Studies*, September, pp. 272–304.

Vidal, Jean-François (1989). *Les fluctuations internationales* (Paris: Economica).

Villa, Pierre (1993). "Une analyse macroéconomique de la France au 20ème siècle," Monographies d'Econometrie (Paris: CNRS Editions).

——— (1994). "Un siècle de données macroéconomiques," INSEE résultats, no. 86–87.

Weir, David R. (1992). "A Century of Unemployment, 1890–1990: Revised Estimates and Evidence for Stabilisation," *Research in Economic History*, pp. 301–345.

Weisskopf, Thomas (1979). "Marxian Crisis Theory and the Rate of Profit in the Postwar U.S. Economy," *Cambridge Journal of Economy*, December, pp. 341–378.

Weisskopf, Thomas; Bowles, Samuel; and Gordon, David (1983). "Hearts and Minds: A Social Model of U.S. Productivity and Growth," Brookings Papers on Economic Activity 1, pp. 381–450.

——— (1989). "Business Ascendancy and Economic Impass: A Structural Retrospective on Conservative Economics, 1979–1987," *Journal of Economic Perspectives*, 3, no. 1, winter, pp. 107–134.

Yates, P.L. (1959). *Forty Years of Foreign Trade* (London: Allen and Unwin).

ABOUT THE AUTHORS

Jacques Mazier is a professor of economics at the Université Paris-Nord since 1984. He studied at Ecole Polytechnique and received a doctorate in economics (Université Paris 1) in 1974. He was research fellow in the Forecasting Department of the Ministry of Finance (Paris), and professor of economics at the Université Rennes between 1976 and 1981. He was also adviser in the Economic Department of the Planning Commission between 1981 and 1984. He has published *Macro-économie appliquée* (Presses Universitaires de France, 1978), and *La compétitivité industrielle* (Editions Dunod, 1988).

Maurice Baslé is a professor of economics at the Université Rennes 1 where he earned his state doctorate in economics in 1974. His publications are specialized in economics of the State, fiscal policy, and policy evaluation. Presently, he holds the Jean Monnet chair in European economics and integration and is a member of the National Scientific Council of Policy Evaluation (Paris). He has published *Le budget de l'Etat* (Editions La Découverte, 1997), and *Changement institutionnel et changement technologique* (Editions du Centre National de la Recherche Scientifique, 1995).

Jean-François Vidal is a professor of economics at the Université Paris-Sud. He received a doctorate in economics from Université Rennes in 1977. His publications are specialized in economic history and international economics. He is the author of *Les fluctuations internationales de 1890 à nos jours* (Editions Economica, 1989). He is the editor of the papers presented at the International Economic History Conference held in Paris, 1994.

INDEX